780.7

36402

Th__ __ __k is to be __ __ed on or __ __re
__ __ __ __ __ __ d be

Composers and the Nature of
Music Education

Ian Lawrence

Composers and the Nature of Music Education

London: Scolar Press
1978

First published in 1978 by Scolar Press,
39 Great Russell Street, London WC1B 3PH

Designed by Alan Bartram
Printed in England by
Western Printing Services Ltd, Bristol

ISBN 0 85967 401 0

Contents

Preface

In this book I have attempted to investigate the contribution made by composers to the understanding of creative and imaginative problems that we constantly encounter in music. It may reasonably be argued that we expect too much of composers if we ask them to illuminate our lives not only with music but also with words, and it is true that some composers have neither found the time nor shown the inclination to channel their energies into what for them must seem an inessential activity.

Nevertheless, there is a surprisingly large store of invaluable material written by composers from a wide range of backgrounds, and their often forceful and incisive manner is nearly always combined with a profound understanding of the nature of music and the difficulties that the learner inevitably meets. Indeed it is not too much to claim that between them they seem to provide a very extensive discussion of all the major current issues. What for me has been the most interesting aspect of their work is the element of continuity. To discover that sixteenth- to twentieth-century composers agree on matters of central importance is, to say the least, reassuring. Time and time again we are made to feel that the questions that perplex us today have already been answered not once, but many times, and with extraordinary confidence and assurance.

As writers, the composers vary in their achievements. At their best, however, they seem to possess a grasp of language every bit as certain as their command of musical resources. Very occasionally they allow themselves to nod, but never for long. Their ideas are never far from the surface, and often burst out with a clarity and radiance that is very exciting. I make no apology for allowing the composers to talk without too many interruptions, for it seems only proper that they should be given the opportunity to make their points with as much emphasis as possible. This is not to suggest, however, that what follows is in any sense an anthology, for in attempting to analyse and classify, I have inevitably drawn on my own experiences as a musician and as a teacher.

The sources that I have used date from the mid-sixteenth to the mid-twentieth century. I have not employed earlier material mostly because it dwells more in the theoretical than the practical, and I have avoided the post-1950 period chiefly in the interests of historical perspective, though a manageable size of book was another factor.

I would not have been able to write this book without the support of a large number of people, among whom I am particularly indebted to Jack Pilgrim of the University of Leeds, Doris Jones and the library staff of the West London Institute, the library staffs of the British Library and the Universities of Cambridge, Edinburgh, Glasgow, Oxford, Leeds and London, and the members of my family, especially my wife Margaret. I am also most grateful to the following publishers for permission to reproduce material in their copyright:

Barrie & Jenkins Ltd, Basic Books, The Bobbs-Merrill Co. Inc., Breitkopf & Härtel, Cassell Ltd, Collet's Holdings Ltd, Cornell University Press, J. M. Dent & Sons Ltd, E. P. Dutton & Co. Inc., Faber & Faber Ltd, Faber Music Ltd, Victor Gollancz Publishing Ltd, Harvard University Press, Heinemann Educational Books Ltd, Ernst Křenek, Macmillan Publishing Ltd, Methuen & Co. Ltd, W. W. Norton & Co. Inc., Oxford University Press, Princeton University Press, Ryerson Music Publishers Inc., Schott & Co. Ltd, Yale University Press, also the Editor of *Psychology of Music* and the Estate of Igor Stravinsky.

List of Abbreviations

BCResMEd	Bulletin of the Council for Research in Musical Education
BritJAesth	The British Journal of Aesthetics
EdT	Education for Teaching
IntMEd	International Music Educator: Journal of the International Society for Music Education
IntRMAesthSoc	The International Review of Musical Aesthetics and Sociology
JAesthArtCr	Journal of the Aesthetics of Art Criticism
JAmMSoc	Journal of the American Musicological Society
JHI	Journal of the History of Ideas
JMT	Journal of Music Theory
JRME	Journal of Research in Music Education
MEd	Music in Education
MEJ	Music Educators Journal
MD	Musica Disciplina
ML	Music and Letters
MQ	The Musical Quarterly
MR	Musical Review
MT	The Musical Times
MMR	Monthly Musical Review
NZfM	Neue Zeitschrift für Musick
PMA	Proceedings of the (Royal) Musical Association
QMIMS	Quarterly Magazine of the International Music Society
RMAResC	Royal Musical Association Research Chronicle

Reference to certain *un-numbered pages* in some early texts employs the system Ai, Aii, Aiii, Bi, Bii, etc.

There is nothing can more advance the
APPREHENSION OF MUSIC
than the reading of such writers
as have both skilfully and diligently
set down the precepts thereof.

John Dowland

The Scope of Composers' Interest in Teaching

1 The Elizabethan Period

Towards the end of the seventeenth century Roger North, English Attorney-General and amateur musician, could look back at a period of considerable change in the development of English music and musical habits; yet when he refers to the teaching of music it is to emphasize the importance of ideas characteristic of the early part of the century:

'The book of Mr. Morley hath sufficiently shewed the rules of musicke in his time, but it is not easy to gather them out of his dialogue way of wrighting, which according to usage is stuft with abundance of impertinences, and also with matters, in our practise, wholly obsolete.'[1]

Thomas Morley's *A Plaine and Easie Introduction to Practicall Musicke* first appeared in 1597. North may have found it antiquated, but the sources which he goes on to mention lean so heavily upon Morley's book that their very existence may be said to have depended upon their authors' close familiarity with that text.

North's first alternatives to *A Plaine and Easie Introduction* are the publications of Christopher Simpson (d. 1669), composer, instrumentalist and teacher.

'I know many serve themselves of Mr. Simpson's books, which are doubtless very good, and worthy as could be expected from a meer musick master, as he was, but they are not compleat' (p. 137).

The books to which North refers are *The Division Viol, or the art of playing ex-tempore upon a ground* (first edition 1659), *The Principles of Practical Musick* (first edition 1665), and *A Compendium of Practical Musick* (first edition 1667). The latter two books were so popular that they both reached an eighth (revised) edition by 1732.

Even more popular was John Playford's *A Breife Introduction to the Skill of Musick* (first edition 1654) which ran to some nineteen editions by 1730, and to which Simpson, Thomas Campion and Henry Purcell all contributed material and revisions. Playford's title is an accurate one,

and his little book is as short as Simpson's *Compendium* and covers only
a very small part of the material in *A Plaine and Easie Introduction*. North
dismisses it in the following manner:

'Nay some make a shift with poor old Playford's Introduction, of which
may be truely sayd that it is but just (if at all) better than none' (p. 137).

Playford, of course, was a publisher and not a composer, although he
had a wide experience as an amateur musician. From his house in Inner
Temple he published a number of important musical works. Besides the
Introduction he is perhaps chiefly remembered for *The English Dancing
Master* (1650) and *A Musicall Banquet* (1651).

It may be felt, however, that North is being less than just about a
publication, which, for all its limitations, served the English musical
public for eighty years at least. Moreover, since it was in the nature of
a compendium, its contents changed a great deal during its lifetime.
The early editions contained a mixture of ideas inherited from Morley
and Campion (partly edited by Simpson). However, the fourth
(enlarged) edition (1664) expanded to include:

'A brief discourse of the Italian manner of singing, wherein is set down
the use of those graces in singing, as the trill and the gruppo, used in
Italy and now in England: written some years since by an English
Gentleman, who had lived long in Italy and being returned, taught the
same here.'

This is in fact a free translation of Caccini's foreword to *Le Nuove
Musiche* (1602). Unfortunately the identity of the 'English Gentleman'
remains a mystery (although he may have been Walter Porter, Gentleman of the Chapel Royal and pupil of Monteverdi),[2] but 'poor old
Playford' is surely to be congratulated for his efforts in widening the
scope of his book.

The twelfth edition (1694) is possibly the most important, since it
contains a substantial revision by Henry Purcell, who demonstrates the
shift in harmonic procedures by recommending his readers to think of
the harmony in relation to the tune in the top part, rather than the
Campion method of working up from the bass. Purcell also shows his
command of contrapuntal techniques with a series of brilliant examples,
which must have proved quite formidable to Playford's beginners.

North's third alternative to *A Plaine and Easie Introduction* is the one
that he recommends with the most confidence:

'But there is a musicall grammar ever to be recommended, compiled by a learned man, and compleat in all gramaticall formes. It was put out by a famous master of sciences Mr. Butler, and I doe not know another in any language comparable to it. And one may be secure that whatever is done persuant to the prescriptions of this work, cannot be irregular or absurd' (p. 137).

Charles Butler, Vicar of Wotton and music teacher at Magdalen College choir school, Oxford, was certainly a 'learned man', and no doubt his work appealed to North for the very reason that he was, like North himself, an amateur musician with wide interests. He was not a composer, however, and the inclusion of any detailed comment on his work at this stage cannot be justified. There can be no doubt, though, that his *Principles* helped in part to fill the gap between the second edition of *A Plaine and Easie Introduction* (1608) and the arrival of the Simpson and Playford books, as also did books by Campion and Ravenscroft.

Among the more important books that North does not mention are Thomas Campion's *New Ways in Making Foure Parts in Counter-point* (*c.* 1614); Thomas Ravenscroft's *A Breife Discourse* (1614), a work very much in the shadow of Morley; John Dowland's *Ornithoparcus, his micrologus* (1609); Robert Dowland's *Varietie of Lute Lessons* (1610); Matthew Locke's *Melothesia* (1673), and Thomas Mace's *Musick's Monument* (1676). From the continent the most extensive books came from Michael Praetorius (1571–1621), whose three-volume *Syntagma Musicum* was published from 1615–19; there were also important essays from Diruta, Sweelink, Carissimi, Bernhard, and Bononcini, as well as the two famous prefaces by Caccini and Frescobaldi, details of which may be found in the Bibliography.

Of these many books, however, there can be no doubt about the crucial position of *A Plaine and Easie Introduction*. Reese refers to it as 'the most celebrated English treatise of the Renaissance',[3] for not only did it (and its imitations) exercise a very powerful influence upon the seventeenth-century musicians, but it also raises matters of principle and practice which are of great importance to those involved in music today.

Morley's book is, moreover, not simply a guide to Elizabethan teaching methods, but represents a breakthrough in the history of music teaching, for it is, as far as is known, one of the first by a composer to emphasize, in the vernacular, the *practical* problems of learning music. There had been earlier examples of 'practical' works, e.g.: Ramos de Pareja, *Musica Practica* (1482); Gafori, *Practica Musicae* (1496); Finck, *Practica Musica* (1556); Zacconi, *Prattica di Musica* (1592); but Morely is the only one of this group known principally for his work as a

composer. This is not to claim a degree of originality for the work
which Morley himself would not have invited, for his debt to various
authorities, especially Zarlino, is considerable; but it is essential to see
A Plaine and Easie Introduction as a landmark; for it both sums up the
teaching achievements of the sixteenth century and indicates the path to
be taken in the seventeenth.

The contribution of other English composers to musical education in
the period immediately following the publication of *A Plaine and Easie
Introduction* should not be overlooked. In 1609 John Dowland (1562–
1626) published his translation of a book by the sixteenth-century
German scholar Andreas Ornithoparcus, published in 1517. In the
introduction Dowland writes as follows:

'My industry and on-set herein if you friendly accept (being now
returned home to remain) shall encourage me shortly to divulge a more
peculiar work of mine own: namely, *My Observations and Directions
concerning the Art of Lute-playing*: which instrument as of all that are
portable, is, and ever hath been most in request, so is it the hardest to
manage with cunning and order, with the true nature of fingering;
which skill hath as yet by no writer been rightly expressed . . .'[4]

In the following year, 1610, his son, Robert Dowland (1586–1641)
published the *Varietie of Lute Lessons* in which the following statement
is to be found in the introduction:

'But whatsoever I have done (until my father hath finished his greater
work, touching the Art of Lute-Playing), I refer it to your judicious
censures, hoping that that love which you all generally have born unto
him in times past, being now grey and like the Swan, but singing
towards his end, you would continue the same to me his son . . .'

The *Varietie of Lute Lessons* contains a selection of lute pieces, mostly
fantasias and dances, 'selected out of the best approved authors, as well
beyond the seas as of our own country', but these are preceded by two
important essays. The title page refers to them as follows: 'Whereunto
is annexed certain observations belonging to Lute-playing; by John
Baptisto Besardo of Visconti. Also a short treatise therunto appertaining: by John Dowland.' This 'short treatise' is apparently the only
further contribution that John Dowland was to make to educational
publishing, although one suspects that 'singing towards his end' or not,
he may have guided the hand of his son in the free translation of the
Besard essay. Whether he felt that the essay in the *Varietie of Lute
Lessons* was sufficient or that he simply tired of his 'greater work' we
may never know.

A year or so later Thomas Campion (1567–1620) published *New Ways in Making Foure Parts in Counter-point*.[5] This consisted of a Preface and three sections, 'Of counter-point', 'Of the tones of music' and 'Of the taking of all concords, perfect and imperfect'. The third section was largely inherited from the *Melopoeia* (1592) of Seth Calvisius (Kalwitz, 1556–1615), who was a director of music at St Thomas Church, Leipzig, for much of his professional life. Campion shares the confidence to be found in all the contemporary publications:

'He that will be diligent to know, and careful to observe the true allowances may be bold in his composition, and shall prove quickly ready in his sight, doing that safely and resolutely which others attempt timorously and uncertainly.' (p. E3iii).

As we shall later observe, this is characteristic not only of the Elizabethans, but a feature to be found throughout the history of textbooks. In each case the author is intent on persuading his clients that with the help of his book remarkable progress can be made by the enthusiastic student.

At the same time that Campion was preparing his book, another English composer, John Cooper, usually known by his Italianized name Giovanni Coperario, or Coprario (*c.* 1570–1626), was writing his *Rules How to Compose*. This text, which is similarly indebted to Calvisius, was never published, but may well have had some limited circulation. Like the *New Ways*, it demonstrated the new seventeenth-century attitude to the teaching of harmony, working extensively with figured-bass ideas.

Thomas Ravenscroft's *A Breife Discourse* (1614) reproduced much of the material to be found in Part One of Morley's book, but it is particularly interesting in the way it is designed. The Dedication occupies three pages; this is followed by six pages of 'Apologie', seven pages of verse, seven pages of preface, twenty-two pages of text, and twenty pages of four-part songs by John Bennet, Edward Piers and Ravenscroft himself. The combination of musical anthology and textbook has already been noted in Robert Dowland's book, and it was to be a characteristic of music publishing for a very long time.

The great importance of these essays is that they help us to understand the growing interest and demand for popular teaching methods in the English language and that they place in perspective some of Morley's ideas. John Dowland is referring to Ornithoparcus when he states that 'Excellent men have at all times in all arts delivered to posterity their observations, thereby bringing Art to a certainty and perfection' (p. A iv), but it could equally apply to Morley or himself; and when he goes on to say '. . . there is nothing can more advance the apprehension of music than the reading of such writers as have both skillfully and diligently set down the precepts thereof' (p. A iv), he is indicating an area of inquiry that is equally important to us. The value of books like Morley's and Dowland's to the modern music teacher is quite different from, say, Playford's. Morley and Dowland are composers of high reputation; what they have to say about the teaching of music is therefore not second-hand, and their ideas about teaching must be given the most serious consideration.

A Plaine and Easie Introduction is dedicated to Morley's own teacher, William Byrd, to whom he refers in the following manner:

'The consideration of this hath moved me to publish these labours of mine under your name, both to signify unto the world my thankful mind, and also to notify unto yourself in some sort the entire love and unfeigned affection which I bear unto you.'[6]

The significance of this close relationship between two musicians who are arguably the greatest composer and the greatest writer on music of their time is apparent in the great command of musical ideas that runs through the book.

The importance of personal contacts between teachers and pupils among composers should never be overlooked, for in music there is so much that cannot be communicated through the medium of words. Examples can be drawn not only from Morley's period (where Italian examples are particularly well known) but throughout the subsequent history of Western European music. Moreover, the sort of evidence that is provided in autobiographical material seems to stress the importance which the younger musician attaches to the personality of his teacher, and to the degree of his influence in matters quite outside the process of acquiring technical skills. Perhaps Morley puts into words the type of ideas that he had encountered as a pupil of William Byrd.

Morley also wishes to make it clear that his teaching is based on his experience of a very wide range of music and contact with a great number of musicians. The 'authorities' he quotes include Josquin, Okeghem, Mouton, Senfl, Clemens, Vecchi, Lassus, de Rore, de Monte, Palestrina, Marenzio, and most of the familiar English names.[7]

The reference to a wide circle of other composers is also found in a most interesting Italian publication, an edition of which appeared in the same year as Morley's book. The author was Girolamo Diruta, and the title 'Il Transilvano; dialogo sopra il vero modo di sonar organi &

instormenti da penna'.[8] The style is similar to Morley's in that Diruta employs the dialogue approach, a discussion between Diruta and Transilvano. Diruta, however, goes further than Morley in citing the works of other composers, for he actually includes examples of toccatas by Merulo, both the Gabrielis, Luzzaschi, Romanini, Quagliati, Bell'hauer and Guami, as well as four of his own works.

The text contains some interesting material on keyboard teaching, and may well be one of the earliest books on teaching keyboard skills. It is, however, very short in comparison with *A Plaine and Easie Introduction*, and does not attempt the comprehensiveness of Morley's book. The format of introduction and substantial musical examples bear obvious comparisons with publications by Robert Dowland and Simpson, and, in the eighteenth century, with those by Geminiani.

Morley writes in what North calls 'his dialogue way of wrighting', a fashion which was not only popular in Morley's time, but was to occur from time to time in later books on music. His intention is clearly to make the course as simple as possible so that his style is 'delivered after a plain and common manner,' (p. 305). The format of master and two pupils does provide the opportunity for plenty of questions to be raised and answered, and although Morley often allows himself to be diverted into the byways of Elizabethan prose, one must agree with him when he says 'my intent in this book hath been to teach music not eloquence' (p. 305).

In a sense, Morley's book is an early example of the Teach Yourself … type of publication which is so popular today, and for that purpose 'to deck a lowly matter with lofty and swelling speech will be to put simplicity in plumes of feathers and a carter in cloth of gold' (p. 305). Perhaps if all such books were of such high standards we could agree with Philomathes when he says to his fellow pupil, Polymathes: 'If my wit were so quick as my master is skilful I should quickly become excellent' (p. 210).

Morley defines his task in a typically straightforward manner: 'to further the studies of them who, being endued with good natural wits and well inclined to learn that divine art of music, are destitute of sufficient masters' (p. 5). Robert Dowland takes up a similar position:

'Take therefore this work of mine in good part, whosoever thou art that readest it, with a mind to profit thyself: yet think not I set it forth to the end to draw thee away from the lively teaching of thy Master (whose speech doth far exceed all writing) or presume to teach those which are masters in the Art these trivial ways, but I offer help to young beginners, and such as oftentimes want a teacher, which it will not be unpleasing for them to use, when they find themselves wearied with those difficulties which lightly befall young learners.'[9]

It is perhapsworth while underlining some of these points: Morley and Dowland are writing for readers 'with a mind to profit' themselves, and can therefore, to use a modern cliché, assume 'motivation'; they do not see their books as substitutes for real teaching, but as available sources when a teacher cannot be found; they have tried to make their books entertaining as well as instructive, and the pace and tone of their books is for the 'young learners'. However tactful such writers may be about their desire not to interfere with the work of other teachers, there can be little doubt that they would also assume that their publications would in fact be used as textbooks by other teachers.

It is perhaps important to stress at this stage that Morley and his fellow writers were not writing for professional musicians. We read that 'when hereafter you shall be admitted to the handling of the weighty affairs of the commonwealth you may discreetly and worthily discharge the offices where unto you shall be called' (p. 299). Here Morley makes an assumption concerning the general values of a musical education which has very important implications, and which we will return to at a later stage.

The full title of Morley's book is, of course, *A Plaine and Easie Introduction to Practicall Musicke*, and it is the practical aspects of music making that he is keen to emphasize. He offers an interesting definition in his annotations to the *First Part*:

'... Music is either speculative or practical. Speculative is that kind of music which, by mathematical helps, seeketh out the causes, proper-ties, and natures of sounds, by themselves and compared with others, proceeding no further, but content with the only contemplation of the art. Practical is that which teacheth all that may be known in songs, either for the understanding of other men's, or making of one's own...' (p. 101).

Although it is clear that Morley's interest is in the latter, there can be no doubt that the Elizabethans still maintained some familiarity with the 'speculative'. John Dowland does not disassociate himself from the following point of view:

'Therefore he is truely to be called a musician, who hath the faculty of speculation and reason, not he that hath only practical fashion of fingering ... He is called a musician which taketh upon him the knowledge of singing by weighing it with reason, not with the futile exercise of practice, but the commanding power of speculation, and wanteth neither speculation nor practice' (*Ornithoparcus*, p. 4).

We may be permitted a faint smile when we also read the following observation, translated without comment by one of the world's greatest instrumentalists: 'For they (which dealeth with instruments) are removed from the intellectual part of music, being but as servants, and using no reason: void of all speculation and following their sense only' (p. 4). It is apparently not only the instrumentalists who are to be regarded merely as 'servants', for under the heading 'Who be called singers' we read: 'The practitioner of this faculty is called a Cantor, who doth pronounce and sing those things which the musician by a rule of reason doth set down' (p. 4).

Since the 1850s there has been a revival of interest in at least one branch of 'speculative' music, and that has been in the area of acoustics.[10] For John Dowland acoustic theory took on a considerable importance:

'Now to place these frets aright, whereby we may make use of these various sounds by them caused, there are two ways: the one is the divine sense of hearing, which those that be skillful do most use ... yet ... the sense of hearing of all others deceiveth most, and cannot discern and judge of the sounds in the smaller intervals ... those sounds must be censured and pondered with natural instruments, and not by the ears, whose judgement is dull, but by wit and reason.'[11]

By 'wit and reason' Dowland is suggesting that a knowledge of acoustics is a valuable possession on the part of the musician; he is very sceptical in any case about the distribution of 'the divine sense of hearing', and suggests that in any group of musicians you will encounter great variations in pitch discrimination. Dowland brings Pythagoras to his support: 'for he would not give credit to man's ears, which are changed partly by nature, partly by outward accidents ...' (p. Diii).

It comes as no surprise to the reader to find that Morley, working as he did in the age of the madrigal and the lute song, devotes a great deal of his attention to the teaching of singing. For Morley, 'practical music' started with singing, as indeed it has done with every generation since. The importance of singing had also been stressed in *The Pathway to Musicke* which had been published a year before Morley's book in 1596. The sub-title proclaims the emphasis: 'An introduction to musicke, how to learn to sing'. This anonymous publication (occasionally linked with Byrd himself) is in question and answer form rather than dialogue form, and contains the following definition: 'Music is a science which teacheth how to sing skillfully; that is, to deliver a song sweetly, truly, and cunningly, by voices or notes, under a certain rule and measure . . .' (p. Aii). It would nevertheless, be wrong to over-emphasize the place of singing teaching in Elizabethan England, for the many instrumental tutors published at the time tend to suggest that playing was of equal significance. In addition to the works by Dowland and Campion already discussed, there are many interesting publications ranging from the early *Brief and Easye Introduction to learne the tablature, to conduct and dispose thy hand unto the lute* by John Alford (1568), which was an English version of one of Adrien Le Roy's treatises, to William Barley's *A new booke of tabliture* (1596), Anthony Holborne's *The cittharn schoole* (1597) and Thomas Robinson's *The schoole of musicke, wherein is taught the perfect method of true fingering of the lute, pandora, orpharion and viol de gamba* (1603). Both Barley and Robinson include in their books additional material for singing; Barley writes 'whereunto is added an introduction to pricksong' and Robinson 'Also a method how you may be your own instructor for pricksong, by the help of your lute, without any other teacher'.[12]

The contribution of Morley and his contemporaries to musical educa-tion was, and is, of considerable proportions. It was, however, imme-diately related to the needs of private lessons rather than the needs of the classroom. This does not mean, however, that their ideas are irrelevant to the school system. On the contrary, unless the classroom teacher can recognize the fundamental importance of these ideas, and adapt class-room conditions to allow these procedures to develop naturally, then the consequent failure to construct a worthwhile musical education must call into question the very existence of music teaching in schools.

From time to time in this book reference will be made to a number of important sources other than those provided by the composers, so that the views of the composers can be seen in a wider context. Particularly important in Morley's period are works like Roger Ascham's *Toxophilus* (1545) and *The Scholemaster* (1570), Sir Thomas Elyot's *The Boke named the Governour* (1531), Sir Thomas Hoby's transla-tion of Castiglione's *Il cortegiano* (1561), Richard Mulcaster's *Positions* (1581) and *Elementarie* (1582), Henry Peacham's *The Compleat Gentleman* (1622), and Richard Braithwaite's *The English Gentleman* (1630), for they show, at least in England, how attitudes to the teaching of music were influenced by social pressures, as well as religious, political and economic factors.

There are many features of Morley's teaching which deserve the very closest attention by anyone concerned with the teaching of music today, not least for the reason that in Morley we may recognize not only a fine composer and a good teacher, but also a man who does not claim infallibility. He writes that '. . . if any man will give me stronger reason to the contrary than those which I have brought for my defence, I will not only change this opinion but acknowledge myself debt-bound to him, as he that hath brought me out of an error to the way of truth' (p. 48), to which Philomathes replies: 'I doubt not but your Master who taught you would think it as lawful for you to go from his opinion as it was for Aristotle to disallow the opinion of Plato with this reason, that Socrates was his friend, and Plato was his friend, but verity was his greater friend' (p. 48).

Let us turn now from the Elizabethan period to the mid-eighteenth century. This is not to suggest that the vast intervening period lacks interest; on the contrary it is full of engaging texts such as Arresti's *Diagolo tra un maestro et un disceplo* (Bologna, 1663), Charpentier's *Règles de composition* (Paris, c. 1692), Locke's various arguments with Thomas Salmon, Couperin's *L'art de toucher le clavecin* (Paris, 1716) and Gasparini's *L'Armonico pratico al cembalo* (Venice, 1708). However, it is clear that if one wishes to see the composers at their best as writers, it is important not to spend too much time with the more minor figures.

2 The Mid Eighteenth Century

Between the years 1752 and 1756 there were published three major contributions to the teaching of music which were not only of great value to the musicians of the second half of the eighteenth century, but are of considerable significance to anyone today who is concerned with the problems of musical education. The first, by Quantz, *Versuch einer Anwisung die Flöte traversiere zu spielen*,[13] was published in 1752 in Berlin. The second, also from Berlin, was C. P. E. Bach's *Versuch über die wahre Art das Clavier zu spielen*,[14] the first volume of which appeared in the following year, 1753. The third was Leopold Mozart's *Versuch einer gründlichen Violinschule*,[15] published in Salzburg in 1756.

When in 1940, in the second year of the Second World War, Willey wrote that 'the eighteenth century can perhaps offer us, not merely escape or refreshment, but even actual guidance in our present troubles',[16] he was suggesting a line of inquiry that is as valuable for us today as it was for him. Our 'present troubles' as far as musical education is concerned are a monumental uncertainty about the objectives of such education, and a consequential uncertainty about the appropriate means to employ in trying to achieve so many varied goals.

Uncertainty is the last thing that these essayists could be accused of.

They see their objectives with amazing clarity, and stride towards them with hardly a look over their shoulders. Where we are indecisive, hesitant, open to discussion, they are single-minded, sure-footed and authoritative; where we are apologetic, insecure and equivocal, they are confident, determined and solid; where we are tolerant of every point of view, they are tolerant only of the informed; where we pursue every byway with equal enthusiasm, they keep to the highway with undivided attention.

What makes the reading of these *Essays* all the more interesting is the fact that they are contemporary with much of the educational writings of Rousseau, whose shadow is so powerfully cast over eighteenth century educational philosophy that most other contemporary voices have been effectively silenced in recent years. Moreover, since Rousseau has been one of the very few modern philosophers who had anything to say about musical education, his ideas have been given what amounts to a rather uncritical attention by his enthusiastic supporters.

Carl Philipp Emanuel Bach (1714–88) and Johann Joachim Quantz (1697–1773) both worked in the court of Frederick the Great of Prussia in the Berlin court, where the reputation of the music was second to none. The English traveller and critic Charles Burney was in no doubt of this when he stated that 'I was impatient to begin my musical inquiries in a place . . . where both theory and practice of music had been more profoundly treated than elsewhere, by professors of great and acknowledged abilities.'[17] In addition to Quantz and Bach, the 'professors' included Agricola, the two Graun brothers, Kirnberger and Marpurg. Not only did they produce important treatises on theory and performance, but also in the case of Marpurg, established the publication of periodicals devoted to the discussion of music. Outside Berlin, other important musical periodicals were produced by Mattheson, Telemann and Scheibe in Hamburg, and by Mizler and Hiller in Leipzig. Graf has written of these men in the following terms:

'The whole development of music, from the Baroque to the Classical period, was accompanied by music critics. Like sappers, they cleared the way by removing the ruins of an obsolete style, and set up signposts at crossroads to indicate the modern way. The portly theoreticians like Mattheson, Marpurg and Scheibe, who were the first music critics in Europe, may seem old-fashioned today. They were slow, profound, combative, quarrelsome, pedantic, conceited and rigid like all dogmatisers. But when they had done their work, trumpeting with the paper trumpets of their magazines, the signals of a new day – nature, reason, clarity, humanity and simplicity – there *was* a new horizon.'[18]

Leopold Mozart (1719–87), the father of Wolfgang Amadeus, was in
Salzburg when his *Essay* was published. All three writers had considerable reputations as teachers throughout Germany and Austria when
their works appeared, and all three were established composers. From
the point of view of the twentieth century there can be no doubt that of
the three, C. P. E. Bach is the most important composer, one whose
stature would appear even greater if he were not the son of the most
powerful figure of the late Baroque.

Quantz is perhaps the least well known as a composer but our
knowledge of his music is growing every day. Of his reputation
Burney says that 'His counsels to young students in Music are built
upon good sense and experience; and though his genius for composition
was not original, he was a keen observer of the beauties and defects of
others, both in composition and performance.'[19] Such an epitaph would
be no mean compliment to a teacher of any generation. Arnold
Dolmetsch calls him 'a philosopher, a deep thinker, and an admirable
teacher'.[20] His *Essay* was well known throughout Europe, and translations of it appeared in French, Italian, Dutch and English. He had
travelled widely and was familiar with most of the musical styles
practised in Europe at that time. Such knowledge led him to the
following conclusion:

'For universal good taste is not to be encountered in single nations, as
each flatters itself; it must be formed and shaped through the mixture
and through the reasonable choice of good ideas and good methods of
playing from different nations. Each nation has in its musical idiom
something both of the agreeable and pleasing, and of the disagreeable.'
(p. 116).

This is clearly not the view of a narrow-minded Berliner!

We have little information about the relationship between Bach and
Quantz in the Berlin court, and when Quantz remarks 'with the permission of my lords the keyboard players' (when he is making a point
about keyboard accompaniments) we have to assume that this is a
smiling reference to his great contemporary (p. 251).

C. P. E. Bach's *Essay* was published in two sections, *Part One* in 1753,
and *Part Two* in 1762, apparently in response to popular demand for
further elaboration of keyboard techniques, especially with reference
to thorough bass and accompaniments. There can be no doubt that, as a
teacher, he felt very strongly about the need to maintain very high
standards in keyboard playing: 'I ask the forbearance of my readers for
repeated mention of divers truths, . . . because I feel that certain
principles cannot be stated too often' (p. 29). The 'divers truths' and

'certain principles' that would lead the pupil to a thorough awareness of the very highest ideals of Bach's techniques are explained with such a wealth of detail and in such a coherent manner that his readers can be left in no doubt about his objectives. For many years, of course, the essays have been used as source books for reliable information on mid-eighteenth-century style. As Mitchell points out in his introduction to Bach's Essay, '. . . Bach presents himself as an analyst. His procedure is to discuss each inflection with relation to its normal behaviour' (p. 14). Such analytical ability is a most valuable asset in any teacher, and when it is accompanied by such a remarkable practical ability as well, we can begin to understand the basis of his reputation. It must be remembered that Bach's Essay appeared some thirty years after Rameau's Traité de l'harmonie, the ideas of which he more or less ignores. But as Mitchell suggests, 'Bach's rejection of Rameau can be traced largely to the fact that the latter had pronounced a *theory*, whereas thorough bass was essentially a *practice*', (p. 17). Bach's teaching can therefore be seen as resulting from his immense understanding of practical problems through years of experience in the best music circles in Europe.

Leopold Mozart (1719–87) published his Essay in 1756, the year in which his son was born at Salzburg. He was perhaps the most important teacher of the violin in Germany and Austria during the middle of the century and his Essay was certainly a successful publication, reaching its third edition by the year of his death, and appearing in Dutch and French translations quite quickly. There can be very little doubt that he was familiar with the Essays of Bach and Quantz, and there are many points in common. Mozart, however, concentrates more intensely on violin technique than Bach does on the keyboard instruments or Quantz on the flute.

As a composer Leopold Mozart's successes were often linked to those of his son, but as the composer of chamber, orchestral and vocal works in the *gallant* style he acquired the compositional experience that was to prove so important to him as a teacher. As is the case with Quantz (and to a lesser extent with C. P. E. Bach), the total picture of Leopold Mozart as a composer remains incomplete.

As has already been pointed out, the Essays have represented important sources of information on interpretation for many years now.[21] They are also valuable introductions to actual techniques for the harpsichord, the flute and the violin.[22] But what makes them of special interest to all those concerned with the problems of musical education is their grasp of problems which are not simply those of the eighteenth century, but are immediately relevant to our present situation.

For this reason substantial reference is made to the three essays throughout this book. It would be wrong, however, not to give some indication at this stage of the range of eighteenth-century sources which relate to musical education. The growth in the publication of teaching material is very marked indeed. Both in England and on the continent publishers seemed very anxious to satisfy a market whose demand was sustained throughout the century.

Perhaps the most important contributions from composers were made during the first half of the century. These include Couperin's *L'art de toucher le clavecin* (1716), Fux's *Gradus ad Parnassum* (1725), Mattheson's several treatises on figured-bass (1719, 1731, 1735), and his *Der Volkommene Kapellmeister* (1739) and Rameau's theoretical works, including the *Traité de l'harmonie* (1722), *Nouveau système de musique théorique* (1726) and *Génération harmonique* (1737).

In the mid-century apart from Tartini's *Trattato di musica* (c. 1754), it is not unreasonable to select Geminiani's English publications as being of special interest, with *The Art of Playing on the Violin* (1751) as the key work. It is ironic that, in contrast with the seventeenth century, the most important English texts should be written by an Italian. Since, however, English composers of the eighteenth century no longer exercised the influence that they had done in the earlier period, it is inevitable that our attention should be mostly confined to the work of continental composers. Nevertheless composers such as William Boyce (1710–90) and Thomas Arne (1710–78) undoubtedly had some influence as teachers; Boyce left a 186-page manuscript treatise on music (which is in the possession of the Royal Institution), and Arne provided the musical examples of *The Compleat Musician* (1760) although the text is definitely by another writer. Charles Avison (1709–70) made an important contribution in the field of musical aesthetics with his *Essay on Musical Expression* (1752), and at the end of the century there are minor contributions by figures like John Calcott (1766–1821) and James Hook (1746–1827) who both commanded some popularity as composers in London.[23]

If we return now to Geminiani we see that he is confident that the music contained in his books will itself instruct the beginner: 'I flatter myself they will find in it whatever is necessary for the institution of a just and regular performer on the violin.'[24] Without apology he goes on to say: 'I have not given any directions for the performing of them [the compositions]; because I think the learner will not need any, the foregoing rules and examples being sufficient to qualify him to perform any music whatsoever.'

Like any other eighteenth-century publication, Geminiani's had several uses: 'This book will also be of use to performers on the violoncello, and in some sort to those who begin to study the art of composition.' This is not the simple commercial gambit that it may appear. The violin parts are, of course, accompanied by figured basses, which provide both interesting 'cello parts and clearly indicated harmonic procedures for the harpsichord. Geminiani clearly shared the idea that a good deal could be learnt about composition through the study and performance of continuo parts.

In another publication, *Rules for Playing in a True Taste*,[25] Geminiani added the sub-title 'on the violin, German flute, violoncello and harpsichord particularly the thorough bass, exemplified in a variety of compositions on the subjects of English, Scotch and Irish tunes'. We must not overlook the emphasis which these writers placed upon the need to study several aspects of music, and in particular that they assumed performance and composition to be twin studies. In the *Preface* to this volume Geminiani shows his knowledge of continuo playing to be as sound as that of Quantz, if not as profound as C. P. E. Bach's:

'Whenever the upper part stops, and the bass continues, he who accompanies must make some melodious variation on the same harmony, in order to awaken the imagination of the performer, whether he sings or plays, and at the same time to give pleasure to the hearer. To conclude I must beg leave to affirm that he who has no other qualities of playing the notes in time, and placing the figures, as well as he can, is but a wretched accompanier' (p. ii).

In the same *Preface* Geminiani further reveals his grasp of the problems of teaching in an amusing aside:

'Indeed those who study with an instinct to please should know the fort and the feeble of the instrument, in order to avoid the error of him, who laboured for a long while to be able to sing play and dance three different airs at once; and being presented to Louis XIV for a wonderful person, that monarch after having seen his performance, said 'what this man does may be very difficult, but is not pleasing' (p. i).

We may share Geminiani's hope that students should learn the 'fort and the feeble' of their instruments, but we might find it impossible to express our ideas with such vigour. In his various texts he offers us the same certainty of manner that we encounter in the *Essays*. As a final example, let us consider his advice to students of composition:

'... although there is not an ordinary performer upon any instrument, in any part of Europe, who does not boast his having composed sonatas, concertos, cantatas etc., yet there are but few modern composers, even of a much higher class, who can be truly said to have produced any thing new with respect to melody, harmony and modulation. What can this be owing to, but imperfect and defective rules? Which instead of guiding the students of harmony, mislead them; instead of assisting, improving, and exalting natural genius, confine and depress it.'[26]

The 'rules' of modulation, which Geminiani then goes on to provide in a most remarkably detailed method, are not, on this occasion, simply the rules of good taste in modulation, but represent a significant analysis of the modulation techniques that were to be employed with growing confidence in the latter half of the eighteenth century. Anton Bemetzrieder, P. J. Fricke and A. F. C. Kollman are examples of other writers who similarly saw modulation as a major enterprise.

A more conventional notion of the rules had been presented by another visiting composer to early eighteenth century London, J. C. Pepusch, the musician who collaborated with John Gay in the production of The Beggar's Opera. Pepusch, under the guise of 'an admirer of this noble and agreeable science', published A Short Treatise on Harmony, 'containing the chief rules for composing in 2, 3 and 4 parts, dedicated to all lovers of music', in 1730. It is a short course in harmony, containing the following definition:

'Composition is that part of music which teaches how to make use of the concords, and of the discords, in a proper manner; so as that the union of the parts shall make good harmony' (p. Bi).

The Beggar's Opera may well have seemed 'modern' to the London theatre, but there was very little in the way of new ideas in A Short Treatise. The use of diagrams and the reference to Guido's Gamut has more of the flavour of the seventeenth century than of the eighteenth. Nevertheless his pupils did include Boyce, Grassineau, Nares and many other musicians whose influence in England was considerable, and we must therefore assume that his teaching was more effective than his writing.

French musical life in the second half of the eighteenth century is curiously paradoxical. After the death of Rameau in 1764, no French composer of similar stature emerged, and yet musical life in Paris continued to flourish, supported by the work of imported composers like Gluck, Piccini, Grétry and Gossec, and a vast quantity of documented argument about the nature of music, or more specifically, opera. This would be of only marginal relevance to our discussion if it were not for the appearance of the encyclopaedias and dictionaries.[27]

The eighteenth century urge towards definition led to the formalization of principles about the nature of music which had important repercussions on nineteenth century thinking about musical education. D'Alembert's and Diderot's twenty-eight-volume *Encyclopédie* (1751–72) employed Rousseau as its principal contributor in the articles on music, although d'Alembert himself also played an important part in this matter.[28] Now the choice of someone who was neither a composer,[29] musical scholar,[30] nor performer can only be regarded as eccentric. Indeed his articles brought him into conflict with Rameau more or less immediately, and are characterized by what has been described as 'a deplorable lack of appreciation of music'.[31]

Rousseau, however, collected his articles together and published his own *Dictionnaire de musique* (Geneva, 1767 and Paris, 1768), and later his *Traité sur la musique* (1781?) published the remainder of his essays. His theories about notation, music as 'heightened speech', and the sole importance of melody, were thus embodied into apparently authoritative contexts.

Waring's English version of the *Dictionnaire* opens with the following words: 'Music is, of all the fine arts, that in which the vocabulary is the most extensive, and for which reason a dictionary is, in consequence, the most useful.' Unfortunately its usefulness was limited by the extent to which it formed a vehicle for Rousseau's propaganda, though it is no less enjoyable to read for that.

Rousseau and Rameau possibly represent the two extremes of the French influence on musical education in the eighteenth century. Where Rousseau, musically untutored and unsophisticated, represents the search for romantic tendencies in both music and education, Rameau is the embodiment of the musical intellectual:

'Music is a science which should have definite rules; these rules should be drawn from an evident principle; and this principle cannot really be known to us without the aid of mathematics. Notwithstanding all the experience I may have acquired in music from being associated with it for so long, I must confess that only with the aid of mathematics did my ideas become clear and did light replace a certain obscurity of which I was unaware before.'

and

'I could not help thinking that it would be desirable (as someone said to me one day while I was applauding the perfection of our modern music) for the knowledge of musicians of this century to equal the beauties of their compositions. It is not enough to feel the effects of a science or an art. One must also conceptualise these effects in order to render them intelligible.'[32]

Rameau believed that 'No rules have yet been devised to teach composition in all its present perfection. Every skilful man in this field sincerely confesses that he owes all his knowledge to experience alone. When he wishes to share this knowledge with others, he is often forced to add to his lessons this proverb, *Caetera docebit usus* (experience will teach the rest)' (p. xxxvi). The *Traité* therefore set out to provide such rules.

In Quantz's *Essay* we are met with a voice that we can immediately recognize:

'If we paid diligent attention to the inclinations of young people, sought to find out how they spontaneously preferred to occupy themselves, and gave them the freedom to choose for themselves that occupation for which they showed the greatest inclination, we would find more happy and truly useful people in the world' (p. 12).

It is the voice of the modern, liberal educationalist: spontaneity, inclination, freedom of choice, happiness; these are all ideas with which we are toiling today. For Quantz, however, freedom to choose always implied knowledge: knowledge of what the choice involved, what learning in a specialized form of knowledge demanded, what society's attitude to its study would be, what, in brief, were its means and its ends.

'Freedom to choose for themselves' must always imply knowledge of the areas of choice. In practice, of course, such freedom is seldom available. Basically, we recognize three choices: modern society (the state) requires *this* sort of man-power to operate, therefore train the child to fit into an appropriate place; or, children behave in *these* patterns, therefore let them grow (naturally?) and see what sort of adults are produced; or thirdly, knowledge of a specialization demands a continuous, directional growth, sustained throughout childhood and adult life.

Quantz, like us, knew that such a choice simply does not exist for most children. How can anyone choose something of which he has no knowledge? How many children are properly introduced to music so that as adults they may exercise a proper choice in the matter? Whichever course is taken, the needs of society, the needs of the child or the needs of the subject, the chances are now, as they were then, that few children are going to be given the possibility of choosing, and many who do choose, do so unwisely.

In whatever way the choice has been made, Quantz now goes on to outline the aims of his *Essay*, which must include 'showing the young people who devote themselves to music how they must proceed' (p. 8). We may compare this with Leopold Mozart's explicit statement of his intention: 'to bring beginners on to the right road and to prepare them for the knowledge of, and feeling for, musical good taste' (p. 225). C. P. E. Bach makes it clear that he is writing for two types of readers, the badly taught adult who still needs proper instruction in the 'foundations of the art', and the beginners, who, with the use of the *Essay*, 'will easily attain a proficiency that they would hardly have believed possible' (p. 29).

It is difficult to be precise in stating at what age the essayists actually recommended that a child should start his musical studies. We know, of course, that C. P. E. Bach began his lessons at an early age with his father, and that the young W. A. Mozart was perhaps the most famous musical child of all time. Quantz also suggests that 'he who wishes to distinguish himself in music must not begin the study of it too late' (p. 24), while Couperin states quite clearly that 'the proper age at which children should begin is from six to seven years'.[33]

This problem poses one of our modern education dilemmas. How can the long-term needs of the child be reconciled with the short-term? If the child who is to learn anything about music cannot be properly taught 'from six to seven years' onwards, how is he to learn at all? The theme of continuity and structure in musical education is one to which the essayists constantly refer.

For the essayists, 'natural gifts' or a 'natural talent' for music were the chief requirements of the beginner. Quantz goes further when he says that:

'Natural gifts are so varied, and are seldom all present in so full a measure in the same person . . . If somebody has the necessary talent for composition, for singing, and for instruments, it may be said, in the most exact sense, that he is born to music' (p. 13).

This division into three skills is characteristic of all three *Essays*, and it is well worth pursuing. The essayists, quite reasonably, make the point that these three aspects of musical education are interdependent. All three demand a singing tone from their instruments, and suggest the use of the voice to help the instrumentalist produce good phrasing and a good tone. All three regard some skill at a keyboard instrument essential for the understanding of harmonic ideas, and compositional abilities are continually referred to. We are all conscious of the lack of balance that has existed in recent music teaching, not only in the schools where the music lesson has often been confined entirely to singing, but also in the conservatoires where composition has often been nothing more than an 'optional extra'.

Gasparini had earlier written in a similar style when he said that:

'You will not deny (whether you are a professional or amateur of music) that to master this noble and beatiful art requires principally three things, namely, resolve, application and a good teacher. But... if a certain natural disposition does not accompany them, the greater part of what is necessary for arriving at the sound practice of correct, well-modulated harmony will be missing ... Of all these things the easiest – and the most difficult – is this natural disposition: easiest, since it is a gift uniquely from God and nature; most difficult ... because at no price is it ever acquired. Resolve is derived easily from one's own direction. Application is the most arduous, since few like to work. A good teacher is the thing most rare, because not all good teachers instruct willingly, not all communicate easily, not all students of music can afford good teachers, nor can these be found everywhere.'[34]

If some are 'born to music', as Quantz remarks, still others are 'useless for music', as Leopold Mozart bluntly put it; he demands that a musician (and especially a string player) shall have a good musical ear: 'If, however, he lacks this, he is useless for music, and it were better he took a wood-axe than a violin in his hand' (p. 62). Such an attitude draws considerable sympathy from many modern teachers, and it is, of course, fundamentally true; but our problem is one of definition. How soon in a child's development is it possible to reach a final statement about the quality of his ear? Can the ear be trained, and if so, how much? Can hard work and perseverance make up for 'natural qualities'? Many research operations have been set up to investigate these questions, but no final satisfactory conclusions have been (some would say, can ever be) drawn.

It is with some force that Quantz turns to the problem of continuous effort on the part of the learner in music:

'No success can be promised to anyone who loves idleness, slothfulness, or other futile things more than music. Many who dedicate themselves to music deceive themselves in this regard. They shrink from the inevitable hardships. They would like to become skilful, but they do not wish to exert the necessary effort. They imagine that music is all pleasure, that to learn it is child's play, that neither physical nor mental powers are needed, that neither knowledge nor experience appertains to it, and that everything depends entirely upon inclination and good natural ability' (p. 18).

Phrases like 'the inevitable hardships', 'necessary effort', 'physical and mental powers', and 'knowledge and experience', may strike a harsh note; they are particularly unpalatable to those who regard music as just 'entertainment' or at best, a mild form of 'self-expression'. But it is a warning that is echoed by all present-day music teachers, for they recognize the essential truth: that if indeed the aim of music may be some form of self-expression (and this is arguable), the means towards achieving such an aim is the whole art, science, craft (or what you will) of music, and that that is a form of knowledge which cannot be acquired as a 'diversion', without the 'inevitable hardships'. Following his point, Quantz goes on to ask:

'Is it not a point common to all sciences ... that without knowledge of them we may also find no pleasure in them? Who can say, for example, whether he would ever have acquired a taste for trigonometry or algebra, if he had learned nothing about them? It is with knowledge and insight that esteem and love for a subject grow' (p. 23).

Knowledge and insight, knowledge and experience, knowledge and taste, knowledge and imagination: these are the themes to which Quantz continually returns, and with which he constantly challenges his readers.

The study of the eighteenth-century composers' views on musical education are important to us in a number of ways, not least among which is the contrast which they form to the more familiar educational ideas of most of the influential thinkers from Locke to Kant. Locke's unsympathetic attitudes hardened into the sort of alienation which was expressed by Lord Chesterfield: 'A taste of sculpture and painting is in my mind as becoming as a taste of fiddling and piping is unbecoming a man of fashion. The former is connected with history and poetry, the latter, with nothing that I know of but bad company.'[35]

Nor was this attitude confined to England. Lecturing in Könisberg towards the end of the century, Kant stated that: 'Some accomplishments are essentially good for every-body – reading and writing, for instance; others, merely in the pursuit of certain objects, such as music, which we pursue in order to make ourselves liked.'[36]

This extraordinary statement is accompanied by other remarkable observations:

'If we estimate the worth of the Beautiful Arts by the culture they supply to the mind, and take as a standard the expression of the faculties which must concur the judgement for cognition, Music will have the lowest place among them (as it has perhaps the highest among those arts which are valued for their pleasantness), because it merely plays with sensations.'[37]

It is perhaps not too improbable to suggest that Kant's experience of music had perhaps been coloured by his exposure to the noise of music (while he was working on the *Critique*?) rather than to music itself:

'. . . there attaches to music a certain want of urbanity from the fact that chiefly from the character of its instruments, it extends its influence further than is desired (in the neighbourhood), and so as it were obtrudes itself, and does violence to the freedom of others who are not of the musical company' (p. 220).

The musician therefore needs to examine the work of Quantz, C. P. E. Bach, Leopold Mozart and their colleagues with the utmost care. Their ideas embody a complete refutation of the popular conceptions of eighteenth-century musical education, and are of major importance to modern readers.

3 The Nineteenth Century

The nineteenth century is perhaps the most obvious period in which one would expect to find a considerable body of literature coming from composers about the teaching of music. Weber, Schumann, Berlioz, Wagner and Wolf all devoted a great deal of their creative energy to writing, and many other composers committed themselves to prose in a variety of ways.

Carl Maria von Weber (1786–1826) contributed articles and music criticism for many periodicals and newspapers[38] and, like Robert Schumann (1810–56), he also wrote for the famous Leipzig *Allgemeine musikalische Zeitung* which had been established in 1798; but the latter was more closely associated with *Neue Zeitschrift für Musik* which began circulation in 1834. Hector Berlioz (1803–69) wrote regularly for many French periodicals,[39] and some of this material reappeared in more permanent form in a number of books. The *Voyage musical en Allemagne et en Italie* and the *Études sur Beethoven, Gluck et Weber* both date from 1843; later came the collection of essays entitled *Les Soirées de l'orchestre* (1853), *A travers chants* (1862), and the *Mémoires* (1870). The only specifically pedagogic work was the famous *Traité de l'instrumentation et d'orchestration modernes* (1841).

Richard Wagner (1813–83) contributed to a number of periodicals in his younger days, but he was later to repudiate musical journalism altogether, and his chief writing is to be found in the vast group of literary works published as a collected edition of ten volumes in German between 1871 and 1885.[40] Among the most important essays in this collection (the ideas of which Wagner returned to again and again) are *Die Kunst und die Revolution, Das Kunstwerk der Zukunft*, and *Oper und Drama*.

Our respect for Wagner in terms of his musical innovations may lead us to expect too much of his prose works. The reader frequently encounters this sort of dense writing:

'If, therefore, music withdraws those portions of the world of phenomena that are nearest related to it into its own peculiar region of dreams, it does this only in such wise that, by means of a wonderful antecedent transformation, the perceptive cognition may, as it were, be turned inwards, where it is now enabled to grasp the essential nature of things, in its most immediate manifestations, and thus, in a manner, to interpret the dream-image which the musician himself beheld in deepest sleep. It is impossible to offer anything more lucid . . .'[41]

No doubt it suffers in translation, but the type of comprehension problem which it poses is found so often in Wagner's writing that it is difficult to reach a very clear impression of its value. As Stravinsky points out, 'he labours mightily to be explicit, but achieves only laboriousness'.[42] He often leans heavily upon the philosophical work of Schopenhauer, whose considerable interest in, and concern for music separates him from Kant and the philosophers of the eighteenth century. However, Wagner seems incapable of Schopenhauer's relative clarity, and in certain respects (which will be discussed later) may be said to have mis-represented Schopenhauer's attitude to music to a significant extent.

It is regrettable that Wagner, supported by Liszt and Wolf, wasted so much time and effort in the attacks on Brahms and his colleagues. Hugo Wolf (1860–1903) worked for a period as music critic for *Solonblatt* in Vienna. Typical of his attacks on Brahms is the following, an extract from his article on Brahms's *Third Symphony*: 'He is a proficient musician who knows his counterpoint, to whom occur ideas now and then good, occasionally excellent, now and then bad, here and there familiar, and frequently no ideas at all.'[43] Today it is possible to admire the work of both Brahms and Wagner without any feeling of conflict.

Perhaps it was Tchaikovsky who best expressed the nature of the Wagner problem:

'I know you are no great admirer of Wagner, and I too am far from being a desperate Wagnerite. I am not very sympathetic to Wagnerism as a principle. Wagner's personality arouses my antipathy, yet I must do justice to his great musical gift.'[44]

It is regrettable also that so little can be learnt about Wagner's music from his prose. As Honegger has pointed out, 'his literary output is considerable, but he reveals nothing in it which touches at all closely on musical composition . . . about his methods as a musician we know nothing'.[45]

It is reasonable, then, to see most of Wagner's prose works as 'only skilful propaganda',[46] and Berlioz's so full of personal anecdotes as to be of only marginal interest in the present discussion. There is, however, a vitality about the latter's prose which occasionally helps us to see a problem from a different point of view. Speaking of the Paris revival of Gluck's *Alceste* in 1861, he stated:

'I incline to think that an appreciable portion of our public is now more capable than formerly of understanding a work of this kind. On the one hand, musical education has made some progress; and, on the other, even if only by dint of indifference, people no longer experience the same dislike for the beautiful.'[47]

There can be no doubt that post-Rousseau French musical education was making some progress, but Berlioz would be the last person to take it very seriously. What we can learn from Berlioz is the direct approach: 'No doubt it is difficult. But art consists in conquering difficulties; and otherwise, what would be the object of study?' (p. 17). Or again: 'It was also requisite to turn a deaf ear to the recriminations of such people as were interested in showing themselves hostile to the revival of great works of art which they dread, as, immediately upon their production, the intelligent public begin to make crushing comparisons' (p. 1).
It is a pity, perhaps, that Berlioz could not find time in his already crowded life to provide more teaching material than his *Traité*, for such a vigorous style would have much to recommend it in the world of musical education.

In the field of textbooks on composition, however, it was not to composers like Schumann, Berlioz, Wagner and Weber that the student looked, but to figures whom we no longer first recognize as composers, although they were undoubtedly so looked upon in their own day. I refer to J. G. Albrechtsberger (1736–1809), who principally interests us as the teacher of Beethoven; to J. G. Weber (1779–1839); and to A. J. Reicha (1770–1836).

Albrechtsberger's *Gründliche Answeisung zur Composition* (Vienna, 1790) was sufficiently popular in the early nineteenth century to be reprinted in Germany in 1818, and to reach England by 1834 in a translation by Arnold Merrick under the title *Methods of Harmony, Figured Bass, and Composition, Adapted for Self-instruction*. It is interesting to note that the English delight in 'self-instruction', firmly established by the Elizabethans, was still recognized by nineteenth-century publishers. This publication appeared in two volumes, with the text in the first, and the musical examples in the second. It is solidly eighteenth-century in its approach, proclaiming on the first page that 'the study of figured base [*sic*] is the first step to the study of composition in several parts', and teaches counterpoint in the Fux manner.

Gottfried Weber's *Versuch einer geordneten Theorie der Tonsetzkunst* (Mainz, 1821) is quite different. Replacing the figured-bass approach with post-Rameau fundamental bass ideas, Weber systematically analyses the harmonic language of Beethoven and his contemporaries. However, after nearly nine hundred pages of closely packed rules and advice, we reach the heading 'To invent a piece of music without anything being given'. Weber then goes on to write:

'The exercises naturally preliminary to this problem having been pretty thoroughly canvassed in what precedes, we may now venture with some degree of certainty upon the business of inventing a piece of music entirely from our own resources – of composing a piece.'[48]

Perhaps Weber shared the exhaustion that his readers would inevitably have experienced at this stage of the course, for he was only able to make two suggestions at this point: either to write a tune and then treat it as a harmony exercise, or alternatively to devise a chord sequence, and write a melody over it.

The first translation into English appears to have been undertaken not in the British Isles, but in the United States, in 1841–2 at Boston, as *The Theory of Musical Composition Treated with a View to a Naturally Consecutive Arrangement of Topics*, translated by J. F. Warner. The interest of the New England intellectuals was sufficient to produce a reprint, and a London edition appeared in 1846. It was apparently in such demand that another publisher employed John Bishop (who was involved in many translations of early nineteenth-century music texts) to edit Warner's translation (while comparing it with the original German text). This 'expanded' edition came out in 1851.

Bishop also edited Merrick's translation of Reicha's *Cours de composition musicale* (Paris, 1818), which was published in London in 1854 as a *Course of Musical Composition*. Born in Prague, Anton Reicha had been an early associate of Beethoven, but his chief influence derived from his long period of teaching in the Paris Conservatoire.

Among the brief, but extremely valuable, contributions by other composers of the period may be mentioned the work of three interesting figures of the early part of the century: Johann Hummel (1778–1837), who studied at times with Haydn, Mozart and Clementi; Louis Spohr (1784–1859), the violin virtuoso; and Carl Czerny (1719–1857), a pupil of Beethoven and a teacher of Liszt. The fame of all three composers was international during their lifetime; it was then all but obliterated by the reaction that set in during the height of the Romantic era. Later generations could not understand how their predecessors could have been so lacking in judgement to have placed these men on the same level as, or in some cases a higher level than, Beethoven. They therefore overcompensated by neglecting a considerable body of music that certainly justifies the revival of interest which is taking place at the present time.

Hummel's ideas on teaching are contained in his *Complete Theoretical and Practical Course of Instructions* (1827), Spohr's in his *Violin School* (1831), and Czerny's in his *Complete Theoretical and Practical Pianoforte School* (1839), his *School of Practical Composition* (1839), and his *Letters to a Young Lady on the Art of Playing the Pianoforte* (1848). To the same period belongs Cherubini's *A Course of Counterpoint and Fugue* (1837), the ideas of which were to be amusingly attacked by Berlioz, who describes his various encounters with the Director of the Paris Conservatoire in his autobiographical writing.[49]

Two interesting works by Russian composers are Tchaikovsky's *Guide to the Practical Study of Harmony* (1871), written while he was professor of composition at the Imperial Conservatory of Moscow (1866–78) and Rimsky-Korsakov's *Principles of Orchestration*, the first complete edition of which was not published until 1912, but which had been intermittently compiled over the previous twenty years. Tchaikovsky's is rather a dull little harmony textbook showing only too clearly that his heart was not in his teaching.[50] Rimsky-Korsakov's work on the other hand ranks with the major works on orchestration by Berlioz, Forsyth and Piston.

In Vienna, Anton Bruckner (1824–96) carried out a certain amount of teaching which has lead to the publication of a useful book containing some of his principal ideas in relation to the teaching of harmony.[51]

It is a more interesting document than Tchaikovsky's, for it contains many indications of Bruckner's own stylistic ideas. Since it was not published in Germany until half a century after the composer's death, and since no English translation has yet become available, it is difficult to estimate the influence that Bruckner has exercised as a teacher.

The full force of the contribution to teaching of English composers was not seen until the twentieth century, when the work of men like Stanford and Parry can be seen in the context of the efforts of Holst and Vaughan Williams. The contribution of William Sterndale Bennett (1816–75), however, is an interesting aspect of the English revival. As Principal of the Royal Academy of Music (1866–75) and Professor of Music in the University of Cambridge (1856ff) he made a vital contribution to the revitalizing of standards in English musical education. The composer's son describes in his biography the sort of situation that Bennett faced in Cambridge:

'In the musical profession, University degrees had for some time been regarded as of no great value, by some even as things to be avoided. Scurrilous suggestions had often been admitted into musical papers, and those who mixed in musical circles often heard doubts expressed in conversation as to the methods by which such distinctions had been obtained . . . It was therefore desirable that the Professor's negotiations with candidates should be conducted with a certain amount of public formality.'[52]

Sterndale Bennett took very seriously his University and Academy work, as indeed he did his work in connection with the examination of music in schools. He was associated from the start with the Cambridge Local Examinations paper in the 'Grammar of Music', putting aside a few days every year for marking papers. It is, of course, possible to argue that these varied educational activities were carried out at the expense of his work as a composer, but it should be noted that the publication of four piano concertos, a symphony, four overtures and a considerable body of piano music was no small achievement for a nineteenth-century Englishman, and that Robert Schumann thought well enough of him to write several reviews of his works, and to go so far as to mention him in the same context as Mendelssohn: 'I look upon Mendelssohn as the first musician of the age, and pay him the homage due to a master . . . Bennett follows in his footsteps.'[53]

Charles Stanford (1852–1924) and Hubert Parry (1848–1918) both exercised considerable influence in English musical education in the latter part of the century. Their careers were remarkably similar in many ways. Stanford was a Cambridge graduate who went on to become Professor there in 1887, and was Professor of Composition at the Royal College of Music from 1883. Parry was an Oxford graduate who became Professor in Oxford in 1900, having become Director of the Royal College in 1894. Like Sterndale Bennett before them, they combined the roles of composer and teacher for much of their working lives, and helped to lay the foundations in both these fields for the major revival that took place in the early twentieth century.

Both composers published books which, although they did not appear until the early years of the twentieth century, clearly reflect the attitudes to music that were characteristic of the later nineteenth century. Parry's *Evolution of the Art of Music* (1893) and *Style in Musical Art* (1900) are frankly wedded to the idea of 'progress' in the arts, and his study of *Bach* (1909) is very much a part of the English/ Mendelssohn view of Bach as a great romantic. Stanford's *Musical Composition* (1911) is possibly a more valuable contribution to teaching, and in relatively few pages affirms many of the principles that we have already encountered in the writings of composers. The view that 'composers are usually reticent as to their methods and experiences, probably because they are too much immersed in creative work to analyse the means which enabled them to write it' (p. i), is one that is common enough, but Stanford achieves his objective of outlining the problems of composition to students with a fair degree of success.[54]

In his autobiography, Stanford shows very clearly how society's attitude to music had undergone a significant change in the nineteenth century: 'After 1875 the atmosphere began to change; the entry of many of my colleagues who were public school and university men into the profession could scarcely fail to raise the standard of music as well as the status of its adherents.' During his professional career he had:

'witnessed a revolution in the quality of the work and in the appreciation of the workers which, at times resisted by short-sighted contemporaries who held that art was only possible in the ranks of Bohemian ignoramuses, and as sturdily fought for by those of wider views and more cosmopolitan experience, must have its effect upon future generations and be rated by them at its true value.'[55]

Stanford's social views, do, of course, raise many questions. The main point, however, is unmistakable: the English upper classes were slowly beginning to change their minds about the place of the musician in society, and were now even ready to believe that a musician could be regarded as an educated person. Thus the English Victorian musical

revival saw educational ideas working hand in hand with new developments in composition, and new standards of performance. Stanford,
however, did not see the improvement in facilities as the only improvement urgently required: 'The lot of the music student in this country
at the present day is a much smoother one than that of his predecessors
of forty years ago . . . It remains to be seen whether the smoothing of
early difficulties will result in a race of hardy men' (p. 138). 'The 'hardy
men' – Elgar, Vaughan Williams, Holst, Britten and the rest – must
surely be seen as fulfilling Stanford's hopes, but another problem that
he raised is still unresolved. Stanford felt that a society should first be
given the facilities to make music – concert halls, opera houses and the
like, not just in London, but in every major city (as on the Continent) –
and then should establish the colleges and schools to supply recognized
demands. He felt, therefore, that the problem was being tackled the
wrong way round, but one wonders what other solution was possible
in a country which had neglected music so seriously in the previous
century.

The relationship of the idea of the critic and the idea of the teacher is
very absorbing. There have been many factors which have led to
making the music critic a figure of fun: it is only too easy to point to
past evaluations of works and contrast them with present day evaluations. It is also easy to confuse the role of the journalist-critic, with his
deadlines to meet, with the more elaborate and time consuming processes of the academic critic. Nevertheless, there is a sense in which, in
at least one aspect of their work, critics and teachers share a common
task, and that is in attempting to bring the listener and the music closer
together.

Notwithstanding their personal prejudices, the composer-critics of
the nineteenth century achieved this objective with a remarkable degree
of success. Their critical works form an important instrument of
teaching throughout the period, and it is a period in which the growth
of a concert-going public is very substantial indeed. In London alone
the demand for concerts led to the use of the Hanover Square Rooms,
the St James's Hall, and the enormous Albert Hall.

Nevertheless, one cannot fail to recognize that the direct rôle of
composer as teacher is one that is less apparent in the nineteenth century
than in the seventeenth and eighteenth. Two factors of a very obvious
nature contribute to this situation. The first is that the composers
themselves tended to see their role in society as somewhat different
from that of their predecessors. The idealization of the 'artistic genius'
concept led the composer away from what he thought to be the more

servile role of the teacher. Secondly, the development of state education systems in many parts of Europe led to the development of a new teaching profession in which the teaching of music was often put in the hands of people specially prepared as music teachers, and who were not composers or performers in the previously accepted sense.

The responsibility of the *Kapellmeister* (who, contrary to popular impression, continued to function for much of the century) changed from the eighteenth-century form of the composer-performer-teacher, to the mid-nineteenth-century conductor type. The growth and wide availability of orchestral music meant that court conductors might easily find their time consumed by the necessity of familiarizing themselves not only with the composition of their own countrymen, but also with the works of foreign composers and, most important, with the works of composers of the *past*. Many composers, therefore, chose not to be employed in circumstances that would seriously curtail their active composing.

Moreover, where there was a need to supplement their income from composition, more lucrative possibilities presented themselves, i.e. as instrumental virtuosi, and as conductors; Chopin and Liszt on the one hand, and Berlioz and Wagner on the other are obvious examples. Further, many composers of the period shared fundamental doubts about the value of, or indeed the possibility of, teaching composition at all, since, in their view, composers might be said to emerge from society by some process not unlike a volcanic eruption, and certainly not by any growth process which could be assisted by a teacher. There was, in any case, a marked conflict between the 'revolutionary' composers and the academic establishment which tended to prevent the former from becoming associated with teaching on any serious level.

The idea of the growth of a music-teaching profession unconnected with composers is one that demands our attention. Any preliminary investigation of the music-teaching methods of the nineteenth century will not bring the reader face to face with the works of the composers, but with the ideas of J. H. Pestalozzi (1746–1827), developed musically by Michael Pfeiffer and H. G. Naegeli; with the ideas of Jean-Jacques Rousseau, especially through the work of Galin, Chevé, and Paris; with L. G. B. Wilhem, Joseph Mainzer, W. E. Hickson, John Hullah, Sarah Glover and John Curwen (all of whose writings are to be found in the Bibliography). The apparent isolation of the composer and the growth of an independent teaching profession is a situation which will be examined in the course of this book. However, it is enough to point out at this stage the obvious contrast between nineteenth-century attitudes and those of the period preceding it. Whereas composers of the earlier period were inevitably drawn into the teaching process, as they were to every aspect of music-making, the composers of the generations succeeding Beethoven found themselves in a position that was very different. The changed situation was one that was to have consequences not only upon their work as composers, but, as we shall see, also upon the nature of music teaching itself.

In the context of nineteenth-century ideas about teaching and learning in music, some may feel surprise that Robert Schumann should be cited as a central figure, for he produced no complete work in the field, and would not have regarded himself as having made any serious contribution to teaching. As a composer-critic, however, his rôle in the apprehension of fundamental principles in musical education and in sound practical advice to those learning basic musical skills is strikingly significant. Schumann's position may, without major distortion, be compared with that of the poet Coleridge, whose work in the field of the education of the literary imagination has been clearly recognized in our own time.[56] Both Schumann and Coleridge bring to their criticism that quality of imagination which illumines the obscure and encourages the beginner. They gain from their individuality as composer and poet a freshness and subtlety of approach which separates them from routine procedures in criticism.

Schumann was himself aware of the type of contribution that the literary critics were making: 'The person who is unacquainted with the best things among modern literary productions, is looked upon as uncultivated. We should be at least as advanced as this in music.'[57] Unfortunately, little has happened to change this position in the period since Schumann's death. Today's raised eyebrows challenge ignorance about the modern theatre, the modern cinema and the modern novel; but ignorance about modern music is almost socially approved. This is, of course, one of the inevitable consequences of an education which is not only language-based, but language-dominated at every level.

Schumann worked for ten years as a critic and editor for the *Neue Zeitschrift für Music* (1835–44), and during this time considered the claims of over eight hundred compositions. Although the level of his concentration is variable, his attitude is always serious: 'Critics and reviewers are not alike; the former stands nearer to the artist, the latter to the mechanic' (I, p. 83).

The 'mechanical' is a characteristic of musicianship that Schumann is utterly opposed to, and it is a characteristic of teaching and learning in music that we may equally regard with suspicion. For Schumann, the musician – whether as performer, composer or critic – must constantly develop his musical imagination, and be alive to the individual identity of musical ideas. He was fond of saying that true criticism can only come from creative minds, and in agreeing with this view today, many would go on to support the additional view that true teaching can also only emerge from creative minds. In underlining the parallels between criticism and teaching, one is pointing to essential conjunctive intentions of the critic and the teacher: between the critic and the reading public on the one hand, and between the teacher and his pupils on the other. In both cases the objectives are the same, that is to bring the music and the public/pupil closer together. In this process Schumann possessed some of the most important qualities that we look for in both the critic and the teacher – disinterest, detachment, objectivity, coupled with enthusiasm, affection and knowledge.

The once popular view that 'the greatest composers have made the greatest blunders in estimating the relative value of each other's work'[58] is simply not true of Schumann. No doubt he thought more of Mendelssohn than we do today, no doubt he could occasionally dismiss with contempt music that seemed unimaginative to him – 'Had I enemies, I would annihilate them in forcing them to listen to music like this. The dullness . . . is indeed extraordinary' (II, p. 449); but he scored so many critical bull's-eyes, especially with Chopin, Berlioz and Brahms, that one must in the end surely come to admire his judgement.

It must be remembered that, in drawing the attention of the German public to the qualities of the *Symphonie Fantastique* of Berlioz, Schumann was relying very heavily on his own judgement. His German readers were in any case suspicious of anything French; the French establishment, in the person of no less a figure than F. J. Fétis, author of the *Biographie universelle des musiciens*, had reacted unfavourably, and the initial purpose of the *Neue Zeitschrift* was, at least in part, to attack the French school. Schumann was able to see the virtues of a work that was very adventurous for its time, and to stand by his opinion. The teacher of music does not, of course, very often find himself confronted by such demanding individuality, but he should, at least in theory, be prepared to recognize and accommodate the unusual in his teaching. It is not necessary, here, to think of the extreme cases, the potentially brilliant instrumentalist, singer or composer; simply to recognize that any group of children demands a variety of methods and ideas, and that the teacher must constantly strive to provide for the individual case. 'The more remarkable and artistic a work is, the more carefully we should judge it' is Schumann's view (I, p. 234); the teacher must apply similar standards, although he will be aware, as Schumann was himself, that it is more difficult to be constructive about work that he admires than to be critical of work that appears inadequate. In an article about a concerto by Field, Schumann could only say 'We are delighted with it, can do nothing more reasonable about it than to praise it endlessly' (I, p. 267). Obviously there will be times when this is all the teacher can do also, but the intention, at least, must always be constructive and forward looking.

It is the experience of most teachers that it is not always possible for them to recapture the excitement that they themselves experienced when they first encountered a great work of art. Yet such excitement is the very quality that they would wish to communicate to those new to the music. Schumann said, 'we regard that criticism as the highest which leaves behind it an impression resembling that awakened by its subject' (I, p. 333). This is equally true for teaching, and must be the objective of every teacher, even though repetition may tend to blunt the enthusiasm. It is as well to remember in this context, however, that there is enough outstandingly good music available today to ensure that the teacher need only repeat his teaching of particular works if he actually chooses to do so.

Schumann was very aware of the problem that the musician faces when he wishes to explain a musical matter to someone in other than purely musical terms:

'In no other art is demonstration so difficult as in music. Science fights with mathematics and logic; poetry wields the golden, decisive, spoken word; other arts have chosen Nature, whose forms they borrow, as their judge, – but music is an orphan, whose father and mother none can name; and perhaps in the mystery of her origin lies half her charm' (I, p. 332).

This element of mystery is an idea that is strong in many writers about music, and Schumann was no doubt aware of Schopenhauer's belief that music was essentially non-representational. Nevertheless, he does attempt to show the kind of ways that the writer or teacher can employ:

'I prefer to go through it . . . according to the four main points of view from which one can consider music, i.e. according to form (of the whole, movements, periods and phrases), according to musical composition (harmony, melody, setting, elaboration, style), according to the special idea the composer intends to convey, and according to the spirit that rules over form, material, and idea alike.'[59]

This important summary of techniques shows very clearly the way Schumann approached the problem of criticism, and how close it is to teaching. The analysis of form is in depth, as is the discussion of the techniques of melody writing and harmony. The 'special idea' refers only to music with a title or programme, and is a matter to which Schumann devoted a lot of thought, concluding generally that he didn't mind knowing the title *after* he had heard the music, so long as he could form his first impressions exclusively about the music. The last, and most important, quality that Schumann looked for was the 'spirit' or imaginative qualities of the music, the 'end' to which the 'means' were directed.

It is easy to overlook the fact that before the age of the gramophone or radio the great problem that the critic faced was one of description. Since only those people who had actually attended the concert in which the subject of the criticism was performed would have heard the music, the first demand on the critic was to describe what he had heard. Schumann felt that such description could either take the form of analysis in strictly musical terms, or be more poetic in nature by attempting to produce verbal images parallel in spirit with the music images contained in the work. A similar situation relates to most art criticism of the nineteenth century. The critic who has seen a painting or sculpture in Florence and wishes to draw to it the attention of his readers in London who have not seen it (and who live in a pre-photographic age) has first to describe the object which he wishes to evaluate.

Schumann regarded this situation with a very great deal of concern, and on many occasions wrote that he wished that he could provide his readers with the actual music so that they could more easily grasp the point that he wished to make about the piece. Fundamentally Schumann saw his principal task as one of bringing his readers' attention to music that he thought was worthy of their attention. For, as he often pointed out, 'it is the listener's duty to find out what a piece contains' (I, p. 233). As far as titles and descriptions are concerned, 'as time passed, Schumann apparently became convinced that if the music itself is really communicative, there is no need for either of them'.[60]

The relationship of these ideas to the teaching of music are apparent in the following ways. First, the teacher's duty is to bring to the attention of the child music which the teacher believes to be worthwhile and which he believes to be appropriate to the needs of the child. Secondly, whether the child is performing the music himself, or listening to others perform it, the teacher cannot do the child's listening for him, nor should he attempt to force the child's mind to follow identical patterns to his own. A piece of music that is worth listening to exists on many levels, and the child's intuitive grasp of the music may take place at any one of these levels. Analysis and description are means to help the listener listen, not just to the parts, but to the whole.

Many teachers of music make the mistake of limiting the child's listening to music which has some sort of verbal attachment, either in the form of a song, or a descriptive title, or a programme. Schumann felt that 'it is not a good sign in a piece of music when we discover that it absolutely needs an explanatory heading; for then we think it is less likely to have sprung from inward depths, than to have been called into being by some outwardly exciting cause' (II, p. 422). If we wish children to learn to understand the 'inward' experiences of music, and not simply the external and the superficial, then it is obvious that we will not help them to do so by bringing them up to see music as a form of illustration.

Schumann's contribution to our understanding of the processes of learning in music covers a very wide field, and his ideas will be found in most of the following sections of this book. He offers plenty of detailed advice on many musical matters, but it is perhaps his ability to get quickly to the heart of a problem that we may most admire:

'At the bottom of all misunderstanding, the unaccustomed novelty of new forms and expression is perhaps the chief hindrance. Too many persons lay stress on details when they first hear a work, with the same result as with the reading of a difficult handwriting; he who, in deciphering it, holds too much to the meaning of every word, needs more time, obtains less results, than he who glances over the whole at once, in order to obtain an idea of its meaning and contents' (I, p. 233).

In order to place the ideas of Schumann and the other nineteenth-century composers in a clearer light, it becomes necessary to compare them not only with the work of professional music teachers already referred to, but also with the contributions of a number of other important writers who have strongly influenced the way we think about music, and consequently the way we teach it. Particularly significant are Arthur Schopenhauer,[61] the philosopher, Edward Hanslick,[62] the music critic, and Edmund Gurney,[63] the psychologist. In the later chapters of this book we shall look more closely at their ideas, together with the suggestions of some less substantial figures.

The nineteenth century is the period in which the pattern of state education was formed in many countries. In the field of music education it is a pattern which is still observable in many schools today. It is therefore very important for us to try to understand the way the pattern was formed, and the consequences of the failure of society to implicate the composer fully in the educational system.

4 The Twentieth Century

If the influence of the nineteenth-century composer in musical education may chiefly be seen in the context of his rôle as composer-critic,
then the contribution of the composer in the first half of the twentieth
century is arguably that of the composer-teacher. This should not suggest, however, that composers gave up their established association
with musical criticism, but rather that their most profound influence in
education resulted from the direct contribution many composers made
as teachers, both in universities and schools.

Indeed the composer who did not teach at one time or another in
this period was very rare. As Gustav Holst pointed out, 'In the music
profession nearly everyone has to teach. The reason is an economic one
– there is a larger demand for teachers than for singers and players.'[64]
While there is undoubtedly some truth in this view, it must not be
overlooked that Holst himself chose to continue teaching at St Paul's
Girls School long after he needed to from a financial point of view, and
that many others, of whom Carl Orff and Zoltán Kodály are the most
obvious examples, deliberately established a firm position in musical
education.

As a consequence of their experience as teachers, many composers
produced major contributions in the field of text-books, but this was
only one way in which their ideas were made generally available.
Several composers carried out pioneer work in making traditional folk
songs available to children, as for example Vaughan Williams and
Holst did in Britain, and Bartók and Kodály in Hungary. Others wrote
works especially for performance by children, including Britten and
Holst in Britain and Weill and Copland in the United States, to cite
only the most obvious examples; still others composed works especially
for child audiences – Prokofiev and Dohnányi; while Orff, through
Das Schulwerk, provided a complete framework for instrumental
improvisation in the classroom.[65]

The vast expansion of educational facilities in the first half of the
twentieth century provided many opportunities for composers to take
part in teaching. This they did with varying degrees of enthusiasm:
there was undoubtedly some expression of regret that composing did
not normally seem able to provide the composer with a steady income,
and that he was therefore forced to look round for part-time employment. In addition to teaching, many composers found opportunities in
conducting, performing, and criticism, both journalistic and academic.
If an occasional atmosphere of nostalgia crept into their remarks on this
subject, it was, in the long term, balanced by the realization not only
that composers in the past had nearly always seen composition as only

one aspect of their varied musicianship (although inevitably the principal aspect), but also that the virtues of a situation which brought the composer into close contact with other people making, and thinking about, music were of a very high level. If the pattern of composing, performing, conducting, teaching and reviewing can be seen as the general pattern of musicianship, and indeed the general objective of a musical education, then the composers of this period may be seen as fulfilling ideal requirements.

Any discussion of the composers' contribution to musical education in this period must inevitably recognize the impact which political factors had on European musical life. In this very complex field it need only be noted at this point that the situation in Europe not only led to the continued interruption of the normal channels of communication between European composers and teachers, but also that the apparent isolation of many leading European figures in their adopted country, the United States (including Stravinsky, Schoenberg, Bartók, Hindemith and Milhaud), had repercussions not only in American education (and by their absence, on European education), but most importantly, on the lives of the composers themselves.

The sources of the study of composers' ideas on teaching and learning in musical education in this period may conveniently be divided into two categories: in the first, essays, articles, letters, teaching material and biographical information; in the second, musical material designed for teaching purposes. The material in both categories is extensive, and there is therefore some need to select only the most important aspects of the subject. Since this involves the discussion of the ideas of such differing personalities as Stravinsky, Schoenberg, Bartók, Busoni, Hindemith, Kodály, Orff, Copland, Holst and Vaughan Williams, there is very little danger of such selection producing a distorted picture of the period.

In very many ways the period is dominated by Igor Stravinsky (1882–1971), in spite of the fact that he was not a teacher,[66] nor did he write any textbooks, nor, apart from some early piano duets, did he compose any music with children specifically in mind. Perhaps no other composer has disturbed attitudes to music on such a variety of levels so profoundly as Stravinsky. This has been achieved almost entirely through his compositions, of course, but the importance of his prose works should never be underestimated.

As far as the discussion of ideas fundamental to musical education is concerned, the chief sources are the two texts that he produced in the 1930s. The first was *Chroniques de ma vie* (Paris, 1935),[67] which presents

most of the basic principles, and the second was the texts of a series of
lectures that he gave in the University of Harvard in the winter of
1939–40, entitled *Poétique musical sous forme de six leçons*.[68]

The later publications, produced with the help of his assistant Robert
Craft, are more in the nature of recollections dating from the years
after the composer's seventy-fifth birthday, and although they sometimes throw more light on his basic ideas, they rarely alter them in any
significant manner.

Stravinsky's vigorous originality was inevitably confused with
'revolutionary' attitudes, but he was determined to rebuff such accusa-
tions:

'In truth, I should be hard pressed to cite for you a single fact in the
history of art that might be qualified as revolutionary. Art is by essence
constructive. Revolution implies a disruption of equilibrium. To speak
of revolution is to speak of temporary chaos. Now art is the contrary
to chaos.'[69]

On the contrary, he was anxious to make people understand how
traditional his approach to musical ideas actually was. By 'tradition' he
did not mean 'habit', as he points out:

'Tradition is entirely different from habit, even from an excellent habit,
since habit is by definition an unconscious acquisition and tends to
become mechanical, whereas tradition results from a conscious and
deliberate acceptance. A real tradition is not the relic of a past that is
irretrievably gone; it is a living force that animates and informs the
present.'[70]

Such a view is supported by the poet T. S. Eliot, who writes: 'Tradition
is not solely or even primarily, the maintenance of certain dogmatic
beliefs; these beliefs have come to take their living form in the course of
the formation of a tradition ... Tradition is a matter of much wider
significance. It cannot be inherited, and if you want it you must obtain
it by great labour'.[71] It is true, no doubt, that Stravinsky was fond of
the paradox, but his claim to be in the main stream of tradition was
made, like Eliot's, with the serious intention of forcing those who
dismissed his ideas as 'revolutionary' to examine them more closely. It
should be remembered that Stravinsky was by then over fifty years old.
Stravinsky used language with great precision, as he pointed out in
another context: 'I am not trying to argue pointlessly over words: it is
essential to know what we deny and what we affirm.'[72]

There is an incisiveness about Stravinsky's writing about music which
could not form a greater contrast than with that of some of his

predecessors, especially with Wagner. Whereas a sentence that began 'We have a duty towards music . . .' in the hands of Wagner might well have been followed by interminable wanderings, in the hands of Stravinsky it is completed with 'namely to invent it'.[73] 'Inventiveness' has a central place in Stravinsky's concept of how a musician behaves, and he differentiates between 'invention' and 'imagination': 'Invention presupposes imagination but should not be confused with it . . . What we imagine does not necessarily take on a concrete form and remain in a state of virtuality, whereas invention is not conceivable apart from its actually being worked out' (p. 69). The creative imagination is 'the faculty that helps us to pass from the level of conception to the level of realization', (p. 71), and it is this creative imagination, and not the adherence to rules and conventionalized practices, that determines the possibility of the learner in music coming to grips with the realities of making music. 'Harmony today in the schools,' Stravinsky wrote, 'dictates rules that were not fixed until long after the publication of the works upon which they were based, rules which were unknown to the composers of those works . . .' (p. 49). He was not against the teaching of harmony as an historical exercise, but did not believe that it helped the composer to be inventive. Theory is 'hindsight', he said, whereas composition was 'foresight'.[74] 'I can follow only where my musical appetites lead me'[75] is a statement of confidence in his instincts, and it is this assertion of the importance of confidence in inventiveness that Stravinsky wishes to pass on to other musicians.

The value for Stravinsky of historical information was not in the provision of a theoretical framework for his compositional techniques. 'My own experience', he wrote, 'has long convinced me that any historical fact, recent or distant, may well be utilized as a stimulus to set the creative faculty in motion, but never as an aid for clearing up difficulties.'[76] The imaginative, not the theoretical, provided him with the means of pursuing his aims as a composer. Furthermore, he felt that much of what was going on in music education missed the point: 'Those tedious commentaries on the side issues of music not only do not facilitate its understanding, but, on the contrary, are a serious obstacle which prevents the understanding of its essence and substance.'[77] Indeed anything which prevented the learner from actively participating in the actual processes of making music, should be avoided: 'Now the musical sense cannot be acquired or developed without exercise. In music as in everything else, inactivity leads gradually to the paralysis, to the atrophying of faculties.'[78] This echo of Thomas Morley, and of the eighteenth-century essayists, emphasizes the view that it is only by complete involvement that the learner begins to understand what the processes of making music really demand:

'The uninitiated imagine that one must await inspiration in order to create. That is a mistake. I am far from saying that there is no such thing as inspiration; quite the opposite. It is found as a driving force in every kind of human activity, and is in no wise peculiar to artists. But that force is only brought into action by an effort, and that effort is work.'[79]

He later added that 'ideas usually occur to me while I am composing',[80] a very different conception from the popular notions of what composing music involves.

Many teachers of music offer their students either the study of composition through the analysis of rules developed from the procedures of composers in the past, or they encourage their students to work in 'free composition'. As we have already seen, Stravinsky did not feel that the teaching of 'rules' in harmony really helped the students to be inventive. But neither did he suggest that the process of composition was 'free' in any sense that might be associated with the undisciplined: 'The more art is controlled, limited, worked over, the more it is free.'[81] This central paradox is crucial in the understanding of Stravinsky's ideas about learning in music. Necessity and freedom are ideas to which he returns many times in the later essays, but they are never more clearly presented than in the *Poetics of Music*:

'So here we are, whether we like it or not, in the realm of necessity. And yet which of us has heard talk of art as other than a realm of freedom? This sort of heresy is uniformly widespread because it is imagined that art is outside the bounds of ordinary activity. Well, in art as in everything else, one can build upon a resisting foundation: whatever constantly gives way to pressure, constantly renders movement impossible' (p. 87).

The assertion that the making of music is 'within the bounds of ordinary activity' is a concept that has been only gradually accepted in educational circles in the present time, but it is one that has the support of most composers of the period.

If, then, the discipline is not to be imposed by external rules, how is it to be provided? Stravinsky answers with another paradox:

'My freedom thus consists in my moving about within the narrow frame that I have designed myself for each one of my undertakings ... Whatever diminishes constraint, diminishes strength. The more constraints one imposes, the more one frees one's self of the chains that shackle the spirit' (p. 87).

Everyone, then, must find his own 'narrow frame', and as long as he does, it doesn't matter how like or unlike it is to other people's.

Stravinsky was aware that the major problem of general musical education is the education of the listener:

'... the listener is called upon to become the composer's partner. This presupposes that the listener's musical instruction and education are sufficiently extensive that he may not only grasp the main features of the work as they emerge, but that he may even follow to some degree the changing aspects of its unfolding' (p. 179).

Unlike many of his colleagues, however, Stravinsky did not attempt to disguise the fact that it is an activity that demands a great deal from the listener, and that consequently the demands made upon organized teaching are equally high. The failure of schools to cope with this problem is mentioned on more than one occasion:

'... the instruction and education of the public have not kept pace with the evolution of technique. The use of dissonance for ears ill-prepared to accept it, has not failed to confuse their reaction ...' (p. 47).

The confused reaction to the unusual is not surprising, of course, but Stravinsky felt that the type of repertoire limitations that were characteristic of the period (i.e. Bach to Brahms) deprived the listener of grasping musical principles that would help him to discover for himself the important features of different styles. In particular, he wanted the listener to understand that:

'All music is nothing more than a succession of impulses that converge towards a definite point of repose ... This general law of attraction is satisfied in only a limited way by the traditional diatonic system, for that system possesses no absolute value' (p. 49).

There is then no attempt in the *Chronicle* or *Poetics of Music* to impose theories of composition or of any other branch of music-making upon the reader. The listener learns by listening, just as the composer learns by composing. What Stravinsky was interested in was width of experience and depth of participation.

The idea of the related functions of the critic and the teacher, already discussed in the context of nineteenth-century thought, is taken up by Stravinsky. Just as he raised many serious objections to what the teacher was doing, or not doing, during his lifetime, so also was he concerned about the contribution of the critics. His principal objection to musical criticism was 'that it usually directs itself to what it supposes to be the nature of the imitation – when it should be teaching us to learn and to love the new reality. A new piece of music *is* a new reality.'[82] He felt that if criticism, and for that matter teaching, could not help us 'to learn and to love', it should confine itself to reporting the facts. It can be seen therefore that Stravinsky felt that if musical criticism and education was ever to be more than just a branch of history, then the critics and the teachers must, to at least a limited degree, be composers as well as performers and historians, in order to be able to grasp 'a new reality' for themselves, and then to help others to grasp it.

In this context therefore he makes a very significant observation, that 'the one true comment on a piece of music is another piece of music'.[83] Our word-dominated educational practices so often try to elicit a verbal response from the learner when a purely musical response is what is appropriate at the time. This topic leads, of course, to the area of musical aesthetics, in which the views of Stravinsky play a very important part.

Stravinsky presents to us a level of questioning about musical ideas related to education that no study of the topic can afford to ignore. At the age of well over eighty he was still able to produce the following type of searching comment:

'It was said to me recently in a certain reviewer's defence that though he may often be wrong, at least he is honest. I find this both illogical and, as an indication of the state of ethics, alarming. It is not the honesty of the opinion that matters but its worth.'[84]

In many respects the contrasts between Stravinsky and Arnold Schoenberg (1894–1951) could not be greater. Stravinsky did not teach professionally, nor did he write any theoretical works. Schoenberg, on the other hand, taught for most of his life, and left a quantity of theoretical material rivalled only by the great theorists of the early eighteenth century. His massive *Harmonielehre* established him as a leading theoretician as early as 1911. Throughout his career he wrote many articles, and these, together with an enormous output of teaching material, were gradually put together and published in the last years of his life and in the period following his death. The essays contained in *Style and Idea* and the musical examples and exercises contained in *Structural Functions of Harmony*, *Preliminary Exercises in Counterpoint*, and *Fundamentals of Musical Composition* form an indispensable body of material for the use of the music teacher.

Schoenberg shared with Feruccio Busoni (1866–1924) a great deal of the responsibility for the break up of romanticism in Germany and Austria. Busoni's *Entwurf einer neuen Aesthetic der Tonkunst* (1911) is, incidentally, an important document in the development of new approaches to music, and indirectly to musical education.

Schoenberg was the teacher not only of Berg, Webern and Wellesz, but of a very large group of composers from every part of Europe and America. Webern said of his teaching:

'Schoenberg educates actually through creating. He follows the traces of the student's personality with the utmost energy, tries to deepen them, to help them break through, in short, to give the student the courage and the strength to put himself in a position from which everything he views becomes, through the manner in which he views it, unique.'[85]

But Schoenberg's teaching must not be seen simply in the light of his successful composition students. The following answers to a questionnaire which the composer completed in 1929 give a very clear view of his broader educational ideas:

1. Are you satisfied with the present educational system?
   'No.'
2. What defects strike you as most serious?
   'The way the young are stuffed with "ready-made" knowledge and acquire only "tangible" qualifications.'
3. What is your idea of good educational methods?
   'Encouraging young people to look at things for themselves, to observe, compare, define, describe, weigh, test, draw conclusions, and use them.'
4. What cultural ideal should modern youth strive to attain?
   '(a) knowledge in the sense of understanding
   (b) skill that is constantly refreshed and enlarged from the depths of the knowledge that is understanding.'
5. Can and should teachers try to influence the young in this direction?
   'Yes.'
6. By what methods?
   'By training the mind;
   by bringing the pupil (according to the stage he has reached) face to face with the difficulties, problems, and inherent terms of the given material;
   by helping him to recognize them;
   by forcing him to help himself in this respect; which means letting

him make his own mistakes and correcting them afterwards, but also being of assistance to him in finding the solution.'[86]

There are many aspects of this important statement of general principles that could be developed: the relationships with the ideas of Pestalozzi, Rousseau and Froebel; the emphasis on what have come to be called 'discovery methods'; the importance of knowledge as understanding as opposed to knowledge as a collection of facts; the value of the teacher, and the nature of his contribution. These general issues have been extensively discussed elsewhere. Two important points of context, however, must not be overlooked. These answers were written in Berlin in 1929 during the rise to power of the Nazis; secondly, they are the answers of a professor of composition, not a professor of education.

The emphasis on the student's need to discover things for himself also makes it clear that, despite their obvious differences, there is an important area of common ground between Schoenberg and Stravinsky in their comprehension of principles in musical education. The following, written by Schoenberg, could equally well have come from Stravinsky's pen:

'Remembering is the first step toward understanding ... Historical facts, biographies of authors and performers, anecdotes of their lives, pathetic, humorous, interesting or instructive, may be of some value to people who are otherwise deaf to the effects of music. But all this cannot help anyone to absorb and remember the content.'[87]

Like Stravinsky, and many other colleagues, Schoenberg wanted students to be taught music, not taught 'about music'. Thus '"Music appreciation" often gives a music student not much more than the perfume of a work, that narcotic emanation of music which affects the senses without involving the mind ...' (p. 147). This emphasis on the thinking musician is a constant theme in Schoenberg's teaching.

As an example of a thinking musician himself, Schoenberg viewed with barely concealed anger much of what he saw going on in musical education:

'Unfortunately methods in music teaching, instead of making students thoroughly acquainted with the music itself, furnish a conglomerate of more or less true historical facts, sugar-coated with a great number of more or less false anecdotes about the composer, his performers, his audiences, and his critics, plus a strong dose of popularized aesthetics' (p. 37).

At one stage he was witness to a lecture in which a student was given the sort of treatment outlined above. Later he wrote: 'In a few years ... she will disseminate what she has been taught: ready made judgements, wrong and superficial ideas about music, musicians, and aesthetics' (p. 38).

What Schoenberg wanted was open-minded students 'thoroughly acquainted with the music itself'. The 'open-mindedness' would lead them to approach all music with an equal interest, and 'thorough acquaintance' (based on many hearings or performances of the work) would lead them away from superficial judgements. The banner that such students should carry would look something like this:

'One should never forget that what one learns in school about history is the truth only insofar as it does not interfere with the political, philosophical, moral or other beliefs of those in whose interest the facts are told, coloured or arranged. The same is true with the history of music ...' (p. 137).

Schoenberg was careful, however, to see that this must be seen to apply to his own teaching as well. Composers 'are in the first instance fighters for their own musical ideas. The ideas of other composers are their enemies.'[88] The obvious balance with which he approached other composers' work, however, is amply displayed in his textbooks on composition, and the 'enemy' was really confined to other people's compositions being written at exactly the same time as he was writing a new work himself.

It is a curious feature of Schoenberg's position in European and American music that, because of his position as a leading figure in the development of serialism, few teachers think of him in connection with the teaching of pre-atonal harmony and counterpoint; and yet his contribution to this field is so valuable that it is overlooked only at the student's risk. It is no doubt arguable that Schoenberg's desire to get things absolutely right tends to make him provide more details than are absolutely necessary, but often this is balanced with a directness that is extremely refreshing:

'I have realized that the greatest difficulty for the students is to find out how they could compose without being inspired. The answer is: it is impossible.'[89]

Ernest Křének (b. 1900), like Schoenberg, left Europe for the United States during the 1930s, and as a result of his teaching, produced an important introduction to the compositional ideas of the period in

Music Here and Now (1939), and a short but illuminating guide to serial techniques in *Studies in Counterpoint* (1940). A collection of his essays was also published in 1966 with the title *Exploring Music*.

The third prominent German (or rather German-speaking, for Schoenberg and Křének were Austrians) composer who exercised an important influence on musical education in the period was Paul Hindemith (1895–1963). He also had the distinction of having his music officially banned by the Nazi government, and like Schoenberg and Křének, settled in the United States, where he became Professor of Music at Yale.

It is arguable that Hindemith's music had more in common with Stravinsky than Schoenberg in terms of style, at least in the mid-1930s when Stravinsky wrote in the *Chronicle*: 'The appearance of Hindemith in the musical life of our day is very fortunate, for he stands out as a wholesome and illuminating principle amid so much obscurity' (p. 169). In terms of their interest in musical theory, however, Hindemith stands much closer to Schoenberg than is sometimes imagined. Moreover, unlike Stravinsky, Hindemith devoted a lot of time to teaching, and his *Unterweisung im Tonsatz* (1937–9), *Elementary training for musicians* (1946) and *A Composer's World* (1952) provide ample proof of his ability in this field.

Hindemith was probably the first composer since the seventeenth century to show off his knowledge of Morley's *A Plaine and Easie Introduction*, and he opens *A Composer's World* with a quotation from Morley's preface: 'It is no marvayle to see a Snayle after a Rayne to creep out of his shell, and wander about seeking the moysture.' Hindemith, like Morley, compared himself to the 'Snayle': 'Is a composer writing a book not like that Snayle, creeping out of his abode of settled professionalism and solid experience, seeking what corresponds to the moysture, looking for readers instead of listeners and forfeiting musical security for doubtful successes in a field through which he can only roam unsupported by professional know-how but at the same time free of professional inhibitions?' (p. v). Like Stravinsky and Schoenberg, he also understood the dangers that faced a composer in this field: 'Musicians producing words instead of notes are too easily apt to fall into this sometimes enticing but mostly insipid kind of gossip with its strictly egotistic or pseudo-profound attitude' (p. vi). The type of 'gossip' to which he refers includes the 'noncommittal aestheticisms, popularizations, and sugar-coated banalities' with which every reader of musical journalism is familiar, and which, regrettably, is often encountered in teaching situations.

In the opening pages of his *Unterweisung im Tonsatz*, Hindemith draws attention to the idea which forms the central theme of this thesis,

when he comments: 'A considerable portion of the responsibility for
the failure of instruction belongs to the instructors themselves. Is it not
strange that since Bach hardly any of the great composers have been
outstanding teachers?'[90]

If we can understand by Bach, C. P. E. Bach, and if we can make an
exception in Schumann, then there is a lot of truth in what he says. Of
course it depends on what is understood by such terms as 'great composers' and 'outstanding teachers', but the failure of the nineteenth-
century educational authorities to absorb the composer into their
investigations of the nature of musical education has already been
noted. What the work of Hindemith and his colleagues represents is the
gradual re-entry of the composer into musical education.

The long-term effects of the teaching of the European composers in the
United States will undoubtedly be the subject of much investigation at
some later date. When Francis Poulenc visited America in the late
1940s he observed:

'How dangerous are the lessons taken from the great composer-
teachers. In Los Angeles the young musicians write like Schoenberg, in
Boston like Hindemith. Milhaud alone, to the gratitude of his students,
maintains in San Francisco a climate of eclecticism.'[91]

What is certain is that neither Schoenberg nor Hindemith set out to
make their students copy their style: quite the contrary in fact, for since
both composers were deeply involved in the study of the theoretical
principles of harmony, their teaching of style was only indirect. Nevertheless, it is entirely true that students do absorb the manners of their
teachers as well as their ideas. The question that later researchers will
have to answer is whether or not the post-war generation of American
musicians were taught in such a way that they grew into independence,
and whether their own individuality was allowed to develop.

The major contributions to musical education by indigenous American composers of the period came from Copland, Sessions and Piston.
Aaron Copland (b. 1900) produced four important books: *What to
Listen for in Music* (1938), *Our New Music* (1941), *Music and Imagination*
(1952) and a collection of essays and articles entitled *Copland on Music*
(1960). Teachers can learn a great many things from his writing, for
Copland's prose style is easier to read than that of the European composers in translations that have been described as 'towards English'. At
the same time, however, Copland, at least in the early *What to Listen for
in Music*, shows how easy it is to fall into the trap of attempting to

simplify musical issues, and end by producing the sort of empty
generalizations that distressed Schoenberg so much.

Nevertheless, Copland often succeeds in presenting important issues
with clarity and vigour. He explains why composers are interested in
writing about their ideas:

'For the composer has something vital at stake. In helping others to
hear music more intelligently, he is working towards the spread of
musical culture, which in the end will affect the understanding of his
own creations.'[92]

But it is not simply a matter of self-interest:

'The composer ought to bring an awareness and insight to the understanding of music that critics, musicologists, and music historians might
put to good use, thereby enriching the whole field of musical investigations.'[93]

This 'awareness and insight' is brought also to the teacher, particularly
through his Harvard lectures where Copland gives himself the room to
develop his major theme:

'An imaginative mind is essential to the creation of art in any medium,
but it is even more essential in music precisely because music provides
the broadest possible vista for the imagination since it is the freest, the
most abstract, the least fettered of all the arts; no story content, no
pictorial representation, no regularity of meter, no strict limitation of
frame need hamper the intuitive functioning of the imaginative
mind.'[94]

There are, however, serious dangers in attempting the evaluation of
elements apparently common to a number of arts, and Copland does
not pursue this sort of comparison too far. That an imaginative mind is
essential in musical composition is, of course, beyond question:

'Music as mathematics, music as architecture or as image, music in any
static, seizable form has always held fascination for the lay mind. But as
a musician, what fascinates me is the thought that by its very nature
music invites imaginative treatment, and that the facts of music, so
called, are only meaningful insofar as the imagination is given free
play.'[95]

The nature of such 'imaginative treatment' is a matter which will be discussed later on, and Copland's valuable contribution to the topic will be fully explored.

Roger Sessions (b. 1896) and Walter Piston (b. 1894) perhaps spent more time than Copland as teachers, and Piston's *Harmony* (1941), *Counterpoint* (1947), and *Orchestration* (1955) have become standard texts. *The Musical Experience of Composer, Performer, Listener* (1950), by Sessions, investigates the same problem tackled by Copland in his *Music and Imagination*, though with a different emphasis. Sessions's later Harvard lectures were published as *Questions about Music* (1970).

English composers of the period found very little time to write about music or the teaching of music. Compared with their contemporaries, particularly those working in America, composers such as Elgar, Delius, Ireland, Bax, Bliss, Walton, Rawsthorne, Rubbra, Tippett and Britten wrote practically nothing, apart from occasional articles. Gustav Holst (1874–1934) and Ralph Vaughan Williams (1872–1958) did, however, produce some important essays. Holst's lecture *On the Teaching of Art*[96] is a brief, but valuable document, and Vaughan Williams's *National Music* (1935), *Some thoughts on Beethoven's Choral Symphony with Writings on other Musical Subjects* (1953), *The Making of Music* (1955), and the collection of letters which Holst published as *Heirs and Rebels* (1959), though often covering the same ground, present a useful picture of the author's basic ideas about music.

Holst, in addition to his teaching at St Paul's Girls School (1905–34) also taught at Morley College, Reading University and the Royal College of Music. As he pointed out, 'Most people who have mastered any form of intellectual activity either are, have been, or are in danger of becoming teachers even for a short time.'[97] Commenting on Shaw's aphorism about teachers ('He who can, does. He who cannot, teaches.'), Holst made his own position very clear: 'That remark of Shaw is not *essentially* true. Teaching is not an alternative to doing. Teaching is doing' (p. 151). Not only was teaching 'doing', but for Holst it meant that learning was 'doing' also:

'In musical circles, a few years ago, we were told: "We cannot make all our children good singers and players, therefore let us make them good listeners". I agree, on condition that we remember that the surest way of becoming a good listener is to first try to sing or play' (p. 152).

Holst, like so many of his colleagues, wanted to make sure that proper use was made of recorded music. Encountering the great impact of records and radio on the listening habits of people between the wars, composers of Holst's generation were acutely aware of the need to teach the public how to listen. Vaughan Williams took a similar position: he required 'creative listening, which cannot exist except as a counterpart of active participation by the hearer. Therefore, before we truly listen we must be able also to create.'[98]

Therefore it was important, in his view, that the child should learn to sing, to play, and in his own terms, compose. Together these formed the ability to hear:

'To educate a child musically is to teach him to hear; then, and then only, is he a musician. I am far from saying that the power to read music, the knowledge of musical history, an intelligent interest in the technique of instruments will not be a great help to him when once he has learnt to love music, but they must never be allowed to take the place of music.'[99]

If the English composers did not write very much about the teaching of music, it should not be thought that they ignored the problem. Perhaps the most valuable aspect of their work in this field is the many fine compositions that they produced with children especially in mind. Works such as Britten's *Young Persons' Guide to the Orchestra*, *Let's Make an Opera* and *Noye's Fludde* are perhaps the most familiar examples, but many other composers have written works of this type.[100]

Books by French composers of the period are hardly more common than those by English composers. However the *Cours de composition musicale* (1903–33) by Vincent D'Indy (1851–1931), is a particularly interesting example of teaching composition with reference to varying historical styles in contrast to 'rules'. Essays by Debussy, Fauré, Dukas and Milhaud are principally of biographical interest, as is the book by Arthur Honegger *Je suis compositeur* (1951). The latter does, however, often recall ideas commonly expressed by composers of the period, and the following is a passage which no teacher should ignore:

'Like all the arts, we have rules which we have learnt, and which have come down to us from the masters. But over and beyond the studied, consciously willed, inherited 'craft' of the profession, there remains a kind of compulsion for which we are not, so to speak, responsible. It is a drive from our subconscious which resists explanation.'[101]

Olivier Messiaen's (1908–) *Technique de mon langage musicale* (1944) has exercised considerable influence in France, particularly on composers of the Boulez generation.

The importance of the two Hungarian composers Béla Bartók (1881–1945) and Zoltán Kodály (1882–1967) in musical education is unlikely to be underestimated. Bartók's influence, though more indirect, has possibly been the greater, simply because of Bartók's status as one of the two or three leading composers of the period. Moreover the *Mikrokosmos* (1926–39) has been used for many years now not only in the preparation of pianists, but also in the teaching of composition, for the *Mikrokosmos* is as useful in this field as the majority of text-books on composition, and is better than most. Although Bartók was never a teacher of composition, believing that such activity would have had a bad influence on his own work, the widespread effect of his music on younger composers was immeasurable. The two volumes *For Children* (1908), based on Hungarian and Slovakian folk songs, provide material of a similar nature. Bartók also wrote a considerable amount of vocal music for children's voices.

'The *Mikrokosmos*, by the very nature of its compilation, is especially suited for illustration of Bartók's activities in music education.'[102] This view of the work is supported by many teachers, and the following comments illustrate the sort of impact it makes:

'In addition to laying a strong and richly varied foundation for the understanding and performance of twentieth-century music, it presents almost unending varieties of situations for facilitating sight-reading and transportation. The work offers virtually every pianistic and musical problem to the student, and interestingly enough, its use gives him increased insight into music of the past as well as of the present.'[103]

The quality of Bartók's teaching was perhaps most clearly described by another of his pupils:

'The primary and most important role of a teacher is to inspire. I have never met anybody who could be more inspiring than Béla Bartók. Words, theories – even the most brilliant words and fascinating theories mean nothing if they are not backed by strong personal convictions and an unwavering moral strength. It is not so much what Bartók said as a teacher – it was what he stood for as a human being that served as a guiding light to me.'[104]

Although Bartók produced no textbooks on composition or performance, he did produce a considerable quantity of papers, articles and other documents. These have recently been edited by Benjamin Suchoff and form a most important contribution to our understanding of musical problems. In particular the essay 'On Music Education for the Turkish People' (1937) makes a number of extremely important points about the teaching of singing which are discussed later on in this book.[105]

Kodály, who collaborated with Bartók in major research projects related to the collection of folk songs, was very much more heavily involved with musical education. He was appointed Professor of Music Theory in the Budapest Academy as early as 1907. Matyas Seiber, who did so much to spread the influence of Kodály (and Bartók) in England, described his teaching in the following way:

'With Kodály, instruction ceased to be merely instruction, and became something quite different. He has that curiously compulsive and suggestive power of drawing out from his pupils all their latent ability. It was not necessary for him to do much talking, and indeed he never said one word too many. But precisely for this reason, everything he did say was all the more significant . . . One such word from Kodály was sometimes enough to change the whole direction of a man's life, suddenly illuminating a field of study that had till that moment been completely obscure.'[106]

Kodály's interest in musical education in schools dated from the late 1920s when he began to work with children's choirs and to write works for them. In an article written in 1929 he said:

'What children are being taught to sing in school is for the most part of no artistic value; and the way they are taught is worse than if they were left to themselves. After such a training they can hardly hope to experience music as an art for the rest of their lives.'[107]

In due course Kodály's interest in teaching children resulted in the publication of a substantial body of material, beginning with *Bicinia Hungarica* (1937-42), an introduction to two-part singing. It was followed by *Let Us Sing Correctly* (1941), two-part exercises for chorus; *333 Reading Exercises* (1943), an introduction to the Hungarian folk song; *Pentatonic Music* (1945-8); *33, 44* and *55 Two-part Singing Exercises* (1954); and *Tricinia* (1954), three-part singing exercises.

Kodály's powerful influence on the musical education of Hungary has established that country in a leading position in Europe. To some extent his influence has spread to other parts of Europe and to the United States, but there is always the problem in vocal music with such strong national links that its very strength in Hungary (which was undoubtedly connected with Kodály's attempts to establish a national identity upon a musical culture soaked in German traditions) may prove to be a weakness in other countries. The difficulties of such a transfer are well illustrated by the evidence of the first English editions of some of the children's songs. In the period which preceded this publishing project the editor wrote an article[108] drawing attention to the merits of the scheme, and ended by giving an example of the type of material that was going to completely revitalize the song repertoire of the four- and five-year-olds:

Hear the rush-es sigh, see the swal-low fly, Dan-ube ri-ver,

Tis-za riv-er, Toss your wave-lets high.

The choice of this vocabulary, remote as it is from the vocabulary of any five-year-old, let alone that of an urban child in Britain, is passed without any comment by the writer.[109] Moreover the difficulties are not confined to the use of language. Kodály's melodic vocabulary is based on the pentatonic scale (as is Orff's), and although British folk songs do enjoy this scale, it is not found in them to the same extent as it is in Hungary, or other parts of the world.

Nevertheless, Kodály's is a remarkable achievement, and one that will be taken up at a later point. There can be no doubt that he had an enormous impact on Hungarian education, and his qualities are made apparent in the following description: 'Kodály's physical activity and his zest for living are combined with a vivid intellectual energy, a splendid sense of humour, and equal zest for learning. In analysis he is shrewd, in exposition direct. In short he has the qualities that one would look for in a teacher.'[110]

The work of Carl Orff (1895–   ) also has strong regional (Munich/Salzburg) connections, but since there is much greater emphasis on instrumental ideas, the music is more easily transferable than Kodály's. Orff had already established a reputation as a composer when in 1924 he joined Dorothee Guenther in the formation of a school in Munich for gymnastics, music and dance. There he 'saw a possibility of working out a new kind of rhythmical education, and of realizing my ideas about a reciprocal interpenetration of movement and music education.' Orff felt that for children the emphasis should not be on harmony (as was characteristic of most piano music) but on rhythm, and that the children should be able to provide their own music for dance purposes. He therefore developed a range of simple, tuned percussion instruments of the xylophone and glockenspiel type (though limited in compass to two octaves or less) which did not call for any advanced instrumental techniques from the players, but which at the same time provided real opportunities for making music. These instruments were combined with singing, recorders, unpitched percussion and a bass stringed instrument (mostly employing open strings) to provide a varied range of timbres. 'The art of creating music for this ensemble', he wrote in the same article, 'came directly from playing the instruments themselves. It was therefore important to acquire a well-developed technique of improvisation, and exercises for developing this technique should above all lead the student to a spontaneous musical expression.'[111]

Since improvisations essentially do not involve printed scores, Orff's principal route of communication was the generations of students who came into personal contact with his teaching. Nevertheless some basic material that could be used for improvisation was published in 1930. The main sources, however, were not published until 1950–54, when together with his collaborator Gunild Keetman, Orff published the five volumes of *Orff-Schulwerk*.

Orff was an outspoken supporter of the need to provide children with a proper musical education.

'It must therefore be stressed that elementary music in the primary school should not be installed as a subsidiary subject, but as something *fundamental* to all other subjects. It is not exclusively a question of musical education . . . it is rather a question of developing the whole personality . . . It is at the primary school age that the imagination must be stimulated; and opportunities for emotional development, which contain experience of the ability to feel, and the power to control the expression of the feeling, must also be provided.'[112]

In the same context as the work of Orff it is not uncommon to find some mention of the work of Émile Jacques-Dalcroze (1865–1950) the Swiss teacher who established the teaching of Eurhythmics in Geneva and Dresden. He studied with Delibes and Fauré in Paris, and with Bruckner in Vienna. Although his work has had a profound effect on the teaching of movement in schools, it is not possible to claim for his work a similar effect on musical education. As a composer, moreover, he is practically unknown outside Switzerland, in spite of the fact that he published a number of works in the orchestral chamber, vocal and operatic fields. His principal book, *Le rythme, la musique et l'éducation* (Paris, 1920, 2nd edn. 1935), is a collection of essays that he had published from time to time in connection with his teaching methods. As it is necessary in the context of the modern writers to exercise a considerable degree of selection in discussing the ideas of composers, it is impossible to place the work of Jaques-Dalcroze in the same foreground as that of Stravinsky, Schoenberg and others.

This summary of the sources of composers' thinking about musical education does not venture beyond the 1950s. I have overcome the temptation to continue the process right up to the present day simply in the interests of space, for the last twenty-five years could provide such a mass of conflicting material that the reader might end up none the wiser. The evidence of the four hundred years up to 1950 does in any case provide such a wealth of material that few will fail to recognize that composers have by no means remained indifferent to the ways by which music has been taught, nor to the analysis of the reasons why it should be taught. The remainder of this book represents an attempt to investigate more closely the actual nature of their ideas.

Notes

1. J. Wilson (ed.), *Roger North on Music* (London, 1959), p. 137.
2. Some speculation has occurred about the possibility of linking the author with Carissimi, whose *Ars Cantandi* may have been in circulation at the time (see J. Coover, 'Music Theory in Translation: A Bibliography' *JMT*, III (1959), pp. 70–96, and Supplement, *JMT*, XIII (1969), pp. 230–48). It is, however, with Caccini that the connection occurs. Ian Spink makes a strong case for Walter Porter as the 'English Gentleman' in 'Playford's Directions for Singing after the Italian Manner', *Monthly Musical Record*, LXXXIX (1959) pp. 130–35.
3. G. Reese, *Music in the Renaissance* (New York, 1954, rev. ed. 1959) p. 792.
4. A. Ornithoparcus (Ger. Vogelsang), *Musica Activae Micrologus* (Leipzig, 1517); Eng. trans. J. Dowland, *Andreas Ornithoparcus, his micrologus or introduction*, (London, 1610), p. Aiv.
5. Campion's book is undated, but it is thought (cf. W. R. Davis, *The works of Thomas Campion*, London 1969), to have been published about 1613–14.
6. P. 3 in the 2nd edition of the modern version edited by R. A. Herman (London, 1963), to which all Morley references apply.
7. Morley, op. cit. pp. 319–22. He was clearly sensitive to the need for academic respectability.
8. 'Dialogue on the true way of playing the organ and quilled instruments' (Venice,

1593 and 1597). It seems unlikely that Morley would have known this work, as he does not list it among the authorities quoted at the end of his book.

9. R. Dowland, *Varietie of Lute Lessons*, (London, 1610), p. Bi.

10. Cf. H. L. F. Helmholtz, *Lehre von den Tonempfindungen* (Brunswick, 1863), and P. Hindemith, *Unterweisung im Tonsatz* (Mainz, 1937).

11. J. Dowland, in appendix to *Varietie of Lute Lessons*, p. Diii.

12. Robinson, like so many of his contemporaries, seems determined to sell his books to a very wide circle of clients. Cf. M. C. Boyd, *Elizabethan Music and Musical Criticism* (Philadelphia, 1962), pp. 153ff.

13. Eng. trans. E. R. Reilly, *On Playing the Flute* (London, 1966).

14. Eng. trans. W. J. Mitchell, *Essay on the True Art of Playing Keyboard Instruments* (London, 1949).

15. Eng. trans. E. Knocker, *A Treatise on the Fundamental Principles of Violin Playing* (2nd ed., London, 1951). All references are to these editions.

16. B. Willey, *The Eighteenth-century Background* (London, 1953), p. i.

17. *The Present State of Music in Germany* (London, 1773–5), p. 159 in P. A. Scholes edition (London, 1959), Vol. 2.

18. M. Graf, *Composer and Critic* (New York, 1947), p. 111. For a detailed account of the Berlin School, see E. E. Helm, *Music at the Court of Frederick the Great* (Norman, USA, 1960).

19. C. Burney, *A General History* (London, 1776–89); ed. F. Mercer (London, 1935), pp. 949–50.

20. A. Dolmetsch, *The Interpretation of the Music of the XVII and XVIIIth Centuries* (London, 1946), p. 23.

21. Cf. F. T. Arnold, *The Art of Accompaniment from a Thorough Bass* (London, 1931); R. T. Dart, *The Interpretation of Music* (London, 1954); R. Donington, *The Interpretation of Early Music* (London, 1963); A. Dolmetsch, op. cit.; H. Keller (trans. and ed. C. Parrish), *Thorough Bass Method* (London, 1966).

22. Cf. F. Couperin, *L'art de toucher le clavecin* (Paris, 1716); J. Hotteterre (Le Romain), *Princeps de la flûte traversière* (Paris, 1707); F. Geminiani, *The Art of Playing on the Violin* (London, 1751); G. Tartini, *Trattato di musica* (Padua, c. 1754).

23. See J. B. Brocklehurst, *Charles Avison and His Essay on Musical Expression*, thesis (Sheffield, 1960).

24. F. Geminiani, *The Art of Playing the Violin* (London, 1751), ed. with an introduction by D. D. Boydon (London, 1953), p. 1.

25. There is some uncertainty about dating the publication of Geminiani's treatises. Grove V gives 1739; the publisher gave it an opus number – op. 8. However, op. 9 is the *Art of Playing on the Violin* (1751) and op. 10 is the *Guida Harmonica*, which Grove V gives as 1742. There is therefore some obvious irregularity about the matter. Some authorities, including Bukofzer, give 1731 as the date of the *Art . . .*, but Boydon has established that the *Art of Playing on the Violin*, 1731, is part five of *The Modern Music Master*, published by Peter Prelleur, and is not by Geminiani.

26. F. Geminiani, *Guida Armonica, o dizionario armonico, being a sure guide to harmony and modulation*, Op. 10 (London, 1742?), p. i.

27. Sebastian Brossard, *Dictionnaire de musique* (Paris, 1703), adapted and trans. J. Grassineau, *Musical Dictionary* (London, 1740); J. C. Walther, *Muskalisches Lexicon* (Leipzig, 1728–32); J. Mattheson, *Grundlage einer Ehrenpforte* (Hamburg, 1740); W. Tan'sur, *New Musical Dictionary* (London, 1746).

28. See A. P. Oliver, *The Encyclopaedists as Critics of Music* (New York, 1947).

29. Rousseau's short one act opera, *Le Devin du village*, hardly justifies the description of composer.

30. Rousseau's paper, later published as the *Projet sur la musique*, had been rejected by the Paris *Académie des sciences* in 1742.

31. A. P. Oliver, op. cit., p. 66.

32. J. P. Rameau, *Traité de l'harmonie* (Paris, 1722); Eng. trans. P. Gossett (London, 1971), p. xxxv.

33. *L'art de toucher le clavecin* (Eng. trans. M. Roberts, 1933), p. 10.

34. F. Gasparini (1668–1727), *L'Armonico pratico* (Venice, 1708), Eng. trans. F. S. Stillings, in an edition by D. L. Burrows, *The Practical Harmonist at the Harpsichord* (London, 1963), p. 9.
35. Chesterfield: *Letters*, Vol. IV (London, 1932), p. 1360: a letter to his son, dated 22 June 1749. The following is similar in tone: 'If you love music, hear it; go to operas, concerts, and pay fiddlers to play for you; but I insist upon your neither piping nor fiddling yourself' (quoted in Raleigh's Introduction to *The Boke of the Courtier* (London, 1900), p. lxxxvi).
36. A. Churton (trans.), *Kent on Education* (London, 1899), p. 19.
37. E. Kant, *Critique of Judgement*, trans. J. A. Bernard (London, 1892), p. 219.
38. These included papers in Leipzig, Munich, Weimar, Berlin, Stuttgart and Dresden.
39. These included the *Revue Européenne*, the *Rénovateur*, the *Monde Dramatique*, the *Gazette musicale* and the *Journal des débats*.
40. *Gesammelte Schriften* (Berlin and Leipzig, 1871–85).
41. R. Wagner, *Beethoven*, Eng. trans. E. Dannreuther (London, 1870), p. 28.
42. I. Stravinsky, *Themes and Conclusions* (New York, 1972), p. 243.
43. H. Wolf, *Musikalische Kritiken* (Leipzig, 1912), Eng. trans. S. Morgenstern, *Composers on Music* (London, 1956), p. 302.
44. Tchaikovsky in a letter to Nadeja von Meck, 1879, Eng. trans. I. Kolodin, *The Critical Composer* (New York, 1940), p. 193.
45. A. Honegger, *I Am a Composer* (London, 1966), p. 77.
46. G. Abraham, 'Weber as Novelist and Critic', *MQ*, XX (1934), p. 27.
47. *Gluck and His Operas*, trans. E. Evans (London, 1914), p. 145–6.
48. *The Theory of Musical Composition*, trans. J. Bishop (London, 1851), p. 896.
49. *Mémoires* (Paris, 1870), trans. and ed. D. Cairns (London, 1969).
50. Nor was it in journalism, although he wrote for the *Moscow Gazette* for a number of years. César Cui (1835–1918) also wrote for a St Petersburg paper.
51. A. Bruckner, *Vorlesungen über Harmonielehre und Kontrapunkt* (Vienna, 1950), ed. E. Schwanzara.
52. J. R. S. Bennett, *The Life of William Sterndale Bennett* (Cambridge, 1907).
53. Letter to de Sire, dated 15 March 1839, trans. M. Herbert, *Letters of Robert Schumann* (London, 1890), p. 209.
54. See also M. Tippett, 'My Kind of Music' (*Observer Magazine*, 7 October 1973), p. 28: '... when I left [school] I was still in the very greatest ignorance as to what the idea of composition would be. So I decided – and it now seems splendidly naïve – to go into a bookshop and find a book on the technique. The book I found was actually called *Composition*, a very remarkable work by Charles Villiers Stanford, which told me immediately, within three or four pages, what I wanted to know, since by discussing the differences between, for instance, harmony and counterpoint, it clarified and channelled processes that were already going on inside me.'
55. *Pages from an Unwritten Diary* (London, 1914), pp. 104–5.
56. See, especially, W. Walsh, *The Use of the Imagination* (London, 1959).
57. *Gesammelte Schriften* (Leipzig, 1854), Eng. trans. F. R. Ritter, *Music and Musicians* (London, 1877), Vol. I, p. 84.
58. Y. Bannard, 'Composer Critics', *ML*, V/III (1924), p. 264.
59. R. Schumann, *Neue Zeitschrift für Musik*, Vol. 3 (1835), p. 33, trans. L. B. Plantigna, *Schumann as Critic* (New York, 1967), p. 237.
60. L. B. Plantinga, op. cit., p. 129.
61. See, especially, *The World as Will and Idea* (1818), trans. R. B. Haldane and J. Kemp (London, 1896).
62. See, especially, *Vom Musikalisch-Schönen* (Vienna, 1854), Eng. trans. G. Cohen, *The Beautiful in Music* (New York, 1957).
63. *The Power of Sound* (London, 1880).
64. G. Holst, 'Lecture at Yale on the Teaching of Art' (1929) in Imogen Holst, *The Music of Gustav Holst* (London, 2nd ed., 1968), p. 151.
65. See Appendix, p. 199.
66. Stravinsky did teach during the winter of 1935–36 in the École Normale de Musique

in Paris, where he joined Nadia Boulanger in a composition seminar. See M. Perrin, 'Stravinsky in a Composition Class', *The Score* (1957), p. 44–6.
67. Eng. trans. (anon.), *Autobiography* (New York, 1936), but it is customary to refer to it in English as the *Chronicle*.
68. Eng. trans. A. Knedel, and I. Dahl, *Poetics of Music* (Cambridge, Mass., 1947).
69. Ibid., p. 15.
70. Ibid., p. 75.
71. *Selected Prose* (London, 1953), pp. 20, 23.
72. *Poetics of Music*, p. 53.
73. Ibid., p. 69.
74. I. Stravinsky and R. Craft, *Stravinsky in Conversation with Robert Craft* (London, 1962), p. 30.
75. I. Stravinsky and R. Craft, *Dialogues and a Diary* (New York, 1963), p. 128.
76. *Poetics of Music*, p. 35.
77. *Chronicle*, p. 163.
78. *Poetics of Music*, p. 181.
79. *Chronicle*, p. 174.
80. *Stravinsky in Conversation*, p. 30.
81. *Poetics of Music*, p. 85.
82. I. Stravinsky and R. Craft, *Expositions and Developments* (New York, 1962), p. 102.
83. *Dialogues and a Diary*, p. 63.
84. I. Stravinsky and R. Craft, *Themes and Conclusions* (New York, 1972), p. 80.
85. A. Webern, *Arnold Schoenberg* (Munich, 1912); Eng. trans. Morgenstern, op. cit., p. 456.
86. A. Schoenberg, *Letters* (New York, 1965), pp. 135–6.
87. A. Schoenberg, *Style and Idea* (New York, 1950), p. 147.
88. *Letters*, p. 265.
89. *Fundamentals of Musical Composition* (London, 1967), p. 215.
90. *The Craft of Musical Composition* (New York, 1941–2), p. 3.
91. F. Poulenc, 'Feuilles Américaines', *La Table Ronde*, 30 (1950), trans. Morgenstern, op. cit., p. 515.
92. *What to Listen for in Music* (New York, 1938), p. viii.
93. *Music and Imagination* (Cambridge, Mass., 1952), p. 3.
94. Ibid., p. 7.
95. Ibid., p. 7.
96. Contained in I. Holst, *The Music of Gustav Holst* (London, 2nd ed., 1968), pp. 150–55.
97. Ibid., p. 150.
98. *The Making of Music*, p. 53.
99. *Some Thoughts on . . .* p. 59.
100. See Appendix, p. 199.
101. Paris, 1951, Eng. trans. W. O. Clough, *I Am a Composer* (London, 1966), p. 74.
102. B. Suchoff, 'Béla Bartók's Contribution to Music Education', *Tempo*, 60 (1961), p. 38.
103. Y. Novik, 'Teaching with Mikrokosmos', *Tempo*, 83 (1967), p. 12.
104. A. Foldes, 'Béla Bartók', *Tempo*, 43 (1957), p. 26.
105. *Béla Bartók Essays*, ed. Benjamin Suchoff (London, 1976). See also Ch. III.
106. L. Eösze, *Zoltán Kodály* (London, 1962), p. 68.
107. Ibid., p. 70.
108. P. M. Young, 'Kodaly as Educationist', *Tempo*, 3 (1962), pp. 38ff.
109. A revised edition of some of the songs, with English words by Geoffrey Russell-Smith, is now available.
110. P. M. Young, op. cit., p. 39.
111. C. Orff, 'Orff-Schulwerk: Past and Future', *MEd.*, 28 (1964), p. 210.
112. Ibid., p. 214.

2

Teaching and the Learning Environment

Composers have thought a great deal about the qualities that should be associated with the teacher of music. Take Hummel, for example:

'Since the whole edifice of instruction depends upon the first principles laid down as a foundation, parents, in the choice of a master, should direct their attention less towards cheapness of instruction, than to ascertaining that he is a man thoroughly conversant with the principles of his art, that his method of instruction is good and intelligible, that he conducts himself towards children with patience and kindness, and employs severity only when it becomes necessary.'[1]

Although he is talking about the fee-paying student with the private teacher, the fundamental proposition should apply with equal force to a public educational system, where, although the parent cannot normally exercise very much direct choice on how individual children are taught, he can, through the available political, social and economic channels, influence the way society thinks about musical education.

Hummel's first point is that a teacher of music should be 'thoroughly conversant with the principles of his art'. This is a view that is supported by every composer: it is pointed out here as a matter of emphasis. Today we might hope that a teacher of music was also 'thoroughly conversant with the principles of education', but unless he is at the same time a musician, he will not be able to provide the specifically musical qualities that are so essential in the teacher.

His second point, that the teacher's 'method of instruction' should be 'good and intelligible' is again an uncontentious statement, but one that stands repeating. It was Berlioz who said of Anton Reicha 'Unlike most teachers, he hardly ever failed to give his pupils the reason for the rules he recommended to them.'[2] Composers, understandably, are reluctant to practise anything that they do not understand: they generally feel that this is a privilege to which every learner has the right. Schoenberg, a teacher for most of his life, put the problem in this way: 'It doesn't take much doing to let smooth talents evolve smoothly. But when you are up against problems; to recognize them; to cope with them and –

last but not least – to do so successfully: that's the mark of the teacher.'[3] 'Good and intelligible' teaching is as demanding as thorough musicianship: only when the two are combined, and applied with 'patience and kindness', is there any chance of the child developing properly.

Composers in general, however, are in favour of individuality and against mass production. They are therefore inclined to place more emphasis on *learning* than teaching. Stravinsky said: 'I learned more through my mistakes and pursuits of false assumptions than from my exposures to founts of wisdom and knowledge.'[4] Although he was prepared to concede the usefulness of teachers sometimes: 'Education, at any rate in its earlier stages, is a trial-and-error process necessarily supervised by beings . . . more experienced and better instructed than one's self. Then as one grows older, older stages of one's changing self must assume the supervising.'[5]

Stravinsky thought that the musician could learn either by 'apprenticeship or by inventiveness',[6] and that of the two inventiveness was the more important. However, there can be no doubt that his own apprenticeship was fairly extensive, even if he quickly outstripped his teachers. Like Stravinsky, Schumann was also much concerned about the failure of many teachers to carry out their work properly: 'Bad teachers . . . are partly the cause of the decline of music. It is almost incredible how long their influence – based on guidance and cultivation, may endure.'[7] He disliked intensely those teachers who produced 'mechanical' musicians, 'for I have often observed that the greatest amount of prejudice and stupidity is to be found among mechanical musicians . . .'[8]

Berlioz was also among those who felt that teachers often did more harm than good:

'I am far from ungrateful to this worthy and excellent man [Lesueur] who watched over the outset of my career with so much sympathy and to the end of his life was a true friend. But what hours I wasted learning his antediluvian theories and putting them into practice, only to have to unlearn them and begin my education all over again from the beginning.'[9]

Nevertheless many composers felt that early contact with a good teacher had enormous advantages for the musician: 'the value of lessons with a great teacher cannot be computed in terms of what he said, or what you did, but in terms of some intangible contact with his mind and character,' wrote Vaughan Williams.[10] Here he draws attention to a characteristic of the teacher that is not simply the sum of his musicianship and his teaching ability, but to that indefinable quality of personality that is associated with good teachers. Fauré found it in his teacher, Saint-Saëns: 'It is not enough for him to initiate us into Schumann, Liszt and Wagner, and thus to open new horizons to us; he also wished to be kept informed about our works in composition. He read them with an interest and care which only masterpieces would merit. He then handed out priase or blame, always with examples and advice.'[11]

The ability of teachers to open the minds of their students to wider circles of experience is a characteristic demanded by many composers. In particular, there is a strong dislike of teaching which is limited to the imparting of rules. Consider Hindemith's view that:

'The teacher must not base his instruction simply on the rules of textbooks. He must continually refresh and complete his knowledge from the practice of singing and playing. What he teaches must have been developed out of his own exercises in writing. For it is his task not only to teach the pupil a correct technique, but also to help him obtain a comprehensive musical education, seeing to it that his work in the practical field is supplemented by an intelligent understanding of the theoretical side.'[12]

Here are many key features: the teacher must continue to be a student; musical education must be 'comprehensive', and so the teacher must himself perform, compose, analyse, enlarge his repertoire, develop his historical awareness, clarify his theoretical understanding.

In *A Plaine and Easie Introduction* Morley wishes to provide his students with an all-round musical education, but he recognizes that a student will prefer certain aspects to others:

'And as there be divers kinds of music so will some men's humours be more inclined to one kind than another; as some will be good descanters and excel in descant and yet will be but bad composers, others will be good composers and but bad descanters extempore upon a plainsong; some will excel in composition of Motets and being set or enjoined to make a Madrigal will be very far from the nature of it; likewise some will be so possessed with the madrigal humour as none may be compared with them in that kind and yet being enjoined to compose a Motet or some sad and heavy music will be far from the excellency which they had in their own vein' (p. 298).

This view of musical education is refreshingly honest. A teacher must be aware of the learner's inclinations not only from subject to subject but also within the structure of a single subject. He therefore has a duty to provide facilities for a student to explore a wide range of musical activities, while at the same time to be conscious of his inclinations.

What of the teacher himself? May he also have inclinations? This is a problem still to be faced in modern teaching. As often as not the teacher of music is expected to have inclinations in every direction of music-making; we cannot be certain that this is possible.

'Some will be so excellent in points of voluntary upon an instrument as one would think it impossible for him not to be a good composer and yet, being enjoined to make a song will do it so simply as one would think a scholar of one year's practice might easily compose a better. And I dare boldly affirm that look which is he who thinketh himself the best descanter of all his neighbours, enjoin him to make but a Scottish Jig, he will grossly err in the true nature and quality of it.' (p. 298)

Perhaps we may hope for the organizers of music teaching, especially in schools, to take some note of the simple truth that Morley is presenting.

The enthusiasm for multi-disciplinary studies which has become academically fashionable in recent years has often led musicians to wonder how they can widen the study of a subject which is by its nature already multi-disciplinary. Musical education is an umbrella for a very wide range of pursuits which include not only performance, vocal and instrumental, but also aspects of acoustics, composition, analysis, history, psychology and sociology. Quantz refers to the student's need 'to explore carefully the area to which his talent most inclines him . . . He who devotes himself to a branch of music for which he lacks the gifts will always remain a mediocre musician in spite of the best instruction and application' (p. 14). Most music teachers today would recognize the need to establish a very firm basis for their teaching which would be broad enough to include all the aspects of a musical education that contribute to the total pattern; but they would most likely also agree with Quantz that later specialization is inevitable. Quantz goes on to make an interesting distinction: 'a special talent is required if one is to become an able and learned musician. By the words "able musician" I mean a good singer or instrumentalist: "learned musician" on the other hand, I apply to someone who has learned composition thoroughly' (p. 14). It is interesting to note that such a division is still with us. Until recently it has been the job of the conservatoire or academy to produce the 'able musician' and that of the university to produce the 'learned musician'.

Such a division, though historically comprehensible is, of course, highly undesirable. It is particularly important that performance and composition are firmly bound together for a substantial part of a student's musical education, so that at no time does one aspect lose contact with the other. Among the implications of such a union is the need for young instrumentalists to compose, not only in the form of improvisations (as in *Orff-Schulwerk*) but also in its complete written forms. It is C. P. E. Bach who points out that 'a good future in composition can be assuredly predicted for anyone who can improvise, provided that he writes profusely and does not start too late' (p. 430).

The eighteenth-century essayists (such as C. P. E. Bach and Quantz) demand very high standards from the teacher. At no time is one encouraged to think that teachers are thought of as separate from performers and composers. Teachers are simply composers and players who have extra abilities, the abilities that we associate with the idea of the good teacher; first prove your musicianship, then learn to teach is a principle that has, in recent times, not always been sufficiently recognized. Quantz outlines in some detail the qualities required of a teacher, but the following short passage gives a fairly clear idea of the sort of demand he makes:

'The student must beware of a master who understands nothing of harmony and who is no more than an instrumentalist; who has not learnt his science thoroughly, and according to correct principles . . . who is not in a position to explain clearly and thoroughly everything that the student finds difficult to understand, and seeks to impart everything by ear, and through imitation, as we train birds; a master who flatters the apprentice, and overlooks all defects; who does not have the patience to show the student the same thing frequently, and have him repeat it . . . who seeks to delay the student; who does not prefer honour to self-interest, hardship to comfort, and unselfish service to jealousy and envy; or who in general does not have the *progress of music as his goal*' (pp. 16–17).

They are powerful and comprehensive requirements. The final 'progress of music' ordinance leaves us in no doubt about his priorities: a musical education must be music-centred before it can be child-centred, or more generally, socially conscious. If such a view has received insufficient support among educationalists in the past it may be in part due to the failure of musicians to bring to the problem the same vigour of expression that we find in Quantz and his contemporaries.

We meet again here the deprecation of the teacher 'who is no more than an instrumentalist.' We may recognize this as a criticism of our own times. Possibly because of the demands now made upon performers, possibly because the serious study of music is so dangerously delayed by the claims of a 'general' education, few instrumentalists have gained much experience in composition, and even fewer have learnt to understand the essential unity that exists between them. There have, it is true, been some encouraging signs that the preparation of a music teacher must take into consideration both accomplishments, but there still remains a very great deal to be done in this direction.

There are many who would suggest that the role of the teacher is essentially concerned with the provision of the appropriate environment. This idea is taken up by Quantz when he indicates that 'many excellent musicians have had no other master than their great natural ability, and the opportunity to hear much music that is good' (p. 17). This is a point of view with which many will have sympathy. The emphasis on 'natural ability' and the 'opportunity to hear much music that is good' raises many questions, of course, but it at least may modify our fears about how to proceed if the paragon previously described proves difficult to encounter.

There is a striking similarity between the following comment by Quantz: 'there are countless things which no master will teach him, or can teach him, and which he must, as it were, 'lift' from' others. Indeed it is this licensed thievery that produces the greatest artists' (p. 18), and C. P. E. Bach's 'study by listening, a kind of tolerated larceny, is the more necessary in music' (p. 28). Such phrases as 'licensed thievery' and 'tolerated larceny' express with some vigour an attitude to learning that is encouraged in many schools today. It is a view that also finds echoes in the writings of many later composers. Vaughan Williams put it this way: 'Cribbing is to my mind, a legitimate and praiseworthy practice, but one ought to know where one has cribbed,'[13] and enlarged on the idea by saying: 'the benefit that one obtains from an academy or college is not so much from one's official teachers as from one's fellow students' (p. 145). Vaughan Williams's own teacher, Stanford, expressed the idea in the following terms: '. . . the absorption of all that is best in other men's work means to the man of genuine invention the accentuation of his own individuality',[14] while Schumann simply said, 'seek among your comrades for those who know more than you do', and 'question older artists about the choice of pieces for study; you will thus save much time'.[15]

In *A Plaine and Easie Introduction* Morley continually refers to the ways in which the student can help himself in the process of learning musical techniques: 'I perceive by this way [example] that if you will be careful and practise, censuring your own doings with judgement, you need few more instructions for these ways; therefore my counsel is that when you have made anything you pursue it and correct it the second and third time before you leave it' (p. 167). This is an illustration of another important principle: that teaching can only go so far in any direction, but the learning goes on when the student has become independent of the teacher. Indeed Morley makes it plain that the test of effective teaching is whether the student is able to continue learning after the formal teaching has been completed. Here is another example: 'I would counsel you to learn to practise them [forms of double counterpoint] till you be perfect in your descant and in those plain ways of canon which I have set down, which will, as it were, lead you by the hand to further knowledge' (p. 201). Morley is confident that if his teaching is properly structured one thing will lead naturally to the next. The whole of *A Plaine and Easie Introduction* is written on the assumption that the total structure which Morley presents is capable of leading the student coherently through the many stages from the very beginning to fairly advanced compositions. By no means, however, does he regard his book as the only source that a student might need: 'whoso will be excellent must both spend much time and practice and look over the doings of other men' (p. 202). He frequently urges the student to listen to and study a very wide range of music; Morley himself was clearly familiar not only with the great wealth of contemporary English music, but also with a lot of the works of Italian composers, especially those who had exercised such a strong influence on developments in England during the last part of the sixteenth century.

Throughout his book Morley shows us that he is well acquainted with the idea of students helping each other. Philomathes says: 'I pray you then, give me some songs wherein to exercise myself at convenient leisure', to which the Master replies, 'Here be some following of two parts which I have made of purpose, that when you have any friend to sing with you, you may practise together, which will sooner make you perfect than if you should study never so much by yourself' (p. 88).

This clear statement of a basic principle in learning techniques may remind us once again that many of the apparently new ideas in teaching are, of course, nothing of the sort. Morley goes on to point out that not only should many practical exercises be worked with other students, but that '. . . there is no way readier to cause you to become perfect than to contend with someone or other, not in malice (for so is your contention your passion, not for love of virtue) but in love, showing your adversary your work and not scorning to be corrected of him, and to amend your fault if he speak with reason' (p. 202). We may compare this advice to that issued by the Open University to present-day students:

'. . . some students expressed concern because other students were discussing assignment questions in study centres before sending in their written work. We cannot stress too strongly that we think such discussion is *highly desirable*. It is not "cheating". It is a natural expression of students' interest in discussing the course objectives and testing one another's grasp of them – in short, of helping one another to learn. Just as you are free to spend as much or as little time as you need on an assignment, and to consult as many or as few source materials as you like, so you must be free to discuss the assignments as fully as you like before completing and sending them for marking.'[16]

The obvious uniformity of approach between Morley as a teacher and our own ideas is not only reassuring: it gives emphasis also to the idea that the principles of teaching music are fundamental to all ages.

The importance of a communal approach has too often been overlooked by musicians. It is perhaps part of our popular nineteenth-century inheritance that very often the ideal figure in music has been characterized as the lone hero, fighting to express his individuality in an alien community. The self-contained pianist and the pianist-composer are obviously central to this idea, but for Leopold Mozart at least, the performer 'has to accommodate himself to others' (p. 216). Throughout the eighteenth century there is a considerable emphasis on the idea of the musician as a member of a group, and it is therefore logical that the essayists should stress the need for group-learning situations in the development of a musical education. Even in the nineteenth century, Schumann's directive was simply 'lose no opportunity of playing music, duos, trios, etc., with others. This will make your playing broader and more flowing. Accompany singers often' (II, p. 413).

Louis Spohr wrote an interesting account of the way a musical environment, in this case his own family, provided him with the necessary encouragement for early growth:

'In Seesen were born my four brothers, and one sister. My parents were musical; my father played the flute, and my mother . . . played on the piano with great ability and sang the Italian bravuras of that time. As they practiced music very often in the evening, a sense and love for the art was easily awakened in me. Gifted with a clear soprano voice, I at first began to sing, and already in my fourth or fifth year I was able to sing duets with my mother at our evening music. It was at this time that my father, yielding to my eagerly expressed wish, bought me a violin at the yearly fair, upon which I now played incessantly. At first I tried to pick out the melodies I had been used to sing, and was more than happy when my mother accompanied me.'[17]

It is, of course, obvious that very few homes could provide those sorts of opportunities for the child to start his musical education: the question that teachers must ask is whether we ourselves can provide anything as good as this in schools with all the resources of the community behind us.

Quantz develops the theme of the importance of listening when he urges that: 'The beginner must therefore seek also to listen to as many good and generally approved compositions as possible. By this means he will greatly facilitate his path toward good taste in music' (p. 116), and C. P. E. Bach similarly remarks that 'Especially recommended are constant listening to good music . . . This will cultivate the ear and teach it to become attentive. Observe how musicians always listen to each other and modify their performance so that the ensemble may reach the desired goal' (p. 174). These comments recall a similar point which Rameau made a quarter of a century before: 'It is often seeing and hearing musical works (operas and other good musical compositions), rather than by rules, that taste is formed.'[18]

Further examples can be found in Schoenberg: 'Of course the best way to train a musical ear is to expose it to as much serious music as possible',[19] and in Wagner: 'A musician's aptitude for his art is best estimated by the impress which other people's music leaves upon him,'[20] and in Berlioz:

'Thanks to [a friend] and the pit tickets he let me have for the Opera, I went to everything that was given there. I took the score with me, and followed it during the performance. In this way I began to grow familiar with the workings of an orchestra and to understand the character and tone of voice, if not the range and mechanism, of most of the instruments. By continually comparing the effect obtained with the means used to obtain it I came to appreciate the subtle connection between musical expression and the technique of instrumentation; but no one had let me into the secret. I analysed the methods of those three modern masters, Beethoven, Weber and Spontini, and made a scientific study of conventional systems of scoring and also of unusual forms and combinations; this and the company of virtuoso players of various instruments, and the experiments I induced them to make, plus a dash of instinct, did the rest.'[21]

Stanford felt that the musician 'must be as well equipped in his literature as the poet or the philosopher. He will not preserve his freshness unless he keeps his ears open and his brains alive to all that is going on round him,'[22] and that in composition the musician's imagination must constantly be fed by the experience of new sounds:

'The secret of obtaining mastery of tints and of mixing well is only gained by a wide knowledge of musical works, and by using every opportunity of hearing them' (p. 126).

Observations on the relationships between performance and listening demand our closest attention. In spite of the considerable efforts of many teachers of what has come to be known as 'musical appreciation', the cultivation of the 'attentive' ear to which C. P. E. Bach refers is perhaps one of our greatest unsolved educational problems. Quantz would have the young musician educated 'in places where he could hear much that was good, and share the society of many worthy connoisseurs' (p. 12), and Bach was in no doubt that he owed much to having spent 'many years of association with good taste in a musical environment which could not be improved' (p. 169). In an auto-biographical sketch, Bach again refers to the Berlin court in the following terms:

'My duties in the Prussian service never allowed me any spare time to travel to foreign countries, so I have always remained in Germany, and have only made a few expeditions in my fatherland. The absence of foreign travel would have been more prejudicial to me in my profession, if I had not from my youth upwards enjoyed the rare good fortune to have at home, and likewise to hear there, the most admirable of all species of music, to make acquaintance with many masters of the very highest class, and to gain their friendship.'[23]

It is difficult to avoid the conclusion that very few people who are not themselves performers have learnt how to listen to music. By listening to music one has in mind the same sort of complete concentration that an educated reader would give to a novel or a play. Like any good novel or play, a good piece of music may encourage the imagination to move beyond the immediate confines of the work itself; but the work itself must first be fully grasped, fully recognized, fully embraced if such imagination is to be more than the mere daydreams which could as easily result from a warm bath. Listening to a piece of music so that the chain of events is clearly distinguished and the relationships properly observed is not as simple as some would suggest. In some ways the popular practice of extracting thematic material from longer works has not helped to achieve any of the many objectives, for a piece of music is more than a collection of tunes, just as a play is more than a collection of speeches.

By taking part in active music-making a person may learn to listen, especially if the opportunity occurs for him to make an individual contribution to a group activity. Quantz, C. P. E. Bach and Leopold

Mozart understood this only too well and regularly urged the young player to avoid the idea that only the soloist is important. Indeed they go so far as to suggest that the demands of ensemble playing are greater.

Bach's 'musical environment which could not be improved' was of course the Berlin court, with Frederick the Great as the chief of the 'worthy connoisseurs'.[24] The teaching of 'listening' as a separate activity was not an eighteenth-century problem, as it is for us today. Unfortunately the steps which led us from the idea of music as a minority upper class activity to music for everyone in a liberal society led us also down an educational cul-de-sac. The musical appreciation movement hoped to teach listening by means of a short cut. By popularizing a few tunes and accompanying other pieces with words and pictures it was hoped to bring non-performers to a participation in the music. There is no doubt that a limited success was achieved; but the real problems of listening were hardly touched upon. It has only been with the steady growth of instrumental teaching in recent years that a proper basis for a musical education has been re-established. It remains to be seen if we possess the courage to pursue the idea of 'good taste' which ranked so high in the essayists' thinking.

If the eighteenth-century essayists demand much of their ideal teacher, they are also painfully aware of the failure of many teachers to live up to their standards. It is Quantz who pronounces the fundamental issue: 'How then can they teach music if they themselves remain in a state of ignorance?' (p. 16) and Leopold Mozart who echoes the question: 'But how can the pupil help it if the teacher himself knows no better; and if indeed the teacher himself plays at random without knowing what he does' (p. 180).

There are, however, limits to the criticism one can make of other teachers if one is to avoid the possible suggestion that most teachers are more trouble than they are worth. It is therefore perhaps with some professional pride that Quantz emphasizes the great need of finding good teachers:

'There are some who have the harmful delusion that at the outset it is unnecessary to have a good master in order to learn the fundamental principles. For the sake of economy they often take whoever is cheapest, and often someone who himself knows nothing at all, so that one blind man leads another' (p. 17).

The blind leading the blind is an image that haunts everyone concerned with the progress of education, nor is the spectre of economic restraint unfamiliar to the present generation. If, however, the little money that is spent on musical education is to be well spent, then the principles outlined by the composers demand the very closest attention. Once established with a good teacher:

'the student with a genuine desire to perfect himself will discover from time to time new benefits that he had been previously unable to perceive, which will stimulate him to further inquiry. Inquiry of this sort must also be warmly recommended to the beginning musician. Industry alone is not enough. He may have good natural ability, good instruction, great industry, and good opportunities to hear much that is beautiful, yet never rise above mediocrity . . . For anything in music that is done without reflection and deliberation . . . is without profit. Industry founded upon ardent love and insatiable enthusiasm for music must be united with constant and diligent inquiry, and mature reflection and examination' (p. 19).

Such reassuring educational sanity will surprise only those readers who imagine that good teaching is a comparatively new invention. 'Diligent inquiry and mature reflection' are qualities that all teachers would wish to pass on to those with whom they work, for they suggest those ways of operating that will allow the process of education to continue long after the pupil is separated from the teacher.

Such inquiry must develop a spirit of independence if it is to lead the student towards a clarity of thinking that is so often missing from learning situations. Bernard Van Dieren gave an example of this problem when he wrote that 'Students, unfortunately, are taught from the tenderest age to honour the pronouncements of so many accepted authors that their opinions become prejudiced before they have had a chance to acquire individuality. The insistent authority with which orthodox critical procedures are impressed on them shields them against early discovery of personal bias in their exponents.'[25] It was Holst who said that 'the last and hardest duty of a teacher is to make himself unnecessary'.[26] The student need not, however, feel abandoned, for the good teacher will, in Holst's view, have connected him with the real world of music: 'If we are teachers our first duty is to make our pupil a child of tradition' and 'we can only do this if we ourselves are its children. Not merely students, but children steeped in the love of our tradition' (p. 151).

The growth towards independence on the part of the student does, of course, place considerable pressures on his teachers: 'When we are old enough to be asked for information by arguing juniors, we learn to dread the strain of ordeal-by-questioning. Hopeful young enthusiasts live in expectation of meeting a man who knows.'[27] Van Dieren points to this unending, unlimited nature of inquiry as perhaps the teacher's greatest problem:

'Must one confess that the old problems remain lifelong companions? That as time has gone on they have only increased one's uncertainties? The questions rarely permit concise answers. Everyone leads a ghostly army of secondary puzzles to which one hardly dares draw attention. Definite replies would require more knowledge than man could possess, be he never so persistent in his studies' (p. 1).

The teacher's task is, then, to participate in inquiry, and to help his students participate also. The composer obviously welcomes such an attitude to teaching, for the nature of his own work is constantly bound up in investigation and exploration.

In attempting to summarize the discussion, therefore, it is perhaps reasonable to emphasize eight principles that the composers have suggested as relevant to the problem: teachers of music should be good musicians; their teaching should be based on sound educational principles; great teachers demonstrate qualities of personality that are more than the sum of their musicianship and their teaching ability; the musical environment in which the learning takes place is of crucial significance; the music student should always be able to work and exchange ideas with other music students; people learning music should always be able to listen to, and study, a wide musical repertoire, preferably in live performance; listening demands active participation; and finally, all teaching, and all learning, should inevitably lead to independence of action.

In conclusion, the following extract from an eighteenth-century document advising French parents how to choose a music teacher, may help us to see the problem in perspective:

'Fathers and mothers or those charged with the education of children deceive themselves when they offer the teacher a lower fee than for teaching an older person. They do not consider that knowledge depends on proper beginnings, which can be given to tender youth only with great care, by devious means, and accomplished by attentions – in short, at considerable pains, which teachers do not have great need of taking with persons more mature, who ordinarily go a part of the way by themselves through their application and judgement.

The Italians are more reasonable or diplomatic in this than the French, for they choose a good teacher, into whose hands they entrust their children; and not satisfied merely with giving them a good fee, at the four great festivals of the year they give them, according to the custom of the country, little presents which re-awaken their attention and encourage the teachers to go beyond their appointed duties. In France, however, people are always eager to find occasion to argue with the teacher over a lesson-fee well earned, with the result that he very often loses it. Can the teacher thus treated retain affection for his task? I say these things more for the profit of the pupils than for that of the teachers and for myself in particular, as I am just about to retire from teaching forever.

There are, moreover, some disagreeable people who wish to make the master a slave, who think they will profit by continually harassing him, and who wish to make him teach in accordance with their caprice.'[28]

Notes

1. J. F. Hummel, *Ansfürliche theoretische practische anweisung zum pianoforte-spiel* (Vienna, 1827); Eng. trans. (London, 1828), p. iii.
2. H. Berlioz, *Mémoires* (Paris, 1870), Eng. trans. D. Cairns (London, 1969), p. 74.
3. A. Schoenberg, *Letters*, ed. E. Stein (New York, 1965), p. 24.
4. I. Stravinsky, *Themes and Conclusions* (New York, 1972), p. 22.
5. Ibid., pp. 21–22.
6. *Poetics of Music* (Cambridge Mass., 1947), p. 31.
7. *Music and Musicians*, trans. F. R. Ritter (London, 1877), Vol. I, p. 83.
8. Ibid., Vol. I, p. 227.
9. *Mémoires*, p. 51.
10. *Heirs and Rebels*, p. 102.
11. *Opinions musicales* (Paris, 1930), Eng. trans. Morgenstern, op. cit., p. 281.
12. *The Craft of Musical Composition*, p. 4.
13. *Some Thoughts on Beethoven's Choral Symphony*, p. 149.
14. *Musical Composition*, p. 126.
15. *Music and Musicians*, Vol. I, pp. 412–13.
16. *The Open University B.A. Degree Handbook* (Bletchley, 1972), p. 15.
17. L. Spohr, *Autobiography*, Eng. trans. anon. (London, 1878), pp. 1–2.
18. *Nouveau système de musique théorique* (Paris, 1726), p. 105; Eng. trans. Morgenstern, op. cit., p. 43.
19. *Style and Idea*, p. 147.
20. *Beethoven*, Eng. trans. E. Dannreuther (London, 1870), p. 35.
21. *Mémoires*, pp. 73–4.
22. *Musical Composition*, p. 126.
23. *Selbstbiographie* (Hamburg, 1773), ed. L. Nohl, Eng. trans. Lady Wallace (London, 1867), p. 52.
24. Frederick the Great (1712–86) of Prussia not only employed many famous musicians, including Quantz, Bach and Agricola, but also took an active part in court music by both playing, and composing for, the flute. See E. E. Helm, *Music at the Court of Frederick the Great* (Norman, USA, 1960).
25. *Down among the Dead Men* (London, 1935), p. 212.
26. 'Lectures at Yale on the Teaching of Art', op. cit., p. 155.
27. B. Van Dieren, op. cit., p. 1.
28. M. P. de Montéclair, *Petite méthode pour apprendre musique aux enfants* (Paris, c. 1730), Eng. trans. W. Wager in M. Pincherle, 'Elementary Musical Education in the 18th Century', *MQ*, 34 (1948), p. 63.

3

Teaching Notation

We have reached the latter half of the twentieth century without arriving at any firm conclusions about the teaching of musical notation. Should children be taught conventional musical notation? If they should, when should it be taught, and how should it be taught? Should the knowledge of notation follow or precede practical experience of music-making? Should conventional staff notation be introduced at the start, or should simplified codes come first?

Composers have answered these questions in different ways at different times. Morley, of course, is essentially a practical teacher, and he expresses concern about teaching which is heavily theoretical: 'I cannot imagine how the teachers (which these thirty or forty years past have taught) should so far have strayed from the truth . . .' (p. 132). His own working division of the study of music is expressed in the following way:

'Music is divided into two parts; the first may be called Elementary or Rudimental, teaching to know the quality and quantity of notes, and everything else belongs to songs of what manner or kind soever. The second may be called Syntactical, poetical or effective, treating of sounds, concords, and discords, and generally of everything serving for the formal and apt setting together of parts or sounds for producing of harmony, either upon a ground or voluntary' (p. 104).

Unlike some of the teaching methods of later periods Morley's teaching of the 'rudimental' is intensely practical, and the learner is given plenty of opportunity to try out his knowledge with practical problems. The teaching pace is carefully thought out, and there is a clear sense of structure throughout the course. Morley starts right at the beginning:

'Master: But have you learned nothing at all in music before?
Philomathes: Nothing: therefore I pray begin at the very beginning and teach me as though I were a child.'

The Master's reply to this request is: 'I will do so; and therefore behold, here is the scale of music which we term the Gam(ut)' (p. 10).

Morley thus plunges us straight away into the hexachords of Guido d'Arezzo (c. 995–1050). Christopher Simpson was later to refer to this procedure in the following terms:

'It is a great hinderance in the learning of an art or science to have its principles delivered in hard words or obscure terms: and no science (I think) has been more unhappy in this particular than music. When I was a boy and learned to sing, the first thing proposed to me was a Gamut, (A re, B mi, etc.), which my master told me was the scale of music, and must be got by rote, to say it rapidly, as well backward as forward. This seemed a hard task; and the rather because I did not understand the meaning of those words; neither did I (then) conceive how such words could anyway conduce to the tuning of a song. Having lately had occasion to instruct a young gentleman in these rudiments . . . I did consider what difficulties had occurred to myself, at the same age, and thereupon did endeavour to render the said rudiments in as plain words as I could express, and is as easy a method.'[1]

Just like Simpson, Philomathes fails to understand the Gamut table, and replies: 'Indeed I see letters and syllables written here, but I do not understand them, nor their order' (p. 10). Morley, however, is careful to explain as fully as possible the implications of his table, and once the first step is negotiated the rest seems to come without too much difficulty. Morley is very fond of using diagrams and tables in order to help him make a point clear, and his book shares with Dowland's *Ornithoparcus* a great collection of such visual aids. Morley, however, avoids 'such fantastical imaginations as it were ridiculous to write . . .' (p. 108), which, apparently, were often associated with the Gamut: 'I will not cloy your mind with unprofitable precepts' (p. 17), and instead leads his pupil through some basic practical lessons: 'Sing then after me till you can tune, for I will lead you in the tuning, and you shall name the notes yourself' (p. 13). The simple practice of singing scales and naming the notes while referring to a diagram thus starts the elaborate structure of Morley's teaching. As long as the student can get as far as that Morley promises him the earth:

'. . . and this much I boldly affirm, that any of but mean capacity so that they can but truly sing their tunings, which we commonly call the six notes, or Ut, Re, Mi, Fa, Sol, La, may, without any other help saving this book, perfectly learn to sing, make descant, and set parts well and formally together' (p. 6).

Clearly Morley might have made a splendid career in advertising.

Matthew Locke (*c.* 1630–77) had a similar attitude. In the conclusion of *Melothesia, or certain general rules for playing upon a continued-bass* (1673) he states:

'By these directions the ingenious practical student who has a thorough knowledge of the scale of music, and hands fitly prepared for the instrument he aims at, may in a short time attain to his desired end of accompanying either voices of instruments: and may with much ease arrive at the rudiments of music.'[2]

The problem of the teaching of rudiments had brought Locke into a fascinating controversy during the period immediately before the publication of *Melothesia*. In 1672 Thomas Salmon had published a 92-page pamphlet entitled: *An essay to the advancement of musick by casting away the perplexity of different cliffs and uniting all sorts of musick, lute, viol, violin, organ, harpsichord, voice, etc. in one universal character.* His idea was to use the F (bass) clef for all parts, employing octave and two-octave transpositions for the higher voices and instruments. His one clef would thus replace eight clefs that were often found in seventeenth-century scores, two G clefs, four C clefs and two F clefs:

Even if, as Salmon points out, only the three most common clefs are used, 'sometimes the lower most line is g, sometimes f, sometimes e, and consequently all other lines and spaces suffer'[3]:

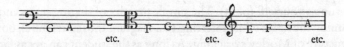

He goes on to say: 'I could not think it feasible to reduce these entangled perplexities into one order, or that such pilgrim notes could be fixed in any constant dwellings, but that the following contrivance shows me the way, and is here already accomplished.' His notation is therefore as follows:

so that M ('Meane') is an octave transposition of the bass clef, and Tr ('Treble') is a two-octave transposition of the bass clef; or

$$B = \;\; \mathbf{9}\!\!: \qquad\qquad M = \overset{8}{\mathbf{9}}\!\!: \qquad\qquad Tr = \overset{15}{\mathbf{9}}\!\!:$$

Another teacher, Étienne Loulié, writing some years after Salmon, also saw advantages in the child concentrating on the bottom line of the stave as a reference point. However, it was not the G clef that he employed but the soprano C clef; the one commonly employed in keyboard music:

$$\text{[clef]} \;\; \mathbf{o \;\; o \;\; o \;\; o \;\; o \;\; o \;\; o \;\; o}$$
C D E F G A B C

Loulié is clearly echoing Salmon when he says that 'I have not followed the usual custom, which is to begin with the scale, to give at the same time all the clefs . . . Knowledge of this is not only useless, but also confusing for beginning students, especially for children.'[4]

In the preface to Salmon's book, his publisher, John Birchensa, puts the case for reform in vivid style:

'There is not any art which at this day is more rude, unpolished, and imperfect in the writings of most of the ancient and modern authors than music; for the elementary part thereof is little better than an undignified mass, and confused chaos of impertinent characters, and insignificant signs. It is intricate and difficult to be understood, it afflicts the memory, and consumeth much time, before the knowledge thereof can be attained; because the clefs are divers, their transposition frequent, the order and places of notes very mutable, and their denominations alterable and unfixed.'

Thomas Campion had expressed a very similar idea:

'There is nothing doth trouble, and disgrace our traditional musician more than the ambiguity of the terms of music, if he cannot rightly distinguish them, for they make him incapable of any rational discourse in the art he professes.'[5]

The central 'ambiguity' for Campion seems to be in connection with the scale:

'In like manner there can be no greater hindrance to him that desires to become a musician, than the want of the true understanding of the scale, which proceeds from the error of the common teacher who can do nothing without the old Gamut . . .' (p. B3ii).

The 'new way' to which Campion refers is the baroque approach to harmony which led the composer to think of the harmony from the bass upwards, rather than from the tenor, as many contrapuntalists would have done. It also refers to the late-Renaissance, early-Baroque growth in understanding of tonality: 'The substance of all music, and the true knowledge of the scale, consists in the observations of the half note . . .' (p. B4i). The positioning of the semitone in the scale is essentially part of the 'new way' which Campion refers to as 'an easy way for him that would either with aid of a teacher, or by his own industry, learn to sing; and if he shall well bear in mind the placing of the half notes it will help him much in the knowledge of the chords which have all their variety from the half note' (p. B4iv). Salmon takes a similar view to Birchensa and Campion:

'That which first of all terrifies a beginner is a long discourse of gibberish, a faddle of hard names and fictitious words called the Gamut, presented to him perfectly to be learned without book, till he can readily repeat it backwards and forwards as though a man must be exact in the art of conjuring before he might enter upon music' (p. 11).

and concludes that he is

'certain if he [the student] can say G, A, B, C, D, E, F, it will do to all intents and purposes as well. For the plain truth is, there are but seven notes in all, only repeated again in double and treble proportion' (p. 11).

Locke replied to this idea with his *Observations upon a Late Book Entitled* . . . by pouring a good deal of abuse on Salmon's head:

'. . . about three years since, our Universal Essayer made his address to me for instruction in composition; but I, never having contrived any method that way, referred him to Mr. Simpson's *Compendium of*

Practical Music for the first rudiments and to Mr. Birchensa (his now Publisher) for his further advance, assuring him I know no man fitter for that purpose, it being in the manner of his whole business' (p. 3).

He went on to accuse Salmon of every type of inadequacy, and to defend the use of various clefs. His main arguments centre round two points: first, that the introduction of new forms of notation might lead to all previous publications becoming obsolete; second, that transpositions were artificial, and deprived the reader of any real sense of pitch.

Locke's angry outburst is a little surprising. He makes great play of his seniority both in age and position – 'Composer in ordinary to his Majesty and Organist of Her Majesty's Chapel' – but his 39-page booklet does not really get to grips with Salmon's arguments. Indeed he devotes over ten pages to publishing a canon, using all the clefs of course, to prove how simple conventional notation is.

Salmon immediately replied with *A Vindication of an Essay to the advancement of music from Mr. Matthew Locke's Observations, by enquiring into the real Nature and most convenient practice of the Science* (1672). There can be little doubt that Locke's attack had put Salmon on the defensive, and he showed that he was not above using the weapons of abuse himself:

'Morefields or the Bear Garden are entertainment only for the rabble: and should I spend my time in wrangling, scratching, pulling by the hair, and such like, the reader would have good reason to think himself but rudely treated. I shall therefore (after I have caressed my good friend and old acquaintance, the Observer) enquire into the nature of music . . . (p. 2).

Salmon then takes each of Locke's objections in turn, repeating the views expressed in the essay.

Much of Salmon's second text, however, has little to do with his new notation, and Locke seized on this fact when in the following year he produced *The Present Practice of Music Vindicated* (1673):

'. . . for no sooner can I cast my eyes on the *Vindication*, but I lose the *Essay*; this proposing a nearer and easier way to the attaining of practical music, that running quite from it to what we have already passed, or to what is merely speculative, or at most, insignificant to us . . .' (p. ii).

The general tone is similar to the first book:

'Though I may without scruple aver that nothing has done Mr. Salmon more kindness than that his books have had the honour to be answered, yet have I been forced to afford him this favour, rather to chastise the reproaches he hath thrown upon the most eminent professors of music, than for any thing of learning that I found in him' (p. ii).[6]

The Establishment was clearly closing its ranks. Locke represents the older generation, and Salmon dares to question its teaching! He continues:

'Those gentlemen he accused of ignorance for not embracing his illiterate absurdities, for which it was necessary to bring him to the bar of reason, and to do him that justice which his follies merited. Though for the fame he gets by this I shall not much envy him; with who it will fare, as with common criminals, who are seldom talked of above two or three days after execution . . .' (p. ii).

There is no doubt some truth in this, for the B-M-T notation (as Locke called it), did not establish itself. Nevertheless, in the interests of accuracy, we may take the opportunity to correct the impression that Locke and Playford (for Playford contributes a whole section of the book himself) were trying to give. In their view the B-M-T notation makes the reading of music harder, not easier. Playford states that the following example:

would be written by Salmon in the following confusing manner:

whereas Salmon would simply have written it thus:

Locke and Playford wish their readers to think that Salmon is advocating a four line stave with no use of ledger lines. This is quite clearly not the case. Salmon uses the five line stave throughout his examples, and merely points out that the scale of an octave does not need five lines. Moreover there is nothing in Salmon's text to suggest that he would jump from one octave to another and then back again; on the contrary he changes octave for *sustained* passages only.

The Locke-Salmon controversy is worth studying for two basic reasons (apart from the light it casts upon Restoration manners): it illustrates well the hold that traditional methods of teaching can exercise, regardless of the value of innovations; secondly, Salmon's use of one clef anticipates the almost exclusive use of one clef by brass bands, where for reasons of simplicity and transferability only the treble clef is used (with the sole, and eccentric, exception of the bass trombone).

There can be no doubt that Salmon's ideas on notation have a lot to recommend them: like changes in spelling, however, changes in notation have obvious economic implications. Composers, moreover, are mostly interested in making musical notation as clear as possible, not to amateurs with an interest in music, but to professional performers who would in any case already have learnt the form of notation traditionally used for their instruments or voice.

In returning to the discussion of Morley's methods for the beginner, it is perhaps as well to emphasize that he taught the notes of the scale by singing and naming the notes, and by requiring his pupils to imitate him. The notes were taught *as sounds*, even if they were given the 'hard names and fictitious words called the Gamut'.[7] It is unlikely that many teachers would today start with the Gamut, but many have until very recently begun by teaching, almost parrot-fashion the lines and spaces of the treble and bass clefs. Many teachers now, of course, prefer to start with two, three, four and five note tunes, and to develop their pupils' pitch vocabulary from there. But it must be remembered that Morley was not writing for a child. Indeed it is reasonable to think of Polymathes and Philomathes as university undergraduates.

After the preliminary work with scales, Morley soon moves from conjunct (scale) passages to disjunct passages:

When you sing imagine a note betwixt them thus (p. 17):

The development of pitch recognition in *A Plaine and Easie Introduction* pursues a course that is not very different from that with which we are familiar today in many elementary books, except for the use of the Gamut names. But the development of rhythmic knowledge is quite strange to modern eyes.

Morley presents a great wealth of information on rhythmic notation, and as usual he brings diagrams and tables to his service. '*A table containing all the usual proportions* is met with this comment:

Phi: "Here is a table indeed, containing more than ever I mean to beat my brains about. As for music, the principal thing we seek in it is to delight the ear . . ." ' (p. 58).

We must not forget that this is Morley himself, for he does not use the Master to deny this proposition. His position is in effect one which acknowledges that 'the principal thing we seek in music is delight', but at the same time recognizes that knowledge of musical techniques may lead the listener more quickly to greater delights.

'A table with all the usual proportions' is also to be found in René Descartes' *Compendium Musicae* (1618). This important theoretical work was translated into English, anonymously,[8] as *Renatus Des-Cartes excellent compendium of musick: with necessary and judicious animadversions thereupon* and appeared in 1653.[9] The 'animadversions' include many pages of tables and reveal Descartes the mathematician as much as the musician, for the *Compendium* belongs essentially to the Tinctoris–Zarlino tradition, more 'speculative' than 'practical'. Nevertheless, we may recognize in the opening statement a feeling that perhaps links the Morley era with the growth of baroque ideas: 'The object of this art is a sound. The end, to delight, and more various affections in us' (p. 1). This text must have been overlooked by Birchensa – in his translation of Alstedt's *Templum Musicum*, a work which dealt with 'both of the mathematical and practical part of musick' that appeared in 1664, for he claimed that there was 'not any book extant in our English tongue'.

Although Morley introduced rhythmic notation after pitch notation, he clearly attaches very great importance to the knowledge of rhythmic devices. The very extensive and detailed information that he introduces to his pupils may surprise the modern reader, for a large number of the techniques that he discusses were already only of historical interest to the Elizabethans. There are perhaps two points that should be made in this context. First, Morley, like most teachers, is a conservator: 'but of myself I am loath to break a received custom' (p. 133). Secondly, our own age has only very slowly become aware of the importance of rhythmic training as an antidote to the effects of too much '*andante*-common-time'.

In Italy the teaching of notation was further developed by Carissimi, whose brief 16-page *Ars Cantandi*[10] shows a movement away from the Guidonian Gamut towards the moveable ut (or later, do) system.

Carissimi used the same method for learning the notes of the hexa-
chord:

But whereas Morley goes on to give examples of plainsong in Gamut
notation, Carissimi now introduces the hexachords on F and C with ut
as tonic in both cases.[11]

The problems of teaching notation do not seem very great to the
eighteenth-century essayists. All of them are confident that the
continuous association of sound and symbol that constitutes the normal
in the learning of an instrument will soon assure the learner of an easy
familiarity with musical notation. Quantz is, of course, writing a book
for flute players, and consequently his notation is mainly in the treble
clef. He therefore gives the letters of the notes as he gives the fingering
required to produce them. This direct procedure he contrasts with the
contemporary French practice which, he claimed, either used the full
Gamut nomenclature, C sol ut, D la re, etc., or simply ut, re, mi, etc.;
he refers to nine possible clefs that the student might encounter:

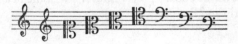

but suggests that three (treble, alto, bass) are sufficient for normal use.[12]
He introduces key signatures up to six sharps and flats fairly early on,
but uses the key of C for most of his examples.

Mozart mentions five clefs as being of importance, treble (violin),
descant, alto, tenor and bass, but again confines most of his examples to
the treble clef (p. 27). At one point he offers, apparently in all serious-
ness, the idea of a moveable G clef for the many transposing wind
instruments of the period, but does not pursue the issue. C. P. E. Bach

has nothing to say about the teaching of notation, and assumes that anyone who reads his book will already be familiar with both the keyboard clefs. 'Those who expected a voluminous work from me' he states in the preface to *Part One*, 'are in error. I believe I deserve more gratitude if through brief precepts I have made practicable, easy and agreeable many things that are quite difficult in the study of the keyboard' (p. 29).

Like other instrumental teachers, Bach knew that learning to read music is a minor problem for beginners: the real problems, the 'many things that are difficult', are tone, phrasing, correct fingering, melodic decoration and improvisation, and the more general problems of style.

It must be remembered of course, that the 'keyboard' clefs that Bach employed were not the treble G clef and F bass clef, but the soprano C clef and the F bass clef:

These clefs were standard keyboard clefs until the middle of the eighteenth century. In the same year as the publication of Bach's *Part Two* (1762), F. W. Marpurg's *Die Kunst das clavier zu spielen* was reprinted in Berlin, and similarly employed the soprano clef throughout the text. It will be recalled that in the earlier discussion of the Locke-Salmon controversy the idea of using a clef whose bottom line was easily remembered was a feature of the argument. The change to the use of the G clef for the right hand of the keyboard reflects the movement towards standardization in the eighteenth century, and also the powerful influence of the violinists who claimed the G clef as their own. Bach was, in any case, not too worried about the choice of clefs, for he points out that the keyboard player 'must be at home in all keys and transpose instantly and faultlessly' (p. 27).

Alternatives to staff notation do not find very great support from composers until recent times. Of course the lutenist composers employed the lute tablatures, and tablatures for both the viol and for keyboard instruments (including the organ) have been used from time to time;[13] and recently alternative forms of graphic notation have been used by an increasing number of composers.

There has, however, been considerable discussion of alternatives to conventional staff notation, particularly in the teaching of music to children, by people with a keen interest in musical education. It is therefore appropriate that a brief outline of the nature of the alternatives be included at this point. The most important development in the eighteenth century was Rousseau's cipher notation. This system, which is arguably an extension of J. J. Souhaitty's *Nouvelle Méthode* (Paris, 1665), was first demonstrated by Rousseau to the members of the Paris *Académie de Sciences* in 1742, and is usually known as the *Projet sur la Musique*.[14] The substitution of numbers for positions on the stave, eg.[15]

(i)

(ii)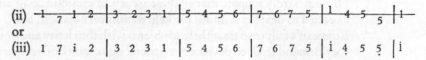
or
(iii) 1 7 i 2 │ 3 2 3 1 │ 5 4 5 6 │ 7 6 7 5 │ i 4 5 5 │ i

(where a dot above or below the note shows a change of octave) has certain limited advantages for single vocal lines (in which Rousseau was chiefly interested), but complex harmonic textures produce increased rather than decreased problems of recognition when the visual patterns of staff notation are replaced with a mass of figures.

Although Rousseau tended to seize every opportunity to talk about his own system of notation, he did in *Émile* discuss more general matters:

'As might be expected, I am no more anxious to have him learn to read music than to read writing. There is no hurry to fix his mind on conventional signs. This I admit seems to raise a difficulty. Even if the knowledge of notes does not appear to be more necessary for singing than a knowledge of letters for writing there is a difference between them. When we talk we are expressing our own ideas, where as in singing we are for the most part expressing other peoples. In the latter case we must read. But in the first instance hearing can take the place of reading: a song is registered more faithfully on the ear than on the eye.'[16]

Few modern teachers would fail to agree that musical notation should follow musical experience in the early stages of a child's development,[17] but Rousseau's answer to the 'difficulty' is hardly illuminating. The important relationship between notation and that reflective, analytical process that must follow in the path of the imagination, is one that has received much attention in recent years. Strangely, Rousseau himself does go on to make a very similar point when he says:

'More than that, to know music well we must compose songs as well as sing them, and the two things must go together if we are ever to know music properly. First train your young musician in the making of regular phrases by a very simple modulation and then to indicate their different relations by a correct punctuation, through a fit choice of cadences and rests. Above all, avoid fantastic tunes and anything with pathos or forced expression. What is wanted in every case is a simple tuneful melody with the bass so clearly marked that he can feel and accompany it without difficulty. This means that for the training of voice and ear the child should always sing with the harpsichord' (*Émile*, p. 63).

One can hardly suppose that all these aspects of music-making are expected to develop without the help of musical notation; but Rousseau's failure to treat these problems with the clarity and honesty they demand tends to devalue the general significance of his assertions. The paragraph quoted above, does, after all, outline a fairly extensive musical education. In addition to the qualities of singing which the child is expected to develop, there are the demands for a good ear, a sense of style and simplicity in composition, a basic knowledge of harmony and a growing awareness of the contrapuntal techniques necessary in the fitting of melodies to basses. As we have seen in the essays of Quantz and his contemporaries, there is a need to recognize that these skills are only developed with great patience over a very long period; if Rousseau understood this, he certainly failed to make it clear. For in *Emile*, where many educational problems are dwelt upon at considerable length, the principles of a musical education are confined to a few unsupported and questionable declarations.[18]

Rousseau repeated the claims for his system of number notation both in his articles in Diderot's *Encyclopédie* (1751–65) and in his own *Dictionnaire de Musique* (1768), and his ideas did influence Galin[19] and the early nineteenth-century French teachers. As a system of notation, however, Rousseau's ciphers did not share the success of the developments which took place in the teaching of the solfeggio systems, particularly with that of the Glover-Curwen moveable Doh. The development of these solfeggio systems both in England and on the Continent have been very fully described by Rainbow[20] who, while warmly supporting the aims of these groups, nevertheless points out that 'the commonest failing of new systems of notation devised to simplify the reading of music has ever lain in the propensity of their various inventors to regard them as *substitutes* for the standard notation' (p. 164). This is a situation that the composers have generally recognized, and when they have supported the teaching of solfeggio systems it has been simply as a preliminary to staff notation.

Perhaps the most important contribution by a composer in this field came from Kodály, who, in addition to his work in developing the use of folk song materials in Hungarian schools, gave considerable support to the initial teaching of singing by tonic-sol-fa means. It is clear, however, that conventional staff notation is essential in instrumental work, and that even in vocal music acute problems occur in compositional styles where scale systems other than major/minor ones are employed.

In spite of the fact that many writers have pointed out the merits of solfeggio systems as initial training methods, the attempts to employ them as *substitute* methods have been fairly common. Mainzer, for example, wrote in the following way: 'in order to impart a general knowledge of the principles of music, it is indispensable that the method employed should be totally different from that employed in giving a purely musical education; and it is a great error to apply to elementary schools, or public classes, methods which are not founded on this rigorous distinction'.[21]

Arguments about the various merits of alternative systems of teaching notation tend to become entangled with extra-musical problems, especially with economic, political and religious ones. Economic problems – to be precise, the lack of financial support for musical education – lead to the defence of inexpensive vocal teaching in preference to expensive instrumental tuition, for all but a small minority. Political and religious reasons are then put forward for this basically economic choice, e.g. 'the growth of a national identity' or 'the value of worship'. The separation of these two basic activities – the instrumental and the vocal – leads to a separation in techniques of teaching them, and finally to a separation in the notational methods of recording these activities. If a musical education is to provide the proper facilities for a child to learn *to be a musician* (and nothing less is a worthwhile educational aim), then they must include the learning of singing, playing, composing and what may be called 'reflection' (i.e. analysis and history).

Curwen has been associated with the 'gradual realization on the part of teachers that learning the symbols of notation *as facts* did not produce the ability to sing from those symbols'.[22] This was not, of course, just a Curwen discovery, but forms part of the general post-Pestalozzian attitude to learning by discovery, which is applicable to all subjects in the school curriculum. Moreover it was an attitude that was very well understood by composers not only in the post-Pestalozzian nineteenth and twentieth centuries, but also by Quantz and his contemporaries in the mid-eighteenth century, and Morley and his contemporaries one hundred and fifty years before that.

The uselessness of teaching any form of musical notation that is not connected directly with the musical experience of the learner is not in dispute. It is, however, important to stress this principle, for it is frequently overlooked. Despite all the efforts of the musical educators in the nineteenth century, the following list of 'easy methods' of learning musical notation, completely detached from the actual processes of making music, were available for purchase in the last quarter of the century: Little May's musical drawing slate, 1873; Musical dominoes, 1877; Mitchell's musical theory illustrated by diagrams, 1878; The Royal game of music made easy, 1879; The fork-lightning system, 1881; Kühne's Grammar of music, 1881; Roylance's Numerical system, 1883; The Pamphonia, 1889; A kindergarten system, 1889; Cyclotone, or scale clock, 1890; The octave family, 1890; and the Fletcher System, 1889.[23]

It was Spohr who wrote that 'in order to render the first dry elementary lessons more agreeable to the pupil, the practical part of violin playing has at once been united with them, instead of being separated as in other works. Hence, according to this method, the violin can be placed in the hands of the pupil from the very first.'[24] Today, Suzuki is doing just that with his young Japanese pupils, and in Europe, Orff is handing out his xylophones and glockenspiels for a similar reason. The principle seems to be, take care of the music-making, and the notation will take care of itself.

Notes

1. *The Principles of Practical Musick* (London, 1665), p. A3.
2. Quoted in F. T. Arnold, *The Art of Accompaniment from a Thorough Bass* (London, 1931), p. 157.
3. T. Salmon, *An Essay to the Advancement of Musick* (London, 1665), p. A3.
4. E. Loulié, *Elements or Principles of Music*, trans. and ed. A. Cohen (New York, 1965), p. xvi.
5. T. Campion, *New Ways of Making Foure Parts in Counter-point* (London, c. 1614), p. B3i.
6. A contemporary 'eminent professor', Giovani Maria Bononcini, published his *Musico pratico* in the same year (1673), in Bologna. He uses Gamut notation and G, C and F clefs.
7. C. Simpson, *The Principles of Practical Musick* (London, 1665), p. A3.
8. Possibly William, Viscount Brouncker.
9. A translation of the original was also made by W. Robert (London, 1961); see also A. W. Locke, 'Descartes and 17th Century music', *MQ*, 21 (1935), pp. 423ff.
10. The original Italian version has not been found. A German version dating from 1693, has been translated into English by J. R. Douglas (Thesis, Union Theological Seminary, New York, 1949).
11. For further discussion of concepts of tonality see W. Atcheson, 'Key and Mode in 17th Century Music Theory Books', *JMT*, 17 (1973), pp. 204–32.
12. Like Carissimi, Quantz and his contemporaries thought that organists should be familiar with all clefs, so that they could play from vocal scores (pp. 60ff.).

13. See W. Apel, *The Notation of Polyphonic Music* (Cambridge, Mass., 1942): keyboard tablatures, pp. 21–53; lute tablatures, pp. 54–86; and the *New Oxford History of Music*, Vol. IV (London, 1968), pp. 773–83.
14. The correct title is *Projet concernant de nouveau signes pour la musique* (Geneva, 1742).
15. Examples given in Rousseau's *Dictionnaire de musique* (Paris, 1768), under 'Notation'.
16. *Emile*, trans. W. Boyd (London, 1956), pp. 62–3.
17. On this principle Mozart seems to be very much out of step. His view is that 'when the teacher, after careful examination, finds that the pupil has understood clearly all that has been discussed up to now, and that it has impressed itself thoroughly on his memory, then comes the time when the violin must be held correctly in his left hand' (p. 54). Rousseau's notion is probably derived from Couperin (op. cit.), who insisted that 'one should not begin by teaching musical notation to children until after they have a certain number of pieces in their fingers . . . moreover the memory improves greatly in learning by heart' (p. 13).
18. Einstein refers to Rousseau as 'this arrogant dilettante' (A. Einstein, *Music in the Romantic Era* (New York, 1947), p. 339).
19. P. Galin, *Exposition d'une nouvelle méthode* (Paris, 1818).
20. B. Rainbow, *Land without Music* (London, 1967).
21. J. Mainzer, *Singing for the Million* (London, 1841), p. 1.
22. B. Rainbow, op. cit., p. 159.
23. P. A. Scholes, *The Mirror of Music* (London, 1947). An important discussion of the use of such devices was written by Annie J. Curwen in *Child Life*, Vol. 1, 1899, pp. 67–72.
24. L. Spohr, *Violin School* (London, 1831), p. i.

4

The Teaching of Singing

Hindemith observed that 'the quality of a society's art of ensemble singing and the value of the composition written to satisfy the demands of the group singers is quite likely the best gauge of a period's musical culture'.[1] It might equally be said that the quality of a school's ensemble singing is quite likely the best gauge of a school's musical culture. The repertoire of vocal ensemble music provides the musician at every level of ability with an extremely rewarding experience which may have important effects not only on his musical development, but also upon his social awareness. There are, however, factors concerning the size of the group which need to be considered in this context. By ensemble singing the musician usually has in mind a group that is large enough to provide a full harmonic texture, but not one that is so large that the individual voice is lost in the sheer volume of sound, as is the position in the full choir. Ensemble singing, in this sense, provides the advantages of participating within the group, without diminishing the possibility of individual, identifiable contributions.

The focus of the educational problem, therefore, is the individual vocal needs of the child, rather than the dubious attempts by some educationalists to involve children in forms of political or sectarian activity. In its turn, moreover, the vocal need may be seen as just one part of the total musical need, and that ensemble singing will therefore combine with other musical activities such as instrumental performance and composition to form the total pattern of musicianship that must be the goal of musical education.

The whole of 'the first part' of Morley's *A Plaine and Easie Introduction* is devoted to singing. At the end of this section the master says 'And let this suffice for your instruction in singing, for I am persuaded that, except practice, you lack nothing to make you a perfect and sure singer' (p. 88). With only the use of the voice, therefore, Morley introduces the beginner to most of the problems of pitch and rhythm. It is, however, entirely singing without words, and the problem of setting words is treated separately later on in the book.

Morley's own teacher, William Byrd, had emphasized the importance of singing in the following way:

'Reasons briefly set down by the author, to persuade everyone to learn
to sing:
First it is a knowledge easily taught, and quickly learned where there
is a good master, and an apt scholar.
2. The exercise of singing is delightful to nature and good to preserve
the health of man.
3. It doth strengthen all the parts of the breast, and doth open the pipes.
4. It is a singular good remedy for a stutting and stammering in the
speech.
5. It is the best means to procure a perfect pronunciation and to make
a good orator.
6. It is the only way to know where nature hath bestowed the benefit of
a good voice: which gift is so rare, as there is not one among thousand,
that hath it; and in many that excellent gift is lost, because they want
art to express nature.
7. There is not any music of instruments whatsoever, comparable to
that which is made of the voices of men, where the voices are good, and
the same well sorted and ordered.
8. The better the voice is, the meeter it is to honour and serve God
therewith: and the voice of man is chiefly to be employed to that end.
    Since singing is so good a thing
    I wish all men would learn to sing.'[2]

Morley, one feels, would have made Polymathes or Philomathes
question the Master on his precise meaning in points one and six. If the
knowledge is 'easily learned' why is it that 'not one among a thousand'
has a good voice? No doubt the answer would suggest that most
people 'want' a good master. Byrd does, however, draw our attention
to a number of benefits derived from singing which it has taken,
apparently, a great deal of research to re-discover in our own times.
Items two, three, four and five of the list are direct statements of extra-
musical benefits associated with singing. Some teachers today believe
that singing can be useful in the treatment of breathing disorders and
speech defects, and there is some evidence that general physical growth
is improved by regular singing activities.

John Dowland similarly attaches much weight to singing, and
concludes his *Ornithoparcus* translation with ten 'precepts by which they
(singers) may err less':

'1. When you desire to sing anything above all things mark the tone . . .

2. Let him diligently mark the scale . . .

3. Let every singer conform his voice to the words, that as much as he can he make the content sad when the words are sad, and merry, when they are merry . . .

4. Above all things keep the equality of measure. For to sing without law and measure is an offence to God himself . . .

5. The songs of the authentical tones must be timed [sic] deep, of the subjugal tones high, of the neutral meanly . . .[3]

6. The changing of vowels is a sign of an unlearned singer . . .

7. Let the singer take heed, least he begin too loud, braying like an ass . . .

8. Let every singer discuss the difference of one holiday [i.e. Holy day] from another, least on a slight holiday, he either make too solemn service, or too slight on a great.

9. The uncomely gaping of the mouth, and ungraceful motion of the body is a sign of a mad [sic] singer.

10. Above all things, let the singer study to please God, and not men . . .'[4]

It is interesting to find the idea of expression, which was to find a place in the writings of composers not only of the seventeenth century, but also in later periods, given such prominence by *Ornithoparcus*. Dowland would clearly have been in sympathy with this attitude, even if some of the other precepts were of less relevance.

Morley encourages his pupils both to be good sight-readers and vocal improvisers, but he does not regard these skills as ends in themselves: 'yet is it a great absurdity so to seek for a sight as to make it the end of our study, applying it to no other use . . .' (p. 215). Only too often do music teachers fail to understand Morley's position when they concentrate on particular skills like improvisation and sight-reading to the exclusion of all the other aspects of what Morley would call 'practical' music-making. John Dowland also demands a balanced approach:

'Wherefor I exhort all practitioners on this instrument to the learning of their prick-song, also to understand the elements and principles of that knowledge, as an especial great help, and excellent worker in this science, and soon attained, if the teacher be skillful to instruct aright . . .'[5]

It would appear to be a fairly simple proposition that a musician must be educated in all the departments of the subject, but there is no doubt that a lot of confusion has arisen about the practical and theoretical aspects of the subject. We have already seen that for Morley and

Dowland the practical side included all those things which we would include under the modern headings of performance, composition, history and analysis. The word 'theory' clearly did not have the associations for them that it does for many people today, and they surely would have regarded the so-called teaching of composition under this heading as literally absurd.

Morley's contemporary, Richard Mulcaster the schoolmaster, also emphasized the need for proper vocal instruction when he wrote that no child 'shall lack whatever is needful . . . for framing the child's voice . . . for in the voice there is a proper pitch, where it is neither over nor understrained, but delicately brought to its best condition, to last out well, and rise and fall within due compass, and so that it may become tunable and pleasant to hear.'[6] The purpose of elementary teaching in singing was to show how the child 'may and ought to proceed regularly from the first term of art, and the first note in sound, until he shall be able without any frequent or serious failure to sing his part in the prick-song (sight-reading), either by himself at first while he is inexperienced, or with others for good practice afterwards'.[7] The emphasis on structured learning which is found in both Morley and Mulcaster is very important. The recognition of long-term objectives is characteristic not only of their writing, but also of most of the composers. Thus, in their view, the selection of appropriate material depends not only on the immediate needs of a particular group of children in a particular environment, but also upon the long term goals of a musical education. It is of course possible and immensely desirable to satisfy both needs, but the tendency of teachers to select vocal music for no other reason than present convenience is one that must be guarded against.

Christopher Simpson draws attention to the basic ideas about singing in tune when he points out that 'tuning is no way to be taught but by tuning, and therefore you must procure some who know how to tune these degrees (which everyone doth that hath but the least skill in music) to sing them over with you until you can tune them by yourself.'[8] The emphasis which Simpson placed on learning by doing is very similar to Morley, but in an age perhaps more instrumentally conscious than Morley's, Simpson can go on to add: 'If you have been accustomed to any instrument that hath frets, as viol, lute, theorbo, etc., you may by help thereof, instead of an assisting voice, guide or lead your own voice to the perfect tuning of them.' The idea of the use of instruments to help with the teaching of singing raises some very interesting points. Simpson is surely right in suggesting that an instrument can be very helpful to a person who is uncertain about singing, and it is therefore appropriate that the learner should be able to seek the assistance which an instrument can provide when he is not working with someone who can immediately help to sing in tune by example. There must remain, however, some uncertainty about the 'perfect tuning' that is based on the stopping of strings on a fretted instrument, for the beginner may in any case be facing difficulties over the tuning of the strings, and the problems of intonation resulting from clumsy fingering.

To help the beginner to sing rhythmically Simpson suggests that 'we use a constant motion of the hand. Or if the hand be otherwise employed we use the foot. If that be also engaged, the imagination (to which these are but assistant) is able to perform that office' (p. 9). This important connection between pitch and rhythm problems for the beginner is emphasized by many writers. Simpson gives an example of the way the singer should count the beats:

Many other seventeenth-century writers discuss matters related to the teaching of singing. The reader who expects much from the *Ars Cantandi* of Carissimi,[9] however, will be disappointed. Although this little book contains some interesting notational ideas (mentioned in the previous chapter), it has little to say about singing as such. More interesting in its way is Christoph Bernhard's *Art of Singing*,[10] which draws attention to many of the baroque attitudes to the art of singing. Bernhard was a pupil of the great German master, Heinrich Schütz, and possibly represents a direct branch of his teaching. Characteristic of Bernhard's writing is the following discussion of the problem of the singer and baroque theories of the affections:

'... the question may here be raised, whether a singer's face and bearing should reflect the affects found in the text. Thus let it be known that a singer should sing modestly, without special facial expression; for nothing is more upsetting than certain singers who are better heard than seen, who arouse the expectations of a listener with a good voice and style of singing, but who ruin everything with ugly faces and gestures.'[11]

Among the composers whose chief concern is with the teaching of instrumental skills, Quantz stands out as a composer worth studying in respect of his views on the teaching of singing. 'A singer must have the strong chest, the long breath, and the ready tongue in common with the wind player . . . and must be gifted with a beautiful voice.' (p. 11). Quantz believed that the physical characteristics of a person should always be taken into consideration in relation to their choice of instruments, and he extends this principle to the use of voice. In his view factors like the length of fingers, the soundness of teeth, the suppleness of joints and similar features, all effect the way a musician works, and for a singer a strong natural voice was indispensable. 'The chief requirements of a good singer are that he have a good, clear, and pure voice, of uniform quality from top to bottom, a voice which has none of those major defects originating in the nose and throat, and which is neither hoarse nor muffled' (p. 300).

A similar point is made by Rousseau in *Émile*, when he states that the teacher should 'make his voice true, even, flexible, sonorous, and his ear responsive to time and harmony, but nothing more'.[12] However, the effect on his readers is necessarily confusing. If the production of a true, even, flexible, sonorous voice were indeed the simple matter implied by the phrase 'but nothing more', then musical education would have few problems; and if it were equally easy to create an 'ear responsive to time and harmony', then our worries would be over. The confusion appears to become greater when he goes on to say that 'Imitative and theatrical music is not suitable for him. I would even prefer him not to sing words; but if he wanted words to sing, I would try to compose songs for him on his own level of interest and ideas.' We may agree that the arias of mid-eighteenth-century Paris opera are not appropriate to the child's 'own level of interest', but why does Rousseau 'prefer him not to sing words' at all? Not only is no explanation offered, but the alternative of teacher-composed songs is quickly brought forward.

From the purely musical point of view Quantz thought that the singer 'must have a good ear and true intonation . . . he must have firmness and sureness of voice, so that he does not begin to tremble in a moderately long hold, or transform the agreeable sound of the human voice into the disagreeable shriek of a reed pipe' (p. 300). Quantz also wants the singer to be able to deliver the words clearly: 'A good singer must also have good pronunciation. He must enunciate the words distinctly, and must not pronounce the vowels a, e and o all in the same way, so that they become incomprehensible' (p. 300). Furthermore, the singer 'must have facility in reading and producing his notes accurately . . . and must not express the high notes with a harsh attack or with a vehement exhalation of air from his chest' (p. 301). As Quantz makes abundantly clear, the matter of breath control and phrasing is as important to the singer as it is to the flute player:

'Taking breath at the proper time is essential in playing wind instruments as well as in singing. Because of frequently encountered abuses in this regard, melodies that should be coherent are often broken up, the composition spoiled, and the listener is robbed of part of his pleasure. To separate several notes that belong together is just as bad as to take a breath in reading before the sense is clear, or in the middle of a word of two or three syllables' (p. 87).

Quantz also felt that the composer must keep all these points in mind when he was writing for singers:

'He must be especially careful to write naturally, vocally, and neither too high nor too low for singers, and to leave them enough time for breathing and for the clear enunciation of the words' (p. 293).

More advice on singing is also found in another eighteenth-century source, Montéclair's *Petite méthode pour apprendre la musique aux enfants*, in which the following requirements are made in connection with the learning of singing:

'1. Not to force the voice in an attempt to make it ascend higher or descend lower than its natural disposition permits.
2. Not to do violence to the voice in an attempt to make it louder and bigger.
3. To sing always in an even voice, never passing from the natural voice to a falsetto, or head voice, unless absolutely necessary.
4. Not to sing near, or in front of, an open door or window.
5. To sing as little as possible during or immediately after a meal.
6. To exercise the voice in the morning before breakfast.
7. Not to tire the voice by singing too long at a time, especially when one is out of practice or has a cold.
8. Not to sing before a great fire without putting something before the mouth.
9. Never to sing at night when the dew is falling. This last bit of advice is most important, as many people have irretrievably lost their voice through not observing this rule.'[13]

Not least among the merits of these recommendations is the useful reminder that although singing is, as Byrd put it, 'good to preserve the health of man', it also requires good health to make its development possible at all. There is, at least, little chance of the modern singing teacher having to worry about Montéclair's last two points!

If there is less emphasis on the teaching of singing in the writing of nineteenth-century composers, it should not be thought that this stems from any lack of interest in the problem. Indeed, one has only to think of the songs of Schubert, Schumann, Brahms and Wolf to recognize in them the keenest interest in singing. Furthermore, the enthusiasm for large choral works that is characteristic of the nineteenth century meant that composers constantly had the problems of writing for amateur voices in front of them. It is true, nevertheless, that the composers did tend to leave the discussion of the teaching of singing firmly in the hands of people like Galin, Chevé, Paris and Wilhem on the continent, and Hickson, Hullah, Mainzer, Glover and Curwen in the British Isles.[14]

It was not really until the twentieth century that composers again exercised a powerful influence in the context of singing in schools. It has already been noted that many composers pursued an active interest in the use of folk-song materials in class singing, and Kodály may be used to demonstrate this involvement as he was perhaps the composer most constantly concerned with the problem.

Kodály showed from the beginning that he was not merely concerned that children should sing, but that they should sing good music:

'What children are being taught to sing at school is for the most part of no artistic value; and the way they are taught is worse than if they were left to themselves. After such a training they can hardly hope to experience music as an art for the rest of their lives. At best, they pass on to the kind of choral society that is nothing more than an adult edition of school singing ... This is the reason why, even amongst educated people, we so often find a disconcerting ignorance of music. A cultivated taste in literature and the fine arts is often accompanied by a childish ignorance of music, so that people who are prepared to fight for higher standards with their right hand actually encourage what is worthless with their left.'[15]

This serious concern with compositional standards separates Kodály from the nineteenth-century Mainzers. It matters to him not only that the children sing well, but that they sing music that is not artistically second-rate. His position is similar to that of Holst when he said: 'I get reams of twaddle sent me periodically ... so I have had some di Lasso and Palestrina lithographed for St Pauls.'[16]

Kodály went on to develop his point of view when he wrote that 'bad taste in the arts is as serious as a mental illness, for it has the effect of cauterizing susceptibility . . . Adults affected by this disease are for the most part incurable . . . it is in school that immunity from the contagion should be provided . . . But today, far from doing this, our schools are actually helping to spread the disease . . . Singing ought to be taught in such a way that children acquire a lasting appetite for the best music.'[17] The conclusion which he went on to draw was, therefore, 'only the best art is good enough for children, anything else will do them harm'.

If the teacher of singing is to be able to judge what is 'only the best art' then his own musical education must be as full as possible. It is difficult to see, therefore, how a teacher with only a little experience in singing, and very little knowledge of music in general, can possess the sort of requirements that Kodály has in mind. Yet generation after generation of children pass through organized education without ever coming into contact with a teacher who has these musical accomplishments; and so the children become adults affected by the 'incurable disease'.

Kodály believed that high musical standards should be introduced at the nursery school stage, 'for it is there while at play, that children will learn what it will be too late to teach them when they get to primary school . . . Modern psychology assures us that, in the education of the child, the period from three to seven years old is of greater importance than the succeeding years.'[18] By the time that Kodály was writing this article a good deal of work had been carried out by psychologists in the area of child development, and at least five of Piaget's major publications were available.[19] Kodály was clearly conscious of this field of work, even if he was not directly familiar with the work of Piaget.

In an epilogue to the above article which Kodály wrote in 1957, he raised the question of whether or not the singing in nursery schools should be accompanied by the piano. In addition to making the usual objections to equal temperament versus pure intonation, he also observed that 'the piano does not correspond to the inevitable fall in pitch of the child's voice. I have heard children's choral works where the choir has dropped two or three tones in pitch while the accompanying piano remained where it was.'[20] This surely must raise an obvious question. Why is there an 'inevitable' drop in pitch if the whole point of the elementary teaching is proper intonation within a limited compass? Even stranger, at least from the point of view of most modern British children, is the idea that 'Though they may have to be sung indoors, children's songs should always convey an illusion of the open air, which the piano makes impossible.' The romantic concept of the child surrounded by nature is surely not appropriate today to most musical activities?

For Kodály, 'not even the greatest talent can ever fully overcome the drawbacks that result from a musical training that has not been based on singing'.[21] He believed also that the early stages should be based upon tonic-sol-fa notation, and also on the pentatonic scale. The latter provided simple access to a great deal of folk-song material, and also, Kodály thought, had the advantage of avoiding the use of the semi-tone.

Although Bartók found far less time than Kodály to devote to writing, he was very heavily involved in the development of singing methods, not only in his own country, but also in other eastern European states. His essay 'On Music Education for the Turkish people'[22] summarizes and reinforces many of Kodály's own statements. Bartók refers to two methods of teaching singing:

'According to one method, the singers are required to memorize their parts by ear, like parrots, at the cost of much effort by student and leader alike . . . The result is that the singers remain musically illiterate – their achievement is almost mechanical labour . . . According to the other method the singers are taught how to read music; a procedure that may be somewhat strenuous at the start but which is in the end more economical, time saving, and above all, closest to the main goal' (p. 512).

Like Kodály, Bartók is very concerned that children should sing worthwhile music. As far as poor music was concerned his view is that 'if we are going to teach only this kind of music to the masses, it would be better not to teach at all' (p. 512). Underlining this point, he went on to say that:

'If the musical guidance of the adults as well as the school children is not performed with the greatest care, forehandedness, and con-scientiousness; if there is no strict endeavour – without exception! – to provide only musical literature of absolute merit; then it would be better not to be concerned with these matters at all. Interest in inferior music is injurious to the taste – it is not only superfluous but directly harmful' (p. 515).

Kodály, in his use of the pentatonic scale, shares a lot in common with Carl Orff. However, Orff made a considerable use of instruments in the development of a child's musical education, and thus is essentially different in his approach from Kodály. Nevertheless, in as far as both

Kodály and Orff use the pentatonic folk song intensively during the initial stages, these two composers shared the responsibility, at least in part, for breaking down the major/minor dominated melodic language that the twentieth century had inherited.

Singing is, of course, an integral part of Orff's *Schulwerk*, and although this also involves instrumental improvisation and movement, the place it provides for singing should never be underestimated. Other modern composers, like Benjamin Britten, have also shown great enthusiasm for writing for children's voices; their works form an important part of the total pattern of thinking by composers about the problems of teaching singing.

Notes

1. *A Composer's World* (London, 1952), p. 172.
2. W. Byrd, *Psalms, Sonnets and Songs of Sadness and Pietie* (London, 1588), Preface. See also W. L. Woodfill, *Music in English Society from Elizabeth to Charles I* (Princeton, N.J., 1953).
3. 'Timed' may be a misprint for 'tuned', but the passage still remains obscure. Similarly in 9, 'mad' should probably read 'bad'.
4. *Ornithoparcus, his micrologus* (London, 1609), p. 89.
5. *Varietie of Lute Lessons*, p. Ei.
6. R. Mulcaster, *Elementarie* (London, 1582), ed. J. Oliphant, p. 39 (The editor has 'modernized' the text.)
7. Ibid., p. 40.
8. *A Compendium of Practical Musick* (London, 1667), p. 4.
9. The original version (Rome?, 1639?) is lost; it cannot be certain that the German version (Augsburg, 1693) is authentic.
10. *Von der Singe-Kunst* (Dresden, c. 1649), Eng. trans. W. Hilse, 'The Treatises of Christoph Bernhard', *The Music Forum*, III (1973), pp. 13–25.
11. Ibid., pp. 21–22.
12. W. Boyd (trans.), op. cit., p. 62.
13. Paris, c. 1750; Eng. trans. M. Pincherle, 'Elementary Musical Instruction in the 18th Century', *MQ*, 34 (1948), pp. 63ff.
14. See Chapter 1, p. 41, and bibliography.
15. Z. Kodály, 'Children's Choirs' (1929), in L. Eösze, *Zoltan Kodály* (London, 1962), p. 70.
16. Quoted in I. Holst, *Gustav Holst* (London, 1968), p. 27.
17. L. Eösze, op. cit., p. 71.
18. L. Eösze, op. cit., p. 72.
19. J. Piaget, *The Language and Thought of the Child* (1926); *Judgement and Reasoning in the Child* (1928); *The Child's Conception of the World* (1929); *The Child's Conception of Physical Causality* (1930); and *The Moral Judgement of the Child* (1932).
20. L. Eösze, op. cit., p. 73.
21. Preface to E. Szonyi, *The Method of Reading and Writing Music* (Budapest, 1952), quoted in L. Eösze, op. cit., p. 80.
22. *Béla Bartók Essays*, ed. Benjamin Suchoff (London, 1976), pp. 511–15.

5

The Teaching of Instrumental Skills and the Use of Improvisation

As it is only a relatively modern idea that composers and performers should be educated in different ways, it will surprise no one that many composers have contributed a great deal to our understanding of the way instrumental skills are acquired. The most direct source of information is contained in the *études* and collections of progressive exercises that composers have completed, varying from the small set of pieces for the vihuela de mano by Luis de Milan called *El Maestro* dating from 1536, to the *Mikrokosmos* of Béla Bartók. For the piano alone, the *étude* repertoire is of considerable proportions, including as it does the studies of Clementi, Czerny, Cramer, Bertini, Hummel, Chopin, Hiller, Liszt, Scriabin and Debussy.

However, as Schumann pointed out, 'in the broadest sense, every piece of music is an *étude*, and the easiest is often really the most difficult'.[1] It is therefore chiefly from the written sources that this survey attempts to examine the composer's point of view. Furthermore, other limitations are obviously necessary. First, since nearly all composers have also been keyboard players, there is a need to restrict the examples related to keyboard instruments, and to balance them with examples from other instruments, such as the violin (Leopold Mozart and Spohr), the flute (Quantz), and the lute (Dowland). Second, since it is not the purpose of this book to pursue the detailed technical advice offered to performers, the matters that are included are of general significance only.

Perhaps the most important issue included in this topic was raised by Hindemith when he wrote:

'We are teaching each pianist or violinist as if he had a chance to become a Horowitz or a Heifetz, although we know that the entire concert life of the civilised world can hardly absorb more than ten or twelve great soloists in each field. Even if for regional demand in each larger country another ten are acknowledged, what in heaven happens to the remaining hundreds and thousands?'[2]

Clearly it cannot be the aim of musical education, as a general principle, to produce virtuoso instrumentalists, even if the possibility of producing such a performer must not be excluded from the total pattern of musical education. It is the development of general musical skills that must be the continuing aim of education, and this will include the development of performing skills alongside all the other musical skills.

The choice of instruments is, for the beginner, a matter of crucial importance, and one for which very little advice seems to be available. A keyboard instrument has obvious advantages in that it is harmonically self-contained, and boasts a very extensive repertoire. Yet, as Hindemith observed, 'keyboard playing in general is of no use for the amateur. Amateurs' music is essentially community music' (p. 216). The choice of an orchestral instrument therefore has serious claims for the beginner. Hindemith emphasized the social significance when he went on to say that '. . . once you join an amateur group, you are a member of a great fraternity, whose purpose is the most dignified one you can imagine: to inspire one another and unite in building up a creation that is greater than one individual's deeds' (p. 217). Hindemith was, of course, a viola player, and this may have influenced his view; but he was also a pianist, and there can be very little doubt that such a combination, of orchestral and keyboard instrument, is the ideal towards which all musical education should aim.

Quantz emphasized the importance of choosing the appropriate instrument when he wrote:

'It is necessary for each person, before he settles upon something in music, to explore carefully the area to which his talent most inclines him. If this matter were always properly considered, there would be less imperfection in music . . . he who devotes himself to a branch of music for which he lacks gifts will always remain a mediocre musician in spite of the best instruction and application' (p. 14).

That the learning of instrumental skills is very demanding is never denied by the composers. Morley wrote: 'I cannot cease to pray you diligently to practise, for that only is sufficient to make a perfect musician' (p. 203). It is because he saw no substitute for the hard work the student must carry out by himself. The 'introduction' may be 'plaine and easie', but the continuation and development of the ideas presented demands some perseverance on the part of the learner.

Morley and his contemporaries, however, did not regard learning as a mechanical process. Robert Dowland was prepared to qualify the 'regular practice' principle:

'. . . it is most necessary at least for the beginner to handle the lute often, yet never but when thy genius favours thee, that is, when thou feelest thyself inclined to music: for there is a certain natural disposition, for learning the arts naturally infused into us, and showing it in us rather at one time than another, which if one will provoke by immoderate labour, he shall fight against Nature. Therefore when thou shalt find thyself aptly disposed, and hast time and opportunity, spare no pains, yet keep this course.'[3]

He also provided good advice to the beginner:

'Whosoever therefore will use these our rules, if he be wholly raw in the art, above all other things let him persuade himself, that the knowledge of this art though it be hard, yet it is easy to be obtained by him that is in this sort conditioned: first if he had no great defect, and have that natural desire towards music, which hath been the founder of excellency in every art: secondly, if he stint himself in his learning with such labour and exercise that is moderate, and continual, not such unreasonable pains as many do weary themselves with: thirdly, if he be patient for a good long time, for commonly this brings us whether we will or not to the highest sciences. To these if he adjoin the industrious and lively instructions of a teacher, that is a good artist, he canno t but hope for a reasonable habit in a short time' (p. Bi).

Here we meet a statement of principles for the beginner: that he must want to learn; that he must be prepared to work regularly for short periods, rather than for long periods occasionally; that he must recognize that it takes time to become a musician, and that patience is therefore of primary importance; and that a good teacher will make the learning process easier. It is difficult to see how such a summary could be improved upon, for these are principles which govern musical education today, and are rightly described as fundamental.

This problem of flexibility in learning provides organized education with one of its greatest fields of enquiry. The precise question for the musician may be presented in this form: can children be provided with regular opportunities for learning and practising within a structure that is flexible enough to allow them to have some choice in the matter of when and where they shall work? At university and college level such choice does exist, at least in part; but in schools, which are wedded to the idea of a compulsory *general* education, not only is the possibility of daily music-making denied to most children but the concept of the individually organized timetable is, as often as not, regarded as a deeply subversive idea.

The principle of inclination on the part of the learner crops up time and again in the writings of composers on education. In a very important sense it must precede aptitude. We are therefore challenged by a common enough situation which may be described in the following way: very few young children who are taught by adults who are both good musicians and good teachers encounter anything other than spontaneous delight in making music; and yet by the time they reach adolescence, for most children the delight has turned to spontaneous agony. Now clearly the inclination was there in the first place: what, therefore has happened in the meanwhile? Has the child encountered 'such unreasonable pains as many do weary themselves with'? Has he failed, not seeing any justification, to 'be patient for a good long time'? Has he failed to meet 'the industrious and lively instructions of a teacher that is a good artist'? Has he been forced to 'provoke by immoderate labour' his interest in music and thus to 'fight against Nature'? There can be little doubt that only the very strongest inclination can survive today's pressures, which include poor facilities, poor teaching, and commercial pressures which Morley and Dowland could not have foreseen.

John Dowland made an interesting point when he wrote that

'When we take in hand to instruct or teach, a man on the Lute, we do suppose that he knoweth before (be he never so rude) what a string, a fret, a stop, a shake, etc. meaneth: therefore it were not convenient for a teacher to stand upon every small point and matter that may be thought appertaining to the art of lute playing, but to leave and let pass over some things, as apparent of themselves, or easy to be discerned of every learner, by Nature, Reason, or common experience ...' (p. Di).

There is, of course, some justification for the view that if we recognize the characteristics of the child's nature, the child's reason, and the child's common experience, that there is equally no need to 'stand upon every small point and matter' in the education of children. If we allow that the child's imagination needs room to exercise itself, we must beware, like Dowland, of being afraid to leave things out, so long as we do not do harm to the overall structure of the process of learning.

Robert Dowland also showed a firm grasp of some of the problems of learning and practising: 'Choose one lesson thyself according to thy capacity, which give not over by looking over others, or straggling from one to another, till thou have got it reasonably perfect ...' (p. Bii). He was thus looking for a balance between the need for the student to exercise some choice over the material he uses, and the importance of concentrated study once he has chosen. He added:

'And although most men do use themselves at the first to the hardest lessons . . . yet would I not persuade young beginners so, for fear lest such difficulties should cause a loathing in them, and consequently a giving over of their practice: but I had rather an easier lesson were set them at first . . . And in this lesson I would not have many or divers changes of the time: for I have known by experience that this hath been more hard to many than all the rest' (p. Bii).

The modern teacher also has to face the problem of the young beginners and 'a giving over of their practice'. He must also be aware that he must provide them with material at the appropriate level, and that they will, in all probability, encounter more difficulties with rhythmic ideas in the early stages than with other aspects of their music-making. But Dowland has more to offer: 'Take this for a farewell: that this divine art, which at this time is by so great men followed, ought to be used by thee with that great gracefulness which is fit for learned men to use, and with a kind of majesty' (p. Civ). The association of gracefulness with learning is an idea that is all too easily overlooked; for the musician, however, a feeling for movement is extremely important. Dowland was writing at a time when dancing was so closely related to everyday music-making that he would be unlikely to separate the problems of the one from the other. As a lutenist, moreover, gracefulness would have had a relevance for Dowland that we cannot ignore. The idea that we should 'use' music 'with a kind of majesty' may at first bring to our minds an image of Elgarian 'nobilmente', but clearly this is not Dowland's meaning. He is inviting us to see music as a serious activity, not as a trivial pastime. For Dowland, music is 'fit for learned men to use', not simply escapist entertainment; and because of this he assumes we will understand that '. . . nothing can be gotten in an instant, and you must not think to play your lessons perfectly at first sight, for that is impossible' (p. Civ).

Dowland, perhaps even more so than Morley, is keen to make us recognize that there is more than one way to learn a skill:

'Neither would I have thee think that in this I detract from the other differing ways, which other men do use, not unfitly, so that there be reason for them, and an easy gracefulness in them. For a man may come to the same place divers ways; and that sweet harmony of the lute (the habit whereof we do daily affect with so great travaile) may strike our ears with an elegant delight, though the hand be diversely applied' (p. Bi).

It is essential that we should note this warning against attaching too much importance to any one method of teaching music. Music teachers have too often fallen into the trap of partisanship in the matter of method; 'schools' have been set up, attitudes hardened, personalities, rather than principles, have been followed, and cults established. Dowland is simply saying that his is but one way.

In the *Elementarie*, Mulcaster, that most enlightened Elizabethan schoolmaster, offered a useful analysis of the teaching situation:

'The training in music, as in all other faculties, has a special eye to these three points: the child himself, who is to learn; the matter itself, which he is to learn; and the instrument itself, on which he is to learn.'[4]

In the development of these points which followed, he showed a clear understanding of some of the basic problems of learning to play:

'And in the training of fingers also, there is regard to be had, both that the child strike the notes clearly, so as not to spoil the sound, and that his fingers run with certainty and lightness, so as to avoid indistinct execution. Of these the first commonly falls out through too much haste in the young learner, who is ever longing to press forward; the second fault comes of the master himself, who does not consider the natural dexterity and order of development in the joints, for if this is rightly attended to, the fingers easily become flexible and master the difficulties of execution without pain' (p. 39).

There is a confidence about Mulcaster's view that is very similar to that which can be found in Morley, Dowland, Ravenscroft and Simpson. Turning to the content of a music course, Mulcaster stressed the need for structure:

'As for the matter of music which the child is to learn, I would set down by what means and degrees and by what lessons a boy ... may and ought to proceed regularly from the first term ... Concerning the virginals and the lute, which two instruments I have chosen because of the full music uttered by them and the variety of execution they require, I would also set down as many chosen lessons for both as shall bring the young learner to play reasonably well on them' (p. 40).

Mulcaster represents part of that informed background in which the work of Morley and his contemporaries must be placed. His vigorous support of music stands as a monument to Elizabethan education.

In the matter of detailed practical advice contained in the essays of Quantz, C. P. E. Bach and Leopold Mozart, the information passed on to keyboard, flute and violin players was abundant. Indeed, it formed the major part of each essay; as instrumental tutors the essays played a major role in the teaching of these instruments beyond the eighteenth century. It is not the purpose, however, of the present discussion to explore these aspects of the works, except where they illustrate general principles. For example '. . . the beginner should at all times play earnestly, with all his powers, strongly and loudly; never weakly, and quietly, and still less should he dally with the violin under his arm' (p. 63). Here Leopold Mozart, in his usual direct manner, draws our attention to the fact that music is a noisy subject, and we may recognize that many of the difficulties encountered in the teaching of music in schools arise from just this fact. The academic mind, brought up to associate intellectual activity with silence, finds it almost impossible to appreciate the value of music as a cognitive process. Consider, for example, the remarks of Kant, writing at the end of the century, on this point: 'Children are fond of noisy instruments, such as trumpets, drums and the like; but these are objectionable, since they become a nuisance to others. It would be less objectionable, however, were the children to learn how to cut a reed so as to play on it.'[5] This alarming ability to miss the point when considering musical education which Kant shares with Locke and with many other writers on education, is a serious matter when seen in the light of the scope of their influence.

Mozart is not suggesting, of course, that the production of a lot of sound is the immediate objective of the instrumental beginner; rather he is inviting the child to learn and act *with confidence*, because only in this way will he form the habit of committing himself to a sound as opposed to waiting for someone else to show him the way at all times. Such practice in the exercise of confidence is of course of general significance, and is not simply a musical problem.

Mozart also reminds us of the great importance of rhythmic accuracy, and the need for the beginner fully to understand its importance: 'Everything depends on musical time-measure, and the teacher must use the greatest patience in seeing that the pupil grasps it thoroughly, with diligence and attention' (p. 30). As every instrumental teacher knows, most pupils will apologize for producing a wrong note, but not for producing a right note at the wrong time. The 'greatest patience' to which Mozart refers in this context is a characteristic demanded of the teacher throughout his work, but in respect of the teaching of rhythm it is one that is constantly to be exercised.

The problem of tonality is also considered in the essays, and there is a particularly interesting reference to it by Quantz in relationship to learning the flute: 'Divining each key in this fashion will become still easier if from time to time he has his master play short passages over for him, so that he may duplicate them without looking at the master's fingers; this exercise he must continue until he can immediately repeat everything he hears' (p. 95). Such a technique of 'echo exercises' has found its way into the classroom today, but, ironically, would often be regarded as a 'new' method. Indeed as one turns the pages of the essays it is with the growing awareness that there is nothing new in musical education.

The essayists give a great deal of thought to the early problems in learning an instrument. The main issue arises from the confusion that may exist between short- and long-term objectives. At one point Bach states that:

'It is dangerous to delay the student with too many easy things for no progress can be achieved in this manner. A few pieces at the beginning suffice, after which the wise teacher will do better to introduce his pupils gradually to more challenging works. It is to accord with the art of teaching . . . that by this means the student will be unaware of the increasing difficulty of his tasks. My deceased father made many successful experiments of a similar nature' (p. 39).

The idea of the structured course is not new to us, but it is often in conflict with the day-to-day needs of the pupil and teacher. However important it may be for a young player to concentrate on a particular aspect of his instrumental technique, the demands of a public concert may temporarily appear greater. But the need for structure in musical education is as important as it is in any other form of knowledge. Bruner makes this apparent when he says:

'. . . the curriculum of a subject should be determined by the most fundamental understanding that can be achieved of the underlying principles that give structure to that subject. Teaching specific topics or skills without making clear their context in the broader fundamental structure of a field of knowledge is uneconomical in several deep senses. In the first place such teaching makes it exceedingly difficult for the student to generalize from what he has learned to what he will encounter later. In the second place, learning that has fallen short of a grasp of the general principles has little reward in terms of intellectual excitement. The best way to create interest in a subject is to render it worth knowing, which means to make the knowledge gained usable in one's thinking beyond the situation in which the learning has occurred. Third, knowledge one has acquired without sufficient structure to tie it together is knowledge that is likely to be forgotten.'[6]

There can be no doubt that Bach and his contemporaries would be less explicit about the structure of their teaching than Bruner would possibly recommend, but the structure is certainly coherent and effective. The great advantage that these teachers possessed was linked with their great experience as players and composers. Structure implies a knowledge of the possible limits of experience within a field of knowledge. If one is among the greatest performers and composers of one's generation, presumably it is relatively easier to define a path towards the summit.

Leopold Mozart is particularly ruthless in this matter. He has no time for culs-de-sac, as the following paragraph makes clear:

'Above all, one should not give a beginner anything difficult before he can play easy things well in time. Further, one should not give him minuets or other melodious pieces which remain easily in his memory, but should let him at first take the middle parts of concertos wherein are rests, or fugal movements; in a word, pieces in which he has to observe all that is necessary for him to know and to read at sight, and he is obliged therefore to show whether or not he has understood the rules which have been taught to him. He will otherwise accustom himself to play by ear and at random' (p. 35).

We must remember that in condemning 'playing by ear' Mozart is in no way objecting to improvisation, which played a central role in eighteenth-century music-making.[7] He is, rather, concerned with the consequence of poor reading abilities on the part of the player. When he goes on to criticize the attitude of some parents, we may recognize a problem which still is as acute today as it was then. Speaking of parents and the need for beginners to play scales, he states:

'Here lies really the greatest error committed by masters as well as pupils. The first often have not the patience to wait, or they allow themselves to be led astray by the disciple, who deems himself to have done all if he can but scratch out a few minuets. Many a time the parents or other guardians wish to hear that sort of untimely little dance at an early stage and then think miracles have happened, and how well the money for the lessons has been spent. But alas! how greatly they deceive themselves. He who does not, right from the beginning . . . by diligent practice of the musical scale arrive at that point where the stretching and contracting of the fingers, as each note demands, becomes so to speak second nature, will always be in danger of playing out of tune and with uncertainty' (p. 61).

This view was later echoed by Hummel when he stated that 'Parents are often so weak as to require their children, in order to attract attention, should play all sorts of little tunes before their tuition is well begun, not considering this leads to nothing advantageous . . .'[8] It may be that the repertoire of the last two hundred years has sometimes made it possible for technique to be learnt in the context of actual pieces of music (e.g. the *Études* of Chopin and Debussy or the *Mikrokosmos* of Bartók), but the fundamental issue cannot change; how is the beginner to master the basic problems of technique *without* tackling them in their most concentrated form for a substantial period of time?

If Leopold Mozart appears to take an extreme position it may be recognized that he did not find himself in the circumstances of compromise that face most music teachers today. His position was the relatively straightforward one of knowing what constitutes good violin playing and how to produce it from his pupils. At one point in the essay he even goes so far as to say, 'Here are the pieces for practice. The more distasteful they are the more I am pleased, for that is what I intend to make them' (p. 88). This is not a point of view that would attract much sympathy today, but the tone of his remarks must not be allowed to disguise his point: which is simply that the struggle with difficult passages is inevitable if the player is to proceed, and to suggest that learning music, or indeed anything worth knowing, is without problems is simply dishonest.

Quantz, though more moderate in his choice of language, makes the same point when he observes that the students' repertoires should be selected on the basis of pieces which 'sharpen their musical discernment' and 'deepen their insight' (p. 19). This may seem to some a statement so obvious that it is hardly worth saying; but such a reader would reveal a lack of familiarity with the institutional requirements of schools and colleges. What may be called the ceremonial of organized education constantly invites the musician to display his wares, forcing many teachers into the difficult choice of pleasing the management or teaching within a carefully structured development from fundamentals to known goals. Of course there are many occasions when the two are not incompatible, and these should be seized upon with the greatest enthusiasm.

It has already been noted that eighteenth-century composers did not wish to see children starting their musical education too late. Couperin suggested that the age of six or seven was the correct point at which to start playing. M. P. de Montéclair, a contemporary of Couperin and famous teacher of the period, stated: 'I have included in this little book the principles in so simple an order that this child [his god-child], but three and a half years old, has made astonishing progress.'[9]

Our present knowledge of the work of Kodály, Orff, Suzuki and other modern teachers would also lead us to believe that too much delay in starting a child's musical education may threaten his future development quite seriously. Many educationalists, of course, assert that early concentration in specialist fields is dangerous for future *general* development. There is, however, some evidence that as long as the general education is properly pursued, the effect of concentrated musical activities will prove of general advantage to the growing child. Instrumental tuition at a reasonably early age offers the child a sense of security in the development of his musical skills. The actual physical contact with the sound source gives the child a concrete experience of music-making from which he can develop not only the rewards of pleasure from the music itself, but also from the social experience of the group musical activities.

Stravinsky once wrote of Czerny: 'I began, therefore, the loosening of my fingers by playing a lot of Czerny exercises, which was not only very useful but gave me keen musical pleasure. I have always admired Czerny, not only as a remarkable teacher but also as a thoroughbred musician.'[10] This 'remarkable teacher', famous for his output of piano studies, underwent a period of some obscurity during the latter part of the nineteenth century, due at least in part to the sort of criticism he had received from Schumann and his colleagues.[11] Nevertheless, as Stravinsky was aware, Czerny has many things to offer the modern musician, and not least among these are the sources of advice on learning to play the piano.

The stated purpose of the *Complete Theoretical and Practical Pianoforte School* (1839) was 'that many young teachers may herein find a desirable and certain guide, to preserve their pupils from falling into errors, and to accelerate their progress towards perfection' (p. ii). Czerny believed that the teacher could not take enough trouble in ensuring that the proper foundations of a musical education were laid:

'Much the greater number of those who begin to learn the pianoforte consist of children of from 8 to 10 years of age; and in truth we ought to commence as early as possible, if we wish to attain to any great degree of proficiency in playing. For this reason, it is necessary to explain the first rudiments [i.e. of playing, not notation] on which in fact everything depends, in a full, clear, and comprehensive manner; for here anything like laconic brevity is more particularly misplaced, since the mere untaught child is not capable of unravelling nor comprehending it, nor indeed are many teachers themselves . . . it requires, months, nay even years, and innumerable repetitions of those rules with practical correctness. These reflections every teacher must have often made. How many pupils sacrifice years to discover and rectify what was misunderstood or erroneous in their first instructions!' (p. i).

In order to make sure that the beginner had a proper chance of acquiring the basic skills Czerny recommended that:

'. . . for the first three months, it is requisite that the learner should receive one hour's lesson every day, or at least four lessons in the week; and in addition to this, that he should daily practise one hour by himself, as it is very necessary to abridge as much as possible the labour of acquiring the first principles of the art' (p. i).

In his later *Letters to a Young Lady on the Art of Playing the Pianoforte* (1848), Czerny was to repeat this demand:

'It is very proper that your teacher gives you an hour's lesson every day. If, in addition to this you daily dedicate another hour – or if possible, two hours – to practising by yourself, you will in a few months have for ever conquered all that is difficult or tedious in the elementary branches of playing; and you will each day see augmented the pleasure which the delightful art of music so richly bestows on its votaries' (p. 9).

The 'young lady' was an imaginary 'talented and well educated girl of about twelve years old residing in the country', which might account for the increased demands upon her time.

Hummel also reinforces Czerny's view:

'For the first half year, and if possible, for even the first entire year, every beginner requires one hour's daily instruction; because the pupil is as yet incapable of assisting himself, and if left too long alone, it is to be feared that, by contracting bad habits, he will rather injure than benefit himself.'[12]

It would be easy to dismiss these requirements as irrelevant to the pattern of modern society were it not for the fact that they are musically justifiable. The beginner does need as much contact with a teacher as possible: this is well understood in, say, the teaching of reading or in elementary mathematics. A teaching scheme which depended upon less than half an hour's contact time per week in either of these subjects would rightly be regarded with contempt. Yet in music, such an allocation of time is regarded as normal, at least in British schools. In countries where a much more generous allocation of time is recognized as essential (e.g. Hungary), higher standards are immediately apparent.

As Czerny's 'young lady' progressed, so did his advice expand:

'You are now arrived at the epoch where the art begins to proffer you true, noble, and intellectual pleasure, and in which the new and continually more and more beautiful compositions with which you will now become acquainted, will give you an idea of the inexhaustible riches and variety in music.'[13]

Nevertheless 'new pieces serve but little, if, on their account, the preceding ones are forgotten . . . If, for example, you forget a piece which it took three weeks to learn, these three weeks are as good as lost' (p. 27). The player should recognize the importance of playing before others, and 'should know how to listen properly to himself, and to judge of his own performance with accuracy' (p. 36). Hummel similarly felt that when 'the pupil has attained a certain degree of improvement, I should myself advise him to play occasionally before others, for this will stimulate his industry and give him courage and certainty' (p. iii).

Hummel issued a series of directives to instrumental teachers which included the following:

'the master should feel the most zealous interest in all that relates to his pupils' progress in the art . . . he must not allow him [the pupil] to contract any bad habits . . . he should accustom the pupil betimes to direct his eyes to the notes only, and to find the keys by the feel of the fingers . . . Let him never allow the pupil to play too fast . . . let him, from the very start, endeavour to give the pupil a clear and correct manner of marking time . . . let the master attend to the proper tuning of the instrument that the ear of the pupil may not be spoiled' (p. iii).

He also showed quite clearly that he was not interested in the pursuit of virtuosity.

'It is no doubt meritorious to overcome great difficulties upon the instrument, but this alone is not sufficient to entitle anyone to the reputation of complete master of it; such dextrous players surprise the ear to be sure (as Ph.Em.Bach expresses himself), but do not delight it; they astonish the understanding without satisfying it' (Bk III p. 40).

Spohr is yet another who felt that there is little point in learning to play an instrument unless a regular period of time can be set aside for practice every day: 'To the amateur, even if endowed with talent, it [the violin] can only be recommended when he is able to set apart from his other occupations, at least two hours every day for practice.'[14] Like his fellow composer-teachers, Spohr saw a good teacher essential from the beginning, because 'faults and bad habits once contracted, if not entirely beyond remedy at a future period, can at least be corrected only by extreme perseverance and with much loss of time' (p. ii). He also felt that parents had a very important role to play in the musical education of their children, for they should encourage the children to practise 'interspersed with the other occupations of the day', and they should take them to concerts 'where the child may have the opportunity of hearing good music' (p. ii).

What Spohr and his fellow composers demand of the parent, we can demand of the school. The provision for the child to have regular, supervised opportunities to practise on a good instrument, in school, is the direction in which institutionalized education must move, if musical education is ever to overcome the social barriers by which it is limited at the present time.

The collection of Schumann's critical essays contains a good deal of advice about playing the piano, and many of his maxims and aphorisms have been presented in the form of rules particularly appropriate for the beginner. 'When you play,' writes Schumann,

'do not trouble yourself as to who is listening. Yet always play as though a master listened to you ... Never strum! Play carefully always, and never try a piece half through ... Try to play easy pieces well; it is better than to play difficult ones in a mediocre style ... Practise industriously the fugues of good masters; above all, those of J. S. Bach.'[15]

Slightly more extended is the following statement of demanding requirements:

'What is it to be intelligently musical? You are not so when, with eyes painfully fastened on the notes, you laboriously play a piece through; you are not so when you stop short and find it impossible to proceed, because some one has turned over two pages at once. But you are so when, in playing a new piece, you almost foresee what is coming, when you play an old one by heart; in short, when you have taken music not only into your fingers, but into your head and heart.

How may we become musical in that sense? Dear child, the principal requisites, a fine ear and a swift power of comprehension, come, like all things, from above. But this foundation must be improved and increased. You cannot do this by shutting yourself up all day like a hermit, and practising mechanical exercises, but through a vital, many-sided musical activity, and especially through familiarity with chorus and orchestra' (1, p. 415).

It has already been noted that Schumann abhorred the mechanical, and this applied, of course, as much to composition as performance. Schumann wants the student to have the 'vital, many-sided musical activity' that is stressed by so many composers. For Schumann even the mechanical practising of scales has its dangers:

'You must industriously practise scales and other finger exercises. There are people, however, who think they may attain to everything in doing this; until a ripe age they daily practise mechanical exercises for many hours. That is as reasonable as trying to pronounce a b c quicker and quicker every day. Make a better use of your time' (1, p. 409).

as also has the mindless pursuit of fashions in playing:

'All that is fashionable again becomes unfashionable; and if you cultivate fashion until you are old, you will become an imbecile, whom no one can respect' (1, p. 412).

Schumann's maxims were partly reiterated by Busoni some fifty years later. They refer to the needs of the more advanced player, but they make an interesting comparison with the ideas of composers already cited:

'1. Practise the passage with the most difficult fingering; when you have mastered that, play it with the easiest.
2. If a passage offers some particular technical difficulty, go through

all similar passages you can remember in other pieces; in this way you will bring system into the kind of playing in question.

3. Always combine technical practice with the study of the interpretation; the difficulty, often, does not lie in the notes but in the dynamic shading prescribed.

4. Never be carried away by temperament, for that dissipates strength and where it occurs there will always be a blemish, like a dirty spot which can never be washed out of a material.

5. Don't set your mind on overcoming the difficulties in pieces which have been unsuccessful because you have previously practised them badly; it is generally a useless task. But if meanwhile you have quite changed your way of playing, then begin the study of the old piece from the beginning as if you did not know it.

6. Study everything as if there were nothing more difficult; try to interpret studies for the young from the standpoint of the virtuoso. You will be astonished to find how difficult it is to play a Czerny or Cramer or even a Clementi.

7. Bach is the foundation of piano playing, Liszt the summit. The two make Beethoven possible.

8. Take it for granted from the beginning that everything is possible on the piano, even where it seems impossible to you and even when it really is so.

9. Attend to your technical equipment so that you are prepared and armed for every possible event; then when you study a new piece, you can turn all your power on to the intellectual content; you will not be held up by the technical problems.

10. Never play carelessly, even when there is nobody listening, or the occasion seems unimportant.

11. Never leave a passage which has been unsuccessful without repeating it; if you cannot do it immediately because of the presence of others then do it subsequently.

12. If possible allow no day to pass without touching your piano.'[16]

Busoni sums up many of the points that have already appeared in this discussion. These and other statements of principle provide the teacher with an absorbing collection of ideas against which he may judge the successes and failures of modern musical education, and particularly instrumental tuition.

Both vocal and instrumental improvisation form an important link between performance and composition, and it consequently plays a very significant part in the total pattern of musical education.

Understandably, therefore, composers have often had occasion to refer to improvisational techniques in their writings, and have indicated the ways in which they can be helpful to the musician. Stravinsky wrote about the way improvisation had formed part of his own musical education when he was a child: 'When I was nine my parents gave me a piano mistress. I very quickly learned to read music, and, as the result of reading, soon had a longing to improvise, a pursuit to which I devoted myself, and which for a long time was my favourite occupation.'[17]

Stravinsky's order of events, that is reading *before* improvisation, is, though common among conventionally taught instrumentalists, not the only way. In class teaching situations both vocal and instrumental (*Schulwerk*) improvisations normally *precede* the reading of notation. A useful description of the latter situation is given by the English teacher Yorke Trotter:

'An examination of intuition as it appears in musical activities may be of service. A child of five or six years of age will respond to a given musical theme by singing an answer to it. As the child grows older these answers become longer and more elaborate. But they are always given without conscious thought, and are not in most cases merely an imitation of what has been sung or played. If the child hesitates or tries to think out his response, the result is failure. The answer must be given without hesitation and immediately after the theme so that there is no break in continuity. These answers are for the most part excellent responses to what is offered. It is idle to say that the child in giving his answer simply reproduces something that he has heard. It is quite impossible to suppose he has stored up in his memory answers to every conceivable phrase. If the same theme is given on different occasions the probability is that the child will give different answers. In a class of fourteen or more children each child will give a different answer.'[18]

This emphasis on improvisation as an agent of the imagination occurs many times. In a sense, the beginner is being persuaded to demonstrate melodic powers which he had no idea he possessed. The continued demands being made upon his melodic intuition help to exercise his musical imagination:

'At first, as soon as the answer has been given it will be forgotten, but as the child grows older, he becomes more and more conscious of what he has sung and is able to write down his ideas. But in all cases the answer is sung without premeditation and without conscious thought. If instead of singing an answer, a child is made to sit down and write a termination of the tune, the result is far inferior to the unpremeditated song response. It would appear that with children the intuition is injured by conscious thought. A child who is made to work slowly and with care loses his power of singing answers to a given theme. If his mind is turned toward what is mechanical his own feeling for what is good disappears. At the outset intuition and conscious thought are antagonistic, though in the end they combine' (p. 24).

The 'conscious thought' must, of course, involve the process of analytical reassessment, and this is an ability which the child only very slowly develops. Improvisation, on the other hand, does not, at least in the early stages, include the analytical process, for, as Yorke Trotter points out, the child very often cannot even remember what he has improvised, let alone how it might be improved. Moreover:

'No doubt, when a child sings his answer, the material out of which the answer is formed must be in his mind. He has heard musical sounds and their effect has sunk into the subliminal part of his mind. But his manipulation of the material is his own intuition. The answers that he sings are not the result of memory associations, but are a putting together in new ways of old material. So strong is the intuition that a child's answer to a theme is often not in the least influenced by hearing other answers' (p. 25).

The 'putting together in new ways of old material' is essentially part of the compositional process, and improvisation, therefore, not only forms an important introduction to composition, but also a constant companion.

For the sixteenth-century composer the use of a plainsong was an essential element of his compositional techniques. It is understandable, therefore, that Morley would wish his students to learn how to improvise on a plainsong as part of their education '. . . for that singing extempore upon a plainsong is indeed a piece of cunning, and very necessary to be perfectly practised of him who meaneth to be a composer for bringing of a quick sight' (p. 215). Christopher Simpson also urges the viol player of the seventeenth century to develop similar skills over a ground-bass:

'A ground, subject or bass, (call it which you please) is pricked down [written down] in two several papers; one for him who is to play the ground upon an organ, harpsichord or what other instrument may be apt for that purpose; the other, for him that plays upon the viol, who having the said ground before his eyes, as his theme or subject, plays such variety of descant or division in concordance thereto, as his skill and present invention so then suggest unto him. In this manner of play, which is the perfection of the viol, or any other instrument, if it be exactly performed, a man may show the excellency both of his hand and invention, to the delight and admiration of those that hear him.'[19]

Improvisation has always been regarded by composers as central to the exercise of the musical imagination. Many teachers on the other hand have tended to regard it with suspicion: some have questioned its value, while others have simply thought it too difficult. Simpson goes on to say:

'But this you will say is a perfection that few attain unto, depending much upon the quickness of invention as well as quickness of hand. I answer, it is a perfection which some excellent hands have not attained unto, as wanting those helps which should lead to it; the supply of which want is the business we here endeavour' (p. 27).

Simpson's point is that 'quickness of invention' can be encouraged by good teaching: 'True it is, that invention is a gift of nature, but much improved by exercise and practice.' Like Morley and Dowland, Simpson clearly believes that sustained effort on the part of the student can overcome many apparent handicaps. As far as improvisation is concerned, however, Simpson feels he must add that: 'He that hath it not in so high a measure as to play extempore to a ground, may notwithstanding give both himself and hearers sufficient satisfaction in playing such divisions as himself or others made for the purpose' (p. 27). Similarly Morley sees no point in a musician simply having the ability to improvise a descant (as many of his contemporaries claimed to be able to do) but who is unable to compose, for descant 'is no longer known than the singer's mouth is open expressing it' (p. 215). Morley recognizes that 'although it be impossible for them to compose without it . . . they rather employ their time in making of songs which remain for prosperity'.

Nevertheless, Morley is convinced that as a preparation for more advanced skills, vocal improvisation should take its part in the musician's training. In *A Plaine and Easie Introduction* the Master asks 'how did you become so ready in this kind of singing [improvisation upon a plainsong]?', to which Polymathes replies:

'When I learned descant of my master Bold . . . he continually carried a plainsong book in his pocket he caused me to do the like, and so, walking in the fields, he would sing the plainsong and cause me to sing the descant, and when I sung not to his contentment he would show me wherein I had erred' (p. 214).

For the composers of the Quantz-Bach-Mozart period improvisation was a very important aspect of their compositional style. Inventions and fancies, or fantasias as they were more often called, represented the most adventurous style of the period, and one that is particularly associated with C. P. E. Bach:

'It is principally in improvisations or fantasias that the player can best master the feelings of his audience ... it is especially in fantasias, those expressive ... of true, musical creativeness, that the keyboard player more than any other executant can practice the declamatory style, and move audaciously from one affect to another' (p. 153).

But when he goes on to say that improvisation requires 'a comprehensive knowledge of composition' (p. 430), we are reminded that Bach would not have us think that such skills are easily acquired.

The most common form of improvisation practised in the eighteenth century was of course the art of the continuo player improvising above a figured bass. As Mitchell points out, 'an accompaniment from a thorough bass demands more than a carefully gathered knowledge of eighteenth-century idioms. It requires in addition a highly creative imagination.'[20] The Essays leave us in no doubt about the need for such 'imagination' but neither do they fail to point out at every turn that the imaginative leaps which the player allows himself to employ depend on the confidence he has gained from knowledge slowly and carefully acquired.

The dangers attached to superficial early successes in improvisation on the part of their pupils are constantly in the minds of the essayists. Their aims are always long-term. Of those musicians with only short-term objectives, Quantz says:

'Frequently they have learned no more than to read notes, and to humbug their listeners with some difficult things poorly executed and in poor taste; and if by chance they have the good fortune to become one-eyed kings in the land of the blind and to receive some applause, their lack of knowledge deludes them into thinking ... they merit preference over other musicians' (p. 24).

We may overlook what is, perhaps, a touch of professional jealousy here, for the basic point that he is making is an important one; it leads to the classical dilemma of how to balance long-term objectives with immediate gains, how the pupils can learn to enjoy doing those things which he must struggle with now if he is to proceed any further.

The 'embellishment' of simple melodies was a technique of improvisation that was constantly demanded of eighteenth-century musicians, and it is one that has its place today in the way a musician learns to elaborate his ideas. For Quantz, 'Almost no one who devotes himself to the study of music . . . is content to perform only the essential graces; the majority feel moved to invent variations or extempore embellishments' (p. 136). This type of improvisation offers the musician who is perhaps not quite confident enough to take advantage of the greater freedom of total improvisation, a framework for melodic invention which may lead him to a much more advanced sense of construction later on. Improvisation is, then, immediately related to performance and composition, and like these two aspects of musicianship, can be improved. This was also pointed out by Kollmann, the German composer who settled in George III's London:

'By *fancy* I understand the extemporary execution of *voluntary thoughts*. Though it is impossible to teach a person *what* he shall fancy, as that would be doing away with the whole idea of *fancy*, or of *voluntary thoughts*, yet his fancy may be assisted in taking a proper direction, by certain *rules*, which tell him: if you fancy *so*, it will be better, or *otherwise*, it will be worse. The said rules I shall attempt in the present chapter.'[21]

C. P. E. Bach promises that 'a good future in composition can assuredly be predicted for anyone who can improvise' (p. 430). In the last chapter in Part Two of his *Essay*, he outlines a number of basic points about improvisation (within his own harmonic language) that are still useful today.

'When only little time is available for the display of craftmanship, the performer should not wander into too remote keys, for the performance must soon come to an end. Moreover, the principal key must not be left too quickly at the beginning nor regained too late at the end. At the start the principal key must prevail for some time so that the listener will be unmistakably orientated. And again before the close it must be well prolonged as a means of preparing the listener for the end of the fantasia and impressing the tonality upon his memory . . .' (p. 438).

The combination of musical imagination and knowledge of harmony is
again emphasized by composers in the nineteenth century. Hummel
wrote that:

'To extemporize freely, the player must possess
a. as *natural gifts*, invention, intellectual acuteness, fiery elevation and
flow of ideas, and the power of improving, arranging, developing, and
combining the subject invented by himself, as well as that taken from
others for this purpose.
b. as the *result of scientific education*, such perfect readiness and certainty
regarding the laws of harmony . . .'[22]

Czerny, with similar earnestness, added that 'it is requisite to commence
this sort of practice [improvisation] at an early period . . . and that we
should learn to apply the experience which we have gained by studying
the compositions of others to our own extemporaneous performances'.[23]

Schumann's point of view is also of interest. He suggests that:

'If heaven has gifted you with lively imagination, you will often, in
lonely hours, sit as though spellbound, at the pianoforte, seeking to
express the harmony that dwells within your mind . . . But beware of
giving yourself up, too often, to a talent that will lead you to waste
strength and time on shadow pictures. You will only obtain mastery
of form and the power of clear construction through the firm outlines
of the pen. Write more than you improvise therefore' (I, p. 417).

While in no way underestimating improvisation's significance, he
makes the point that it is not a substitute for composition, but a
preliminary to it. Many students with a talent for improvisation fail to
observe Schumann's warning, and the result can be that their creative
imaginations never meet with the 'power of clear construction' that is
necessary in the organization of larger compositions. Schumann,
though often conveying an improvisatory freshness in his piano compositions, does not wish to be misunderstood: composition is altogether
a more complex process than improvisation.

   Improvisation was also a great source of ideas for Stravinsky: 'on
the one hand it contributed to my better knowledge of the piano, and,
on the other, it sowed the seed of musical ideas'.[24] Developing this
point, he wrote that 'fingers are not to be despised: they are great
inspirers, and in contact with a musical instrument, often give birth to
subconscious ideas which might otherwise never come to life' (p. 82).
In opposition to the often expressed view that composition should be

done away from the piano, Stravinsky said: 'I think it is a thousand times better to compose in direct contact with the physical medium of sound than to work in the abstract medium produced by one's imagination' (p. 5). Improvisation was, then, a basic need which Stravinsky retained all his working life.

Carl Orff's introduction of group improvisatory techniques into the classroom represents one of the most significant direct contributions by a composer to musical education in recent times. From its beginnings in Austria and Germany in the inter-war period, *Schulwerk* techniques have spread to practically every part of the world. Orff described his basic idea in the following way:

'My idea was to take my students so far that they could improvise their own music (however unassuming) and their own accompaniments to movement. The art of creating music for this ensemble (pitched percussion, other percussion, recorders, some open-stringed instruments) came directly from playing the instruments themselves. It was therefore important to acquire a well-developed technique of improvisation, and the exercises for developing this technique should above all lead the students to a spontaneous, personal, musical expression.'[25]

The points of emphasis are the association with dance rhythms, *ensemble* improvisation, the Stravinskian physical contact with the instruments, and the development of technique to be directed towards the gaining of freedom of expression.

Orff employed the word 'elementary' to describe the nature of this type of music-making, and he used the word in the sense of 'pertaining to the elements, primeval, rudimentary, treating of first principles'. For him 'elementary' music was:

'. . . never music alone, but forms a unity with movement, dance and speech. It is music that one makes oneself, in which one takes part not as a listener, but as a participant. It is unsophisticated, employs no big forms and no big architectural structures, and it uses small sequence forms, ostinato and rondo. Elementary music is near the earth, natural, physical, within the range of everyone to learn it and to experience it, and suitable for the child' (p. 212).

The speech rhythms were formed into songs which always retained the natural verbal rhythms, rather than the more complex setting techniques usually employed by composers. This type of music was for everyone, not simply the musically gifted child:

'I did not think of an education for specially gifted children but of one on the broadest foundations in which moderately and less gifted children could also take part. My experience had taught me that completely unmusical children are very rare, and that nearly every child is at some point accessible and educable; but some teachers' ineptitude has often, through ignorance, nipped musicianship in the bud, repressed the gifted, and caused other disasters' (p. 212).

The improvisatory techniques of *Schulwerk* are therefore intended for the general class teaching situation, rather than specialist musical education (although even in this context it has been recognized that such methods have their value). It would be a mistake, however, to overlook some of the problems associated with this type of teaching. The major difficulty is contained in the very nature of improvisation. An improvisation, once written down, takes on the nature of a composition. Compositions can be rehearsed, and performed, if necessary, in concert-like conditions. Now the publications which Orff and Keetman produced as a result of their series of programmes on Bavarian Radio can, and are, easily mistaken for actual *playing scores*. The result is that many teachers who have had no direct contact with the Orff-Schulwerk Institute do not involve their pupils in basic improvisations which contain real opportunities for individual, imaginative musical ideas, but rather a sort of reproduction of wax models.

In order, therefore, to provide the opportunities for spontaneous improvisations, the teacher must himself understand the essential nature of improvisation, and even for a trained musician, this is not as simple as it may sound. He must, for example, be able to pick up quickly the germ of an idea which any child in the group may produce; he must be able to see immediately the directions in which the idea may be developed; when the group is not providing its own materials, he must be able to provide the right sort of embryonic sources himself; he must be able to give some sort of structure to the work, without imposing too heavily his own musical personality; he must be able to listen to the whole sound of the improvisation, and help the performers to achieve some sort of balance. In other words, the teacher's role in *Orff-Schulwerk* is not unlike, in a certain sense, the combined role of composer-performer. It is obvious, therefore, that the teacher who is to do this type of work adequately must be a musician, and one who has himself experienced the problems of improvisation and composition.

As Quantz said: 'How can they teach music if they themselves remain in a state of ignorance?' (p. 16).

Other problems, however, arise for teachers who, though musically able to cope with many of the demands of improvisation, have little experience of the dance-movement aspect of *Schulwerk* which is in Orff's view, fundamental. In British education at least, there is an invisible barrier between the teaching of music and the teaching of dance and movement, so that few musicians know anything about the problems of teaching dance, and most dance teachers simply put on a record when they need music. The full rewards of *Schulwerk*, however, are only obtained when music, dance and speech are combined, and until such time as this is properly understood, the real advantages of the system cannot be appreciated.

Orff described the use of improvisation as a stimulus to the imagination in the following way:

'It is at the primary school stage that the imagination must be stimulated; and opportunities for emotional development, which contain experience of the ability to feel, and the power to control the expression of that feeling, must also be provided. Everything that a child of this age experiences, everything in him that has been awakened and nurtured is a determining factor for the whole of his life. Much can be destroyed at this age that can never be regained, much can remain undeveloped that can never be reclaimed' (p. 214).

Moreover, he felt that 'only when Primary Schools have laid the foundations can Secondary Schools build up a successful musical education'; through improvisation, therefore, the whole structure of a child's musical development may be built.

There are, then, several aspects of musical improvisation with which composers have been concerned: improvisation as a means of developing vocal and instrumental techniques; improvisation as a means of developing composition; as a performing *tour de force*; and as a basic, all-round, teaching method. In the period after 1950, and therefore outside the scope of this book, the use of improvisation and composition in musical education has increased; it is to be hoped that some of the fundamental principles outlined in this chapter have not been overlooked.

Notes

1. L. B. Plantinga, *Schumann as Critic* (New York, 1967), p. 141.
2. *A Composer's World*, p. 176.
3. *Varietie of Lute Lessons*, p. Ei.
4. R. Mulcaster, *Elementerie*, in *The Educational Writings of Richard Mulcaster*, ed. J. Oliphant (London, 1903), p. 39.
5. A. Churton (ed.), *Kant on Education* (London, 1899), p. 63.
6. J. Bruner, *The Process of Education* (Cambridge, Mass., 1960), p. 31.
7. Improvisation was fundamentally associated with *basso continuo*, ornamentation, cadenzas, etc.; cf. Mattheson *Grosse General-bass schule* (1731); Gasparini, *L'Armonico pratico al cembalo* (1708); Heinichen, *Der Generalbass in der composition* (1728); Tartini, *Trattato di musica* (*c.* 1754). Tartini also encouraged his pupils to 'play extempore [passages] as many as you please, and in every key, which will be both useful and necessary'. *Lettera* (1760) in *Trattato*, ed. R. Jacobi, p. 137.
8. J. F. Hummel, *Complete Theoretical and Practical Course* (London, 1828), p. iii.
9. *Petite méthode pour apprende la musique aux enfants* (Paris, *c.* 1730) trans. M. Pincherle, 'Elementary Musical Instruction in 18th Century', *MQ*, 34 (1948), p. 62.
10. *Chronicle*, p. 113.
11. E.g. '. . . the weeds still flourish that have flourished at all times; but Czerny [etc.], have lost much of their former favour with the public. Since as little can be said of a certain type of music, as of a very similar style in circulating library literature, this merely deserves a very cursory mention in an art paper.' (*Music and Musicians*, Vol. 1, p. 281.)
12. J. F. Hummel, *Complete Theoretical and Practical Course*, p. iii.
13. *Letters*, p. 26.
14. *Violin School* (London, 1831), p. i.
15. *Gesammelte schriften* (Leipzig, 1854); Eng. trans. F. R. Ritter, *Music and Musicians* (London, 1877–80), Vol. 1, pp. 411–13.
16. F. Busoni, from a letter to his wife, 1898, in *The Essence of Music*, Eng. trans. R. Ley (London, 1957), pp. 81–2.
17. *Chronicle*, p. 5.
18. T. H. Yorke Trotter, *Music and Mind* (London, 1924), p. 23.
19. *The Division Viol* (London, 1659), p. 27.
20. W. J. Mitchell, *Preface* to translation of Bach's *Essay*, p. 21.
21. A. F. C. Kollmann, *An Essay on Musical Harmony* (London, 1796), p. 120.
22. *Complete Theoretical and Practical Course*, Bk 3, p. 73.
23. *Letters to a Young Lady on the Art of Playing the Pianoforte*, trans. J. A. Hamilton (3rd ed. London, 1848), p. 76.
24. *Chronicle*, p. 5.
25. 'Orff-Schulwerk: Past and Future', *MEd*, 28 (1964), p. 210.

6

The Place of Composition

In the conversation that begins the second part of Morley's *A Plaine and Easie Introduction*, the Master says that he thought Philomathes wished only to learn to sing, and the pupil replies:

'Indeed when I came to you first I was of that mind, but the common proverb is in me verified that "much would have more", and seeing I have so far set foot in music I do not mean to go back till I have gone quite through all; therefore I pray you now to discourse to me what Descant is, what parts and how many it hath, and the rest' (p. 140).

Morley thus draws our attention to a very important feature of the learning situation: a person who is well taught in the early stages will normally wish to develop his knowledge. We are therefore faced with the problem of continuity in education, and the question Morley poses for us may be presented thus: do we sufficiently realize the importance of trying to understand the overall structure of the subject we are teaching? Do we agree that for the student 'a curriculum should involve the mastery of skills that in turn lead to the mastery of still more powerful ones'?[1]

It is not surprising that composers should believe that the teaching of composition should form an essential part of musical education, and that the gradual 'mastery of skills' should include the mastering of compositional techniques as well as those of singing and performing on instruments. It is, however, as a part of a *general* musical education, rather than as an isolated specialism, that they wish to see the teaching of composition proceed. Hindemith, for example, believed that the object of musical education was the development of general musicianship, and that:

'this vast stock of general musical knowledge was the hotbed in which the germs of composing grew ... Composing was not a special branch of knowledge that had to be taught to those gifted or interested enough. It simply was the logical outgrowth of a healthy and stable system of education, the ideal of which was not an instrumental, vocal, or tone-arranging specialist, but a musician with a universal musical knowledge . . .'[2]

Composition as 'the logical outgrowth of a healthy and stable system of education' was as basic an idea to Hindemith as it was to Morley. If, therefore, it should not be seen, at least in the early stages, as a 'specialism' it was important that the methods of teaching composition were properly conceived: 'Don't teach composition in the way it is usually done. Teach musicians' (p. 186).

'The way it is usually done' meant, as often as not, both the habit of separating the teaching of composition from other musical skills, and the habit of confusing terms like 'theory', 'harmony', and 'composition', so that often a course in composition became nothing more than a course in analytical harmony. Hindemith wished to provide the pupil with 'an all-round technique of general validity, on which his talents may thrive' (p. 184). The all-round musicians are those '. . . who are useful players, not of one instrument, but of several; who sing acceptably, who know how to handle classes, choirs and orchestra; who have a decent knowledge of theory, and beyond all, who certainly know how to compose' (p. 185).

It was Schoenberg who provided a convincing answer to the question 'why teach composition to people who will never try it again after their student days?'[3] His view was that, as it is 'possible to make people with even less than mediocre gifts use the means of musical composition in a sensitive manner', the teacher must employ these means of helping the student in 'understanding the fine points' (p. 148). Schoenberg felt that 'composing trains the ear to recognize what should be kept in mind, and thus helps the understanding of musical ideas' (p. 151). In these circumstances, the purpose of teaching composition 'is to help them [the students] understand music better, to obtain that pleasure which is inherent in the art' (p. 152). The teaching of composition, then, as a means towards general musicianship and increased sensitivity, is an important element of Schoenberg's theories of musical education.

It is essential, therefore, to emphasize the main purpose which the composers attached to the teaching of composition: it was *not* to create more composers. Most composers, one feels, would have agreed with Stravinsky when he said 'a composer is or isn't; he cannot learn to acquire the gift that makes him one, and whether he has it or not, in either case, he will not need anything I can tell him.'[4] Rather, it was the urgent belief that the various aspects of musicianship are interdependent, and that consequently a musical education which failed to incorporate some experience of composition was in a very real sense unbalanced, and incapable of providing the appropriate pattern of growth that is essential to the musician.

Perhaps the major problem which the composers discuss in relation to the teaching of composition is the matter of freedom and restraint. There seems to be two main aspects of this question with which they are concerned. The first is the restraint of tradition, and the second is the restraint of actual musical resources. In the first case, composers have naturally tended to attach a great deal of importance to originality as far as their own work is concerned, but at the same time to stress the importance which the beginner should attach to tradition. According to Stravinsky: 'No matter what the subject may be, there is only one course for the beginner; he must at first accept a discipline imposed from without, but only as the means of obtaining freedom for, and strengthening himself in, his own method of expression.'[5] In the second case composers have largely agreed that limitations in respect of numbers of voices or instruments, length of composition, variety of forms, even in the scope of harmony and counterpoint, are essential in the early stages of learning composition. Again, Stravinsky points to the advantages that he found in the limitations imposed by the discipline of strict counterpoint:

'This first contact with the science of counterpoint opened up at once a far vaster and more fertile field in the domain of musical composition than anything that harmony could offer me. And so I set myself with heart and soul to the task of solving the many problems it contains. This amused me tremendously, but it was only later that I realised to what an extent those exercises had helped to develop my judgement and my taste in music. They stimulated my imagination and my desire to compose; they laid the foundation of all my future technique, prepared me thoroughly for the study of form and orchestration' (p. 15).

The paradox of finding freedom in strict limitations is, of course, a constant theme not only in Stravinsky's writing, but also that of his contemporaries, Schoenberg and Hindemith.

In relation to the idea of tradition, the teacher of composition has always had to strive to find a balance between teaching what might be called the 'rules', and encouraging his pupil's imagination to run freely. The 'rules' are, of course, nothing more than his analysis of how composers have worked in the past, and their value depends upon factors which included not only the quality of the analysis, but also the

relevance of the information thus produced to that particular pupil at
that particular time. Tovey emphasized this point when he said that
'the orthodox rules of musical grammar are generalizations from the
experience of composers. They are completely misunderstood if they
are regarded as *a priori* principles to which the composers were bound
by authority.'[6] Similarly Hindemith questioned the 'faith in the magic
power of the old rules of harmony';[7] and pointed out that 'the teaching
of music theory, intended to acquaint the student with the composer's
working material and its treatment, has in our teaching system been
degraded to a tedious educational by-product, which is presented
without any relation to practical music and is accepted listlessly and
practised drearily.'[8] Hindemith was particularly resentful of the class
of music teacher whose '. . . representatives are those who drive the
intelligent student into the wilderness of pseudomusical problems.
Such a student cannot avoid seeing our teaching system's sole purpose:
the perpetuation of a composing and teaching mediocrity, its leading
up to a certain point of superficial traditional training and then, as an
act of self defense, its refusal to give satisfactory answers to justified
questions.'[9] By way of comparison he suggested that 'It is remarkable
that people who are improving their households by buying the newest
models of refrigerators, washing machines, television sets, and cars,
are in their teaching profession clinging to old Goetschius and Kitson
and many similarly antimusical textbooks which in an age of the
aforementioned appliances are as outmoded as kerosene lamps.'[10]
'Those industrious ones', he remarked, 'who think that by memorizing
and working hard at rules and precepts they will come by a recipe for
producing convincing music had better give up the search.'[11]

When Quantz wrote that 'none should imagine that I demand that
every piece must be composed . . . in accordance with the rules . . . the
listeners should perceive no laborious industry, but nature alone
shining forth everywhere' (p. 22), he was speaking for his contemporaries clearly enough; and if the next generation appeared to care less
for the 'rules'–

'Art is free, and not to be confined by technical fetters. The ear –
naturally the cultivated ear – must be the judge, and I feel myself as
authorized as anybody else to make up rules. Such artificialities have
no value; I should rather someone try to write a truly new minuet.'[12]

– that generation certainly would not have wished to be associated with
unstructured abandon:

'Once I had captured the idea, I strove with all my might to develop and sustain it in conformity with the rule of art. In this way I tried to help myself, and this is where so many of our newer composers fall short: they string one little piece onto another and break off when they have scarcely started.'[13]

But it was Grétry who perhaps expressed the position the most vividly:

'Woe to the artist enslaved by rules who does not dare yield to the flight of his genius... However, only the man who is familiar with the rules may sometimes violate them for he alone can know that, in certain cases, the rule is not enough.'[14]

Earlier in the eighteenth century the same point had been made by Rameau when he stated that 'while composing music is not the time to recall rules which might hold our genius in bondage. We must have resource to the rules only when our genius and our ear seem to deny what we are seeking.'[15]

Quantz, however, is always at pains to warn us that the composer's task is not an easy one:

'Anybody who imagines that everything in composition depends upon luck and blind fancy errs greatly... It is true that inventions and fancies are fortuitous and cannot be acquired through instruction; but the nicety and propriety, and the choice and mixture of ideas are not fortuitous, and are learned through knowledge and experience' (p. 45).

Similarly Brahms states that: 'There is no real *creating* without hard work. That which you would call invention, that is to say, a thought, is simply an inspiration from above, for which I am not responsible, which is no merit of mine. Yea, it is a present, a gift, which I ought even to despise until I have made it my own by right of hard work.'[16] Moreover, Stravinsky emphasizes that it is the *task* itself which gives the composer his pleasure, not simply the completion of the task:

'The idea of work to be done is for me so closely bound up with the idea of the arranging of materials and of the pleasure that the actual doing of the work affords, that should the impossible happen and my work suddenly be given to me in a perfectly completed form, I should be embarrassed and nonplussed by it, as by a hoax.'[17]

Quantz usefully elaborates some of the qualities he thinks are demanded of the musician, and also makes some precise recommendations for the student of composition:

'He who wishes to devote himself to composition must have a lively and fiery spirit, united with a soul capable of tender feeling; a good mixture, without too much melancholy, of what scholars call the temperaments; *much imagination, inventiveness, judgement, and discernment*; a good memory; a good and delicate ear; a sharp and quick eye; and a receptive mind that grasps everything quickly and easily' (p. 13).

We are here plunged into the whole complex business of eighteenth-century theories of the 'affections',[18] 'passions', 'sensitivity' and the 'temperaments', many of which, of course, were linked with ideas prevailing in philosophical thinking in previous centuries. The 'affect' of music is a matter which deeply concerns all three essayists, and it is a matter that we will return to at a later point. But we may recognize at once that here Quantz is clearly stating that the knowledge of the 'rules' is not enough, not even when it is enlarged in concept to knowledge of the 'rules of good taste'; the composer at least must have 'imagination, inventiveness, judgement and discernment'.

These are powerful demands; they reach out to the heart of the composer's inner world where the needs of the music and the needs of the musician are one. Lest his reader should be still in doubt of the requirements of a composer, Quantz goes on to mention the 'good memory', the 'good and delicate ear', and the many other necessities. We do not feel, however, that he, or indeed the other essayists, are constructing a high fence around their territory. They are simply making it as clear as possible that the pursuit of music must not be entered upon lightly.

The composers of the essayists' generation were inclined to accuse their fathers of too great an adherence to what they often described as the 'learned style', coupled with what they obviously thought of as a certain lack of imagination. In a telling phrase Quantz states that '. . . the nicety, coherence, order, and mixture of ideas . . . require new rules in almost every piece' (p. 21). What rules? Clearly not rules that could be found in a textbook, but the rules of 'good taste'; and what, then, is 'good taste'? It is certainly not an externally imposed set of values as far as Bach, Quantz and Mozart are concerned. If pressed one feels they would have to admit it was their own 'taste' that they were talking about, and as leading composers and performers of their generation, who was there to argue with them? The 'new-rules-in-every-piece' requirement is a call to the imagination in the most direct terms. Quantz observes that he disapproves of composers who 'bring along their inventions not in their heads but in their luggage' (p. 20). What he requires of a composer is an imagination, informed of the methods of the past, but vigorously alive to the needs of the present, which can only be perceived by a receptive mind, not explained by the rules brought along 'in their luggage'.

We are, perhaps, at first disturbed by the idea that if Quantz, C. P. E. Bach and Leopold Mozart could not see the enormous worth of the music of the previous generation, the music of J. S. Bach, and of Handel, there must be something fundamentally unsound about their own concepts of value. But such concern must be short lived, for the development of what we might call the 'historical sense' is comparatively recent. The first growth of it is not really found until the last quarter of the eighteenth century,[19] and it flourished only weakly throughout much of the nineteenth. In our own century the phrase 'early music' has been employed to describe in turn the eighteenth, seventeenth, sixteenth, fifteenth, fourteenth and thirteenth centuries. Our great gains in historical perspective have of course to be seen in the light of our failure to know the present, and the great dangers of a 'museum culture'.

Of the many linguistic ambiguities that are encountered in musical education, the word 'academic' perhaps attracts the greatest uncertainty. Used in directly opposed senses, the reader cannot always be certain whether the writer is offering praise or blame. It is in the pejorative sense, however, that Stravinsky employs the word when he stated that 'academicism results when the reasons for the rule change, but not the rule'.[20] Similarly Schoenberg wrote:

'I have so often shown . . . how to develop one's own talent in the way most suited to it. I do not force anyone to compose in the modern manner if he does not feel in a modern way, but he will learn to understand classical music more thoroughly than he would if taught by the dyed-in-the-wool academicians.'[21]

Stravinsky was prepared to grant 'academicism' limited support –

'A work is called academic when it is composed strictly according to the precepts of the conservatory. It follows that academicism considered as a scholastic exercise based on imitation is itself something very useful and even indispensable to beginners who train themselves by studying models. It likewise follows that academicism should find no place outside of the conservatory.'[22]

– although he was not very enthusiastic about learning from models himself.

Tchaikovsky believed that the talented pupil should be encouraged to follow his musical instinct, but the '. . . less talented student, however, who is in need of definite and concisely expressed theoretical principles should work in strict accordance with the rules, troublesome and unbending though they be. These rules have sprung empirically out of the musical promptings of man's nature.'[23] Perhaps Cherubini was also thinking of the 'less talented student' when he wrote that 'it is necessary that the pupil should at first be obliged to adhere to very vigorous precepts, in order that afterwards, when he is composing in the free style, he may know how and wherefore his genius, if he possesses any, shall have compelled him to break through the severity of these early rules'.[24] There are, however, very great dangers associated with such attempts to categorize pupils' activities. Berlioz, who Cherubini undoubtedly regarded as a poor student, appeared to gain nothing from his lessons in counterpoint, and were it not for his powerful individuality, might never have developed as a composer. How can the teacher, then, so structure the learning situation in composition that those who need the support of 'rules' are provided with the appropriate models, and those for whom 'rules' are irrelevant or harmful are given the freedom to develop in their own ways?

In answering this question the composers have, of course, assumed that the teaching of composition should be based on individual teaching, even when it is in the class situation. Furthermore, they have emphasized the importance of the relationship between listening to, and studying other people's music as a way of helping the student in composition to develop his own awareness of musical standards. It is perhaps in Schumann that we can see this process most clearly at work.

Characteristic of Schumann's approach is the following comment on an immature work:

'I would not think of alarming you with such words as "tonic", "dominant" or "counterpoint", for you would only laugh, and say, "that is the way I wrote it, and I shall not alter it"; and one must be indulgent with you. Were I your instructor, however, I would put Bach and Beethoven in your hands very often, to sharpen your eyes and ears, to give a safe shore to your tender feelings, to impart certainty and form to your ideas' (II, p. 248).

Or again:

'To be sure, he has yet much to accomplish; if he asks us, what? we answer: keep your head clear, and play your own sonata after one by Mozart or Beethoven, and then find out where the difference lies' (II, p. 283).

It must be recognized that in mentioning Beethoven, Schumann is referring to a composer of the immediately previous generation; thus today the examples might be Bartók or Stravinsky or another of their contemporaries. Schumann's point is that 'the study of the history of music, and the hearing of masterworks of different epochs, will most speedily cure you of vanity and self-adoration' (I, p. 414). At the same time, Schumann was aware that too much comparison with master-pieces might lead many students to give up in despair, and so he was quick to give approval to the student who '... writes down what sounds well to him, and considers the ear the highest court of appeal. We have nothing to say against this principle. Whatever sounds well mocks all grammar, whatever is beautiful may scoff at aesthetics' (II, p. 182). Moreover, he certainly did not wish the student simply to imitate the style of the works he analyzed: 'He who constantly confines himself to the same forms and circumspections, finally becomes a mannerist and a Philistine; nothing is more injurious to an artist, than long-continued repose within a convenient form' (II, p. 327). He wishes rather, to increase his understanding of the principles of structure and development. Schumann, no doubt, would have agreed with Stanford when he said that: 'In composition *per se* there is no rule save that of beauty, and no standard save that of taste.'[25]

Stanford, the teacher of Vaughan Williams and many other English musicians, added a good deal of clarity to the discussion on teaching composition when he wrote:

'To tell a student how to write music is an impossible absurdity. The only province of a teacher is to criticise it when written, or to make suggestions as to its form or length, or as to instruments or voices for which it should be designed. He can thus keep impatience within bounds when invention is outpacing experience, develop by sure, if sometimes necessarily slow, means the experience to equal the inven-tion. For the rest his functions must be ... to give hints as to what to avoid, leaving the constructive element to the pupil's own initiative' (p. 1).

Furthermore, Stanford wished the student to develop his sense of self-criticism, and felt that the best way of doing this was to provide him with the opportunity to hear his own works performed:

'Young composers were taught abroad upon paper and only the most picked and finished examples of their work ever reached the point of a hearing. We went on the principle that a hearing of a composition is the best lesson the writer can get, and that the perspiration agony from which a composer suffers when he hears the sounds of his own inexperience is the most valuable part of his training.'[26]

In these circumstances the young composer also has to copy out the parts, arrange the rehearsals and conduct the performance. The general educational value of such a process is considerable, and applies both to the child who composes a sixteen bar piece for recorder, glockenspiel and drum, and to the student who composes a full scale orchestral work.

Stanford also believed in the process of intuitive leap followed by analytical reassessment. 'Some young composers think too little', he wrote, 'others too much. The one extreme is as dangerous as the other. Let the imagination run, and criticize it for youself after it has had its fling.'[27] Moreover he was well aware that originality was not a characteristic that should be looked for in the beginner: 'There is nothing so dangerous to a young composer as to criticize him for lack of originality. The truest originality is, and has always been, a gradual growth and not a sudden phenomenon' (p. 188). As far as Stanford was concerned, 'a beginner must not think about originality. If he has it in his nature, it will come out as surely as the world goes round the sun' (p. 189), provided, it might be stressed, his teacher does not destroy it.

It was not uncommon, according to Stanford, to encounter the situation in which:

'. . . teachers often overlook the natural tendency of a young and ardent inventive brain to chafe under advice which at the moment seems merely formal, irksome and dry. This impatience of temperament . . . can only be moulded . . . by the sympathetic method of explaining why those rules were laid down and by clearly showing their origin' (p. 3).

Such a 'sympathetic method of explaining' is found throughout Morley's *A Plaine and Easie Introduction*. For Morley, success in dealing with a single melodic line leads naturally to an investigation of the problems of counterpoint: 'Now I pray you set me a plainsong and I will try how I can sing upon it' (p. 144). We may note that the teaching of counterpoint is essentially a *practical* activity for Morley, and he employs the simple procedure of improvising one part above another. One wonders how often in our own times the teaching of counterpoint is seen in such practical terms?

Philomathes' observation on the need for limitations gives a very clear picture of Morley's attitude: 'You use me as those who ride the great horses, for having first ridden them in small compass of ground, they bring them out and ride them abroad at pleasure' (p. 152).

The idea of expanding from limitations, and not the reverse, is in this way vividly presented. If we see the child's imagination as something growing and expanding, then this point of view will be familiar to us; but if we were to see it as a quality that needs to be severely restrained in order to fit the child into predetermined modes of behaviour, then we would oppose such expansion.

At the same time, however, it is clear that Morley believes very strongly that the development of musical ability only comes through continual practice: 'This is well; but I will make another [example], that all my faults may come out at the first and so I may have the more time to mend them.' 'Do so, for the rules and practice joined together will make you both certain and quick in your sight' (p. 157).

John Dowland also refers to the development of practice when he comments: 'Again, though the master be never so diligent, painful and industrious, yet three things are required in the scholar, necessary for the obtaining thereof, viz: Nature, Reason and Use; because this harmony dependeth of science and human art, which the understanding retaineth by musical habit.'[28]

Morley's emphasis on 'musical habit' is drawn to our attention on several occasions, as the following examples may show: 'By working we become workmen, therefore once again set down a way of this kind of descant.' 'That was my intended purpose before and therefore here is one, and I pray you censure it without flattery.'

At a later point Morley states: 'In your music seek to please the ear as much as show cunning' (p. 217), indicating a common enough proposition. In introducing the idea of the intellectual and the emotional in music, Morley makes it very clear that he sees no reason for separating the two in real music by stating that '. . . it be greater cunning both to please the ear and express the point than to maintain the point alone . . .' (p. 217), and going on to criticize those '. . . that seeking to show cunning in following of points they missed the mark whereat every skilful musician doth chiefly shoot, which is to show cunning with delightfulness and pleasure' (p. 220).

This amiably concise statement of a composer's aims would surely have given satisfaction to musicians throughout the seventeenth century, and as a teaching goal it has much to recommend it in today's complex situation.

As an illustration of the point Morley shows how a composer may use both his knowledge and his imagination. A knowledge of cadential procedures might be assumed, but the discovery of others 'particular to yourself' opens up the possibility of showing 'cunning with delightfulness and pleasure'. In making this point Morley touches upon a central issue, namely that a composer's knowledge needs to take him only as far as it brings him into the fullest appreciation of his own imagination.

It has already been made clear that *A Plaine and Easie Introduction* is an outward looking work. One of its objectives is to send the reader searching for a wider experience of music: 'If you would compose well the best patterns for that effect are the works of excellent men' (p. 276), or again: '... of all this you shall find examples everywhere in the works of the good musicians' (p. 291). Until the last twenty years or so composition, in twentieth-century England at least, tended to be taught without reference to examples of real music, and inevitably the sort of unconvincing, synthetic product which emerged had very little in common with the works of composers actually writing at the time.

The authorities whom Morley cites are carefully listed at the end of his book and include both the authors 'such as have written of the art of music' and the 'practitioners, the most part of whose works we have diligently persued'. This list has always been of interest to historians since it has provided valuable cross-references to the study of the period; but it is also interesting as an example of Morley's thoroughness as a teacher, for he was clearly determined to bring before his readers as vividly as possible the need for studying sources outside those immediately available. These qualities have led one recent writer to the view that the '*Plaine and Easie Introduction* is in fact a remarkably comprehensive composition tutor, containing features – notably the use of improvisation as an aid to learning – that might well be incorporated into our modern curricula'.[29]

Morley's contemporary, Richard Mulcaster, also supported the idea that it was important that composition should be incorporated into musical education at a reasonably early stage. His first thought is that he should '... postpone the study of composition and harmony till further knowledge and maturity are attained, when the whole body of music will demand attention'.[30] But, with the need for structure and continuity in mind, he goes on to say that '... since the child must always be advancing in that direction, I would set him down the rules of composition and harmony, which will make him better able to judge of singing, just as in language he who is accustomed to write can best judge of a writer' (p. 153). Some teachers today might venture a little further, and through improvisational techniques at least, begin to develop the child's ability to compose for the very reason that Mulcaster suggests, that one skill helps another. However, in fairness to Mulcaster, it must be admitted that many teachers of music today would not, or could not, introduce their children to composition at any stage, let alone at the elementary stage.

The composition teaching of Morley and his contemporaries is understandably based on counterpoint rather than harmony. Although the two techniques are closely related, it is important to recognize the emphasis which composers have placed upon the teaching of counterpoint as a basic compositional procedure. Presented in its simplest form, the common assertion has been that once a beginner has mastered the most elementary procedures in making melodies, he should then move on, not to adding chords to his melody, but to adding a second or counter-melody to his original. This attitude is regularly encountered in the seventeenth and eighteenth centuries, and is particularly characteristic in the work of the composer-teacher of the first half of the twentieth century. As Vaughan Williams pointed out, '... at a recent meeting of modern composers the only thing they all agreed on was that the only sure foundation for musical composition was strict counterpoint'.[31]

Hindemith (*Ludus Tonalis*), Bartók (*Mikrokosmos*), Stravinsky and Schoenberg have all stressed the value of teaching counterpoint. Indeed Schoenberg's *Preliminary exercises in counterpoint* (1963) provides a very extensive coverage of the technique. Inevitably a book on strict or species counterpoint reminds the reader of Fux's *Gradus ad Parnassum*, but as the editor points out:

'... it will soon become apparent that only the most tenuous relation exists between the two works, the former providing merely a point of departure, as it were, for Schoenberg goes far beyond the usual application of the species in many significant ways. First of all, Schoenberg's examples provide many more problems and situations than those encountered in traditional texts based on Fux. Secondly, discussions and criticisms in the form of *comment* appear at the end of each main section as a directive to the student himself to examine, criticise, and improve his own examples.'[32]

Counterpoint also forms a central principle of Kodály's singing methods (where he suggests that the best accompaniment to a single vocal line is another vocal line), and in Orff's *Schulwerk*, where chords are only introduced after the children have gained considerable experience in combining melodies.

It would be quite inaccurate, however, to give the impression that composers in general saw the teaching of counterpoint as the sole basis of the teaching of composition, for this would be to overlook the great significance they saw in the development of rhythmic skills, harmonic textures and instrumental and vocal timbres. Their enthusiasm for counterpoint, and particularly strict counterpoint, is for the advantages which it provides as a discipline. It must, however, be a *practical* discipline, both in the sense of Morley's students improvising vocal counterpoint against a *cantus firmus*, and in the sense that work in counterpoint must never be left on paper, but performed on every occasion. Moreover, the essential demand which the composers make upon the teaching of composition is that the student's musical imagination shall be given the opportunity to develop, and that although the application of strict limitations usually provides the right sort of forcing ground for such growth, the nature of such limitations may vary from composer to composer, and from generation to generation.

Brahms, for example, felt that an essential discipline was involved in the process of constantly editing a new composition –

'One ought never to forget that by actually perfecting *one* piece one gains and learns more than by commencing or half-finishing a dozen. Let it rest, and keep going back to it and working at it over and over again, until it is completed as a finished work of art, until there is not a note too much or too little, not a bar you could improve on.'[33]

– while Schumann thought that 'the first conception is always the most natural and the best' (I, p. 74). Some composers thought that song writing provided the beginner with a clear framework for his ideas, while others felt that the words got in the way of the notes:

'It is also a dangerous rut in the composer's road. It seems to him smooth enough to progress in, but is likely enough to upset him when he tries to get out of it. To write a good melody or theme in absolute music by the suggestion of music itself will be doubly and trebly more difficult when the crutches of suggestive poetry are not there to lean on. The wisest plan is to keep song writing for an occasional and experimental amusement, and to eschew it as a practice until the power over writing absolute music is assured.'[34]

Vaughan Williams even suggested that writing music for films provided an excellent discipline: '. . . film composing is a splendid discipline, and I recommend a course of it to all composition teachers whose pupils are apt to be dawdling in their ideas, or whose every bar is sacred and must not be cut or altered.'[35]

'The creative imagination of a musician', wrote Schumann, 'is very different [from other artists], and though a picture, an idea, may flow before him, he is only happy in his labour when this idea comes to him clothed in melody' (II, p. 60). Composers have naturally been very concerned about the ways the musical imagination can be stimulated. Hindemith felt that: 'If imagination is the agent that, over and above the acquirement of a reliable technique, ought to direct a future composer's instruction, we must accuse the majority of our teachers of a lack of this quality.'[36]

Stravinsky believed that technical problems actually '... developed and exercised my imagination'[37] and that the 'direct contact with the physical medium of sound'[38] was a primary stimulus. Vaughan Williams agreed. 'Does not the actual shock of sound,' he wrote, 'help to fertilize the imagination and lead him [the composer] on to still further musical invention? The answer is that everyone must use the means which enable him to do the best. If a composer finds inspiration in the bass trombone or the accordion, by all means let him use them.'[39] Schumann on the other hand wrote that 'when you begin to compose, do it all with your brain. Do not try the piece at the instrument until it is finished. If your music proceeds from your heart it will touch the hearts of others' (I, p. 417). Clearly then, there is more than one way to set the imagination in action; as Tovey pointed out, 'every musical activity has its proper part in training the imagination'.[40] He felt, however, that he must also add that every musical activity equally has 'its danger of warping or starving the imagination by misuse' (p. 340). Thus for some students, the constant use of an instrument while composing would only 'warp' their imagination, while for others the constant absence of an instrument would 'starve' their imagination.

Teachers of music are understandably interested in discovering ways by which they can stimulate the musical imaginations of those they teach. It is, unfortunately, only an occasional glimpse of the answer that can be found in the composers' writings:

'Most music lovers believe that what sets the composer's creative imagination in motion is a certain disturbance generally designated by the name of *inspiration* ... [however] inspiration is in no way a prescribed condition of the creative act, but rather a manifestation that is chronologically secondary ... an emotion which invariably follows the phases of the creative process.'[41]

Thus Stravinsky draws us closer to the nature of the problem. He believed that 'all art presupposes a work of selection' (p. 89); therefore, we may conclude the teacher's task is to immerse the student in musical experiences from which he can begin to select and identify those resources which he may wish to employ in his own creative processes. Stravinsky goes further, however:

'The very act of putting my work on paper . . . is for me inseparable
from the pleasure of creation. So far as I am concerned, I cannot separate the spiritual effort from the psychological and physical effort; they
confront me on the same level and do not present a hierarchy' (p. 67).

And also:

'The appetite that is aroused in me at the mere thought of putting in
order musical elements that have attracted my attention is not at all a
fortuitous thing like inspiration, but as habitual and periodic, if not as
constant, as a natural need' (p. 67).

These comments provide us with some sense of the sort of environment in which composition may develop. In trying to provide a similar
environment for his pupils, the teacher of music may recognize at least
three basic requirements: first, that the student can work in a musically
enriching atmosphere; second, that he is encouraged to observe
(analyze) the musical resources around him; and third, that he is allowed
to develop regular habits of work. However, regular habits of work
should not be confused with routine habits. 'Routine and fashion,'
wrote Hindemith, 'are the worst snarls that can entangle the creative
mind.'[42] There is no fundamental reason why such conditions should
not be provided in schools. Regular, daily facilities for study are provided as a matter of course in what are regarded by many as the 'basic
elements' of the curriculum. What is not usually recognized is that
musical education equally needs such regular provision of teaching,
observation and practice.

If Hindemith also 'cannot establish laws which govern the way a
creative mind works',[43] he can, like Stravinsky, help us to clear our
minds a little:

'Each individual has to develop his own procedure. Nevertheless people
have their notions about a composer's activities. To most of them . . .
factual knowledge and imaginative composition seem to be two
irreconcilable opponents . . . Certainly those people are right who look
at a perfect composer's craft as something that for the average man is
strange and inapproachable. But why this strangeness precludes
consciousness, exactitude, and rational working methods is a mystery.
In music, as in all other human pursuits, rational knowledge is not a
burden but a necessity, and it ought to be recognized as such by all.'[44]

Moreover, he can help to reduce the obscurities that are sometimes
attached to compositional techniques:

'The true work of art does not need to wrap any veil of mystery about its external features. Indeed the very hallmark of great art is that only above and beyond the complete clarity of its technical procedure do we feel the essential mystery of its creative power.'[45]

Furthermore, he regarded it as essential that the teaching of composition should not be confined simply to problems of a technical nature, but that a broader view should introduce problems like the size and location of the place where the music was to be performed, the level of the performer's skills, and even the possible listening capacities of the audience.

Schoenberg believed that the experienced composer tended to 'conceive an entire composition as a spontaneous vision', but equally he believed that this information was of very little use to the beginner: 'No beginner is capable of envisaging a composition in its entirety; hence he must proceed gradually, from the simpler to the more complex ... It will be useful to start at building musical blocks and connecting them intelligently.'[46] A similar view is also found in Czerny's writings:

'Often ... the plan of the whole piece is presented to the imagination of the composer ... Most composers, however, and particularly beginners, would act very wrong if they were always to wait patiently until this enthusiasm sprang up of itself.'[47]

Schoenberg's 'building brick' method is therefore the most obvious way in which the beginner will learn the basic principles of musical construction. Another illuminating comparison he made is contained in the following passage:

'A piece of music resembles in some respects a photograph album, displaying under changing circumstances the life of its basic idea – its basic motive ... In contrast to the chronological succession in a photograph album, the order of motive-forms is conditioned by the requirements of comprehensibility and musical logic. Thus, repetition, control of variation, delimitation and subdivision regulate the organization of a piece in its entirety, as well as in its smaller units.'[48]

'The life of its basic idea' is a phrase that might also have been found in Schumann's writings, for he laid considerable stress on the need for the beginner in composition to learn the virtues of simplicity. The sort of work that pleased him was one in which: 'Nothing on the whole, is out of place; there is nothing in the work that does not appear inwardly related to its fundamental plan' (I, p. 212), or one to which he could respond: 'How delightful it is to find an organic, living whole amid the trash of student work' (I, p. 213). On another occasion he observed that 'the first movement is the most musical of all: everything in it is organically and happily connected' (II, p. 157), and of a song he wrote: 'Harmony – pure and choice; melody – clear, not without originality, easily singable; accompaniment – natural, enhancing the effect; choice of texts – judicious, earnest. Can one desire a better passport into the kingdom of musicians?' (II, p. 137).

Schumann felt that early attempts at composition nearly always suffered from trying to be too ambitious. 'Nearly all of them,' he wrote, 'are injured by a sort of superabundance, which in young composers is partly caused by technical uncertainty, and partly by a desire to do everything equally well. These faults will, we hope, be greatly modified at a riper age by self-knowledge and practice' (II, p. 142). He was particularly worried by the student who 'tries to deceive us as to the superficiality of his work with various harmonies; he strives to dazzle us; he seizes something quite dissimilar, or suddenly breaks off with a pause' (I, p. 336).

Structural simplicity is also a feature of Bartók's *Mikrokosmos*. As a textbook for composition it has the great virtue of demonstrating in a multitude of examples the principles of simplicity and unity of construction. Moreover, with its great emphasis on rhythmic variety and its use of modal and chromatic scales, it provides a viable alternative to the major/minor tonalities usually encountered in models written for young composers.

It is possible, then, to see certain fundamental principles, associated with the incorporation of the teaching of composition in musical education, contained in the critical and pedagogic works of composers. They are, that composition is a *normal* part of musical education, closely related to performing and listening; that composition is a musical activity which enriches, and is enriched by, other musical activities; that composition provides a major opportunity for the musical imagination to develop; that compositional limitations and restrictions tend to encourage the *growth* of the musical imagination, and *not* to damage it; that the critical study of works by established composers is a vital means towards developing powers of self-criticism in composition; and that the essential contribution of the teacher is (over and above the provision of a structured learning environment) the help he gives the student towards the critical analysis of his work. These are principles, surely, well worth the consideration of every teacher of music.

Notes

1. J. Bruner, *Toward a Theory of Instruction* (Cambridge, Mass., 1967), p. 35.
2. *A Composer's World*, p. 178.
3. *Style and Idea* (New York, 1950), p. 148.
4. *Stravinsky in Conversation with Robert Craft* (London, 1962), p. 145.
5. *Chronicle*, p. 20.
6. D. F. Tovey, *Essays and Lectures on Music* (London, 1949), p. 378.
7. *A Concentrated Course in Traditional Harmony* (London, 1943), p. iii.
8. *A Composer's World* (Cambridge, Mass., 1952), p. 188.
9. Ibid., p. 189.
10. Ibid., p. 190.
11. *The Craft of Musical Composition* (New York, 1941), p. 10.
12. Joseph Haydn (1732–1809), quoted in S. Morgenstern, *Composers on Music* (London, 1958), p. 69.
13. Ibid., p. 69 (quoted in Greisinger's *Biographische Notizen*, Vienna, 1809).
14. André Ernest Modeste Grétry (1741–1813), quoted in S. Morgenstern, op. cit., p. 75.
15. Jean-Phillippe Rameau (1683–1764), quoted in S. Morgenstern, op. cit., p. 42, from *Le Nouveau système de musique théorique* (Paris, 1726).
16. G. Henschel, *Personal Recollections of Johannes Brahms* (London, 1907), p. 22.
17. *Poetics*, p. 69.
18. See Johann Mattheson (1681–1764), composer and theorist, especially *Der Volkommene Kapellmeister* (Hamburg, 1739); cf. M. F. Bukofzer, *Music in the Baroque Era* (London, 1948), pp. 382–93; also P. Kivy, 'What Mattheson Said', *MR*, 34/2 (1973), pp. 132–40.
19. One is thinking of the actual performance of older music. There were, of course, examples of historical inquiries, e.g. M. Praetorius, *Syntagma Musicum* (1614–19), and M. Marsenne, *Harmonie Universelle* (1636).
20. *Stravinsky in Conversation with Robert Craft* (London, 1962), p. 241.
21. *Letters* (New York, 1965), p. 27.
22. *Poetics of Music*, p. 109.
23. *Guide to the Practical Study of Harmony* (Leipzig, 1900), p. 57.
24. *A Course of Counterpoint and Fugue* (London, 1837), p. 1.
25. *Musical Composition* (London, 1911), p. 3.
26. *Pages from an Unwritten Diary* (London, 1914), p. 219.
27. *Musical Composition*, p. 165.
28. *Varietie of Lute Lessons*, p. Ei.
29. P. Le Huray, 'The Teaching of Music in Sixteenth-century England', *MEd.*, 30 (1966), pp. 75–7.
30. *The Educational Writings of Richard Mulcaster*, ed. J. Oliphant (London, 1903), p. 152.
31. *The Making of Music* (New York, 1955), p. 24.
32. *Preliminary Exercises*, ed. L. Stein, p. xii.
33. G. Henschel, *Personal recollections of Johannes Brahms* (London, 1907), p. 39.
34. C. V. Stanford, *Musical Composition*, p. 34.
35. *Some Thoughts on Beethoven's Choral Symphony, with Writings on Other Musical Subjects* (London, 1953), p. 107.
36. *A Composer's World*, p. 188.
37. *Chronicle*, p. 101.
38. Ibid., p. 5.
39. *Some Thoughts on . . .*, p. 60.
40. 'The Training of the Musical Imagination', *ML*, 17 (1936), p. 340.
41. *Poetics of Music*, p. 65.
42. *A Composer's World*, p. 125.
43. *A Composer's World*, p. 44.
44. Ibid., pp. 44–5.
45. *The Craft of Musical Composition*, p. 157.
46. *Fundamentals of Musical Composition* (London, 1967), p. 1.
47. *School of Practical Composition* (London, 1850), p. 2.
48. *Fundamentals of Musical Composition*, p. 58.

7

The Problem of Aesthetics

In attempting to investigate the view that composers have much to offer us on *how* music is learnt, we have discussed ideas about the quality of teachers, the teaching environment, the introduction of notation, the teaching of singing, instrumental skills, improvisation and composition. In each of these aspects, we have encountered the composers writing about techniques with which they necessarily have intimate familiarity. In the remaining major question, how we should approach the problem of musical aesthetics, the composer is necessarily venturing into philosophical territory and into extra-musical ideas.

Matters of aesthetics do, however, concern the composer, performer and listener. It is, nevertheless, only since the mid nineteenth century that composers have turned their attention towards matters of musical appreciation peculiar only to the listener, since most of their earlier publications were intended for people who were learning to sing or to play or to write their own music. Schumann and the other composer-critics may be said to represent, therefore, the first major attempt by composers to discuss musical aesthetics for the *general* reader. In musical education in the more limited sense however, composers have generally confined themselves to matters directly related to the principles of musicianship, and it is usually only through indirect means, if at all, that their ideas have been absorbed into the fabric of musical education. Moreover, those indirect means, which are sometimes merely anecdotal, do not often appear in easily verifiable sources, and tend to acquire second-hand additions and modifications which may bear only slight similarity to the composer's original point of view.

Matters of aesthetics impinge upon all levels of musical education, and it is therefore important that the teacher be familiar with the main doctrines of aesthetics that composers have employed in their critical writings. These may usefully be examined within the context of four differing viewpoints: Morley, the eighteenth-century essayists, Schumann, Stravinsky and their contemporaries.

In *A Plaine and Easie Introduction* Morley refers to the idea of 'expression' only in the context of word setting, where it is appropriate 'to dispose your music according to the nature of the words you are therein to express' (p. 290). Commenting on an example of complex contrapuntal writing, Morley says: 'This hath been a mighty musical fury which hath caused him [Renaldi] to show such diversity in so small bounds. True, but he was moved to do so by the words of the text . . .' (p. 60). He does, however, devote only a small part of the last section of the book to 'rules to be observed in dittying', and not only are these mostly developed from Zarlino, but also they appear without musical examples. This lack of emphasis on word setting techniques may suggest that Morley felt that the important thing for the learner to acquire was the technical contrapuntal skills to which most of the book is devoted, and that the techniques of word setting could be superimposed upon such a compositional technique, once it was developed.

Nevertheless, in the space he allows himself, Morley provides the student with what he sees as the essential points. 'If you have a grave matter,' he writes, 'apply a grave kind of music to it; if a merry subject you must make your music also merry, for it will be a great absurdity to use a sad harmony to a merry matter or a merry harmony to a sad, lamentable, or tragical ditty' (p. 290).

This may be compared with a similar view expressed by Christopher Simpson: 'When you compose music to words, your chief endeavour must be, that your notes do aptly express the sense and humour of them. If they be grave and serious, let your music be such also: if light, pleasant, or lively, your music likewise must be suitable to them.'[1] For seventeenth-century writers the 'affections of the mind' are clearly at the mercy of the accomplished composer when he brings together the combined forces of music and words. It therefore becomes very important to them that there should be a common language of associations in music, and that this should be passed on from generation to generation. Morley urges that:

'. . . you must have a care that when your matter signifieth "ascending", "high", "heaven", and such like you make your music ascend; and by contrary when your ditty speaketh of "descending", "lowness", "hell", and others such you must make your music descend; for as it will be thought a great absurdity to talk of heaven and point downwards to the earth, so will it be counted great incongruity if a musician upon the words "he ascended into heaven" should cause his to descent . . . '(p. 291).

As far as phrase structure is concerned Morley insisted that one '. . . must not make a close (especially a full close) till the full sense of the words be perfect' (p. 292), and as a general principle in harmony there must be 'an harmonical consent between the matter and the music . . .' (p. 292). Morley provides his pupils with fairly precise specifications for word setting:

'You must then when you would express any words signifying hard-ness, cruelty, bitterness, and other such like make the harmony like unto it . . . you must cause [the parts to] proceed by whole notes, sharp thirds, sharp sixths, and such like; you must also use cadences bound with the fourth or seventh which . . . will exasperate the harmony' (p. 290).

By way of contrast '. . . when any of your words shall express com-plaint, dolour, repentence, sighs, tears, and such like let your harmony be sad and doleful . . . then must you use notions proceeding by half notes, flat thirds and flat sixths . . .' (p. 290). He also indicates the proper use of chromaticism –

'so that those natural motions may serve to express those effects of cruelty, tyranny, bitterness, and such other, and those accidental motions may fitly express the passions of grief, weeping, sighs, sorrows, sobs and such like.' (p. 290)

– and tempo:

'Also if the subject be light you must cause your music to go in motions which carry with them a celerity or quickness of time . . . if it be lamentable the notes must go in slow and heavy motions . . .' (p. 290).

Music historians have been interested for many years in this section of Morley's work because it can be said to provide them with some assistance in the analysis of a composer's technique, especially in madrigal and song forms. What, however, can be learnt from this section about the teaching of music?

Our attention must focus on the fact that Morley, in providing his students with what amounts to a collection of acceptable solutions to certain word-setting problems, is attempting to make things easier for them. The words may give the composer not only an instant structure, a sort of mould into which he can pour his musical ideas, but also, in most cases, a series of reference points where he can employ known techniques; and they will be known, of course, not only to the composer, but also to his audience, thus bringing the two parties into closer communication. A teacher is always justified in simplifying ideas and techniques for his students, provided that the process of simplification does not do harm to the students' ability to perceive the real nature of the ideas, or develop the full possibilities of the techniques. For the Elizabethans, and indeed for most composers during the following three hundred years, vocal music had to be 'framed to the life of the words' because that was the only acceptable style. (Morley strongly disapproves of the word setting techniques of medieval and early renaissance composers, for which composers of our own time show considerable enthusiasm.) The teacher therefore had a duty to introduce his pupils to this way of writing in order that he should recognize the points of immediate contact with his listeners before he develops the ability to surprise them.

There is a sense, also, in which Morley may have thought of word setting composition as easier, at least for the student, than writing in instrumental forms:

'The most principal and chiefest kind of music which is made without a ditty is the Fantasy, that is when a musician taketh a point at his pleasure and wresteth and tuneth it as he list, making either much or little of it according as shall seem best in his own conceit. In this may more art be shown than in any other music because the composer is tied to nothing, but that he may add, diminish, and alter at his pleasure' (p. 296).

Since 'in this may more art be shown', it follows that the Fantasia could also reveal 'less art' in the hands of an inexperienced or unimaginative composer, for the simple reason that it is a more exposed form and the composer's ideas cannot be held together by words. He would, therefore, be anxious to help his students with the 'easier' forms in the earlier stages.

In his section on word setting in the madrigal Morley raises an issue which crops up many times in later writers. His proposition is that 'in no composition shall you prove admirable except you put on and possess yourself wholly with the vein wherein you compose' (p. 294). This may be compared with Quantz, who says of the performer:

'A beginner must therefore be constantly attentive when he plays, and must take care that he hears each note as he sees it with his eyes, and as its value and expression require. Inner feeling – the singing of the soul – yields a great advantage on this regard. The beginner must therefore seek gradually to arouse this feeling in himself. For if he is not himself moved by what he plays he cannot hope for any profit from his efforts, and he will never move others through his playing, which should be his real aim' (p. 117).

– and then C. P. E. Bach, who follows with:

'A musician cannot move others unless he too is moved. He must of necessity feel all of the affects that he hopes to arouse in his audience, for the revealing of his own humour will stimulate a like humour in the listener. In languishing sad passages the performer must languish and grow sad. Thus will the expression of the piece be more clearly perceived by the audience' (p. 152).

and lastly with Leopold Mozart, who concludes:

'In a word, all must be so played that the player himself be moved thereby' (p. 218).

In as far as the essayists are demanding that good performance demands *feeling* on the part of the performer, they are simply expressing an idea, which if commonplace, is nonetheless important. But Bach goes much further. It is not enough to express the feeling within the music, but apparently, the feeling must be externalized to the extent that the performer must 'languish and grow sad'.

Such a view of the role of the performer is one which, from time to time, has received a good deal of popular support, but it is one that clearly does not stand up to analysis. The following questions present themselves: how can a performer cope with all the actual physical requirements of playing his instrument while giving similar attention to the theatrical demands of conveying the 'affect'? (How, for example, could one of Quantz's flautists manage while maintaining his embouchure?) Why should a performer feel so unsure about the quality of his performance that he must also convey the feeling through non-musical means? Why should it be thought that an audience is so insensitive to the music that it has to be accompanied by a visual commentary? How is it possible to reduce the vast range of feelings possible in response to a piece of music to a series of symbolic gestures?

In this context, Quantz, C. P. E. Bach and Leopold Mozart are specifically referring to performers; Morley, however, is specifically referring to the composer. His suggestion is that, in order to convey to the listener the closest possible association between the words and the music, the composer must himself be so involved in the emotions expressed in the words, that his music will inevitably reflect this involvement. This is a very popular view of the role of the song writer, and one to which Quantz and his colleagues subscribed. Moreover, it is a view that they carried over to instrumental music which had no verbal associations whatsoever, such as the sonata and the symphony. It is impossible to say just how far Morley believed that his instrumental compositions really had definite emotional associations. Although he says 'in no composition shall you prove admirable except you put on and possess yourself wholly with that vein wherein you compose' (p. 294), he is writing within the context of the madrigal, and in the section on the purely instrumental forms (fantasias, pavans, galliards, almans and the rest of the dances), he makes no reference to the need for the composer to 'possess himself of the vein wherein he composes', except, of course, that the dance forms necessarily possessed very strong *rhythmic* associations. In the case of the fantasy, as we have already seen, Morley believed that the composer could 'show more art than in any other music' and aim at 'the mark whereat every skilful musician doth chiefly shoot, *which is to show cunning with delightfulness and pleasure*' (p. 220). For this reason 'the more variety of points be showed in one song, the more is the madrigal esteemed' (p. 282). Thus Morley may be seen as applying general compositional standards to music, whether or not it involves word setting. Morley's reference to the relationship between the composer's feelings and the emotional associations experienced by the listener is a theme which will be further developed later on.

At this point, however, it is appropriate to look at another aspect of the problem: the development of 'good taste'. The conception of art as a means of satisfying the demands of taste has unfortunate associations with the idea of satisfying the demands of fashion – 'routine and fashion ... the worst snarls that can entangle the creative mind'.[2] But, as it has already been pointed out, mid-eighteenth-century musical taste was not so much imposed upon the composer, as the composers imposed their taste upon society. As Stravinsky noted: 'The artist imposes a culture upon himself and ends by imposing it upon others. That is how tradition becomes established.'[3] Through their position in the Prussian court, Quantz and Bach were able to exercise a considerable influence on the 'taste' of at least the German speaking parts of Europe.

The process associated with musical composition in the middle of the eighteenth century is essentially that of simplification. The Berlin school, the Mannheim school, the rise of 'opera buffa' leading to the Gluck reforms, Arne and Boyce in England, Monn and Wagenseil in Vienna, all represent a style which is less complex than either the high baroque which preceded it or the full classical forms which followed it.

The reasons put forward for this simplification are commonplace enough: in order to convey 'feeling' more directly, simpler compositional technique must be employed. The echoes of the Council of Trent, and the Florentine Camerata are loud in our ears; indeed one might go far enough to suggest that a generation which did not express the need to present its ideas more directly was very rare indeed. It is characteristic also that the new generation should, in claiming to have the expression of feeling as uppermost in its style, accuse the previous generation of a certain lack of feeling. Gluck, a central figure in this process of simplification, refers to the problem in the following way: '. . . my most strenuous efforts must be directed in search of a noble simplicity, thus avoiding a parade of difficulty at the expense of clarity.'[4] The whole of this process of simplification, which saw the replacement of the baroque style with the rococo and classical styles, became the 'good taste' of the mid eighteenth century, to which the essayists continually refer.

In each eighteenth-century essay the writer directs our attention to this topic. Leopold Mozart wishes 'to pave a way for music loving youth which will guide them with certainty to good taste in music' (p. 6), and there is continuous reference to what C. P. E. Bach calls 'our present elegant taste' (p. 373). Quantz makes no apology for the fact that he had 'ventured rather extensively into the precepts of good taste in practical music . . . I must try not only to educate his lips, tongue and fingers, but must also try to form his taste, and sharpen his discernment' (p. 7). He is speaking of the 'lips, tongue and fingers' of the flautist, but the principle naturally applies to all 'practical music'. He has very little patience with the mechanical player, and looks for all-round skills: '. . . if talent, technical skill, and experience are combined, they will form an almost inexhaustible source of tasteful invention' (p. 21). This is a point of view echoed by C. P. E. Bach: 'No one can be content any longer with . . . one who memorizes all the rules and follows them mechanically. Something more is required . . . I aim to instruct those who . . . desire to follow the precepts of good taste' (p. 173). Leopold Mozart also emphasizes the point when he states that 'taste' and 'technique' must run together from the start of a musician's education (p. 123).

The problem of good taste had also received the attention of Geminiani, who believed that it consisted of *expressing with strength and delicacy the intention of the composer*. This expression is what everyone should endeavour to acquire, and it may be easily obtained by any person, who is not too fond of his own opinion, and doth not obstinately resist the force of true evidence.'[5] It is clear that Geminiani employs the same directness in his writing that we find in the other essayists, and as a teacher he joins in their demands that the performer must learn to study the composer's intentions with the very greatest care.

Geminiani also approaches the problem of expression with the same firmness that we encounter in Quantz, Bach and Mozart:

'Men of purblind understandings, and half ideas may perhaps ask, is it possible to give meaning and expression to wood and wire; or to bestow upon them the power of raising and soothing the passions of rational beings? But whenever I hear such a question put, whether for the sake of information, or to convey ridicule, I shall make no difficulty to answer in the affirmative, and without searching over-deeply into the cause, shall think it sufficient to appeal to the effect. Even in common speech a difference of tone gives the same word a different meaning. And with regard to musical performances, experience shows that the imagination of the hearer is in general so much at the disposal of the master that by the help of variations, movements, intervals and modulation he may also stamp what impression on the mind he pleases.'[6]

Like Quantz, Bach and Mozart, there was 'no difficulty to answer in the affirmative' concerning questions of expression as far as Geminiani was concerned. The question that is raised for us is not whether it is 'possible to give meaning and expression to wood and wire', but if 'meaning and expression' imply more than *musical* meaning and *musical* expression, and how the idea of 'meaning and expression' can be introduced to those learning music.

Geminiani was clearly pleased with his efforts to put his ideas into prose, for he was to repeat the above extracts word for word in *The Art of Playing on the Violin* (1751). This volume, perhaps the most well known of Geminiani's publications, opens with the following challenge: 'The intention of music is not only to please the ear, but to express sentiments, strike the imagination, affect the mind, and command the passions' (p. 1). Like the essayists, however, Geminiani is careful to point out that this does not provide the performer with unrestricted freedom, for 'the art of playing the violin consists . . . in executing every piece with exactness, propriety, and delicacy of expression according to the true intention of music' (p. 1).

The eighteenth-century composer, then, seemed inevitably drawn into a line of argument that appears to demand from music the same criteria of assessment as the verbal and representational arts. Since music is essentially non-representational (except in a purely onomato-poeic context), and only has verbal associations in the context of singing

and descriptive words, composers tried to justify their purely instrumental compositions by transferring to them the sort of associations
their music had in verbal and representational situations, such as the
opera, and thus attempted to encourage the view that music was as
worthy of the educated man's attention as the work of writers and
painters.

It is C. P. E. Bach who says that 'it can be seen from the many
affects which music portrays, that the accomplished musician must
have special endowments and be capable of employing them wisely . . .
Nature has provided music with every kind of appeal so that all might
share in its enjoyment' (p. 153). Leopold Mozart also observes that 'one
must throw oneself into the affect to be expressed' (p. 216), and
Quantz adds that the composer 'must express the different passions for
the soul properly' (p. 23).

The three essayists are united in their desire to emphasize the
importance of *feeling*, and in this respect they share the position that
we associate with the writers and painters of the period, with Grey and
Cowper, with Goldsmith and Sheridan, and with Gainsborough and
Reynolds. Quantz goes on to make an interesting comparison:

'Musical execution may be compared with the delivery of an orator.
The orator and the musician have, at bottom, the same aim in regard to
both the preparation and the final execution of their production,
namely *to make themselves masters of the hearts of their listeners*, to arouse
or still their passions, and to transport them now to this sentiment, now
to that. That it is advantageous to both, if each has some knowledge of
the duties of the other.'

The idea of the communication of feeling is here placed in a slightly
unconvincing context. The art of oratory includes the improvisatory,
while the requirements of good performance demand that the performer communicate the composer's intentions to the best of his
ability. C. P. E. Bach makes this clear when he asks: 'what comprises
good performance? The ability . . . to make the ear conscious of the
true content and affect of a composition . . .' (p. 148). The implication
of a similar remark by Leopold Mozart is that he imagined the expression of feeling to be a special feature of the mid-eighteenth-century
style: 'The good performance of a composition according to modern
taste is not as easy as many imagine . . . who have no sensitiveness
whatever for the affect which is to be expressed in the piece' (p. 215).
Three further references may also be noted at this stage. First Quantz:

'The good effect of a piece of music depends almost as much upon the performer as upon the composer himself. The best composition may be marred by poor execution, just as a mediocre composition may be improved and enhanced by good execution' (p. 120).

Second, C. P. E. Bach:

'In order to arrive at an understanding of the true content and affect of a piece . . . it is advisable that every opportunity be seized to listen to soloists and ensembles . . . Above all, lose no opportunity to hear artistic singing . . . the keyboardist will learn to think in terms of song. Indeed, it is a good practice to sing instrumental melodies in order to reach an understanding of their correct performance' (p. 150).

Third, Leopold Mozart:

'. . . every care must be taken to find and to render the affect which the composer wished to have brought out' (p. 218).

All three attitudes are complementary, for it is indeed the duty of the performer to reflect the composer's intentions, and thus the performer does indeed shoulder a very heavy responsibility, both to composer and audience. Moreover, he must, in order to fulfil these demands, produce, if he is an instrumentalist, the singing tone-quality that Bach prizes so highly.

There can be no doubt that the essayists were in agreement in placing the requirements of expressiveness in performance above that of technical virtuosity. Bach insists that players 'whose chief asset is mere technique are clearly at a disadvantage . . . They overwhelm our hearing without satisfying it and stun the mind without moving it' (p. 147). This is a criticism which we would readily associate with certain trends in the nineteenth and twentieth centuries; it is particularly interesting in its mid-eighteenth-century context.

The identification of feeling in vocal music is made easy by the verbal associations of the text. Thus Quantz was able to ask, in reference to opera: 'whether the majority of listeners have been transported into the passions represented in the spectacle, so that they quit the theatre with a desire to hear the opera frequently?' (p. 308). But in the case of purely instrumental music the problem is slightly different. As we have already seen, the essayists thought that there was the same responsibility on the part of the performer to capture the precise feeling required by the composer. Some years earlier Johann Mattheson had referred to the problem in the following terms:

'An instrumental player or composer must observe the rules which lead to good melody and harmony much more clearly and assiduously than a singer or a choral composer, because when singing, the singer or composer is aided by the great clarity of the words, while the latter are always missing in instrumental music.'[7]

Quantz takes up this idea when he says:

'Vocal music has some advantages that instrumental music must forgo. In the former the words and the human voice are a great advantage to the composer, both with regard to invention and effect ... Yet instrumental music, without words and human voices, ought to express certain emotions, and should transport the listeners from one emotion to another just as well as vocal music does ... And if this is to be accomplished properly, so as to compensate for the lack of words and the human voice, neither the composer nor the performer can be devoid of feeling' (p. 310).

It is possible here to detect a slightly defensive attitude on the part of the essayists, and it must be remembered that in an age dominated by the opera, the establishment of instrumental forms of composition was achieved only slowly.

In the same year (1752) in which Quantz's work was published, Charles Avison (c. 1709–70) published *An Essay on Musical Expression.* He was organist of Newcastle-upon-Tyne, probably a pupil of Geminiani, and a composer, chiefly of instrumental music. The following extract from his book focuses on the problem:

'The force of harmony, or melody alone, is wonderful on the imagination. A full chord struck, or a beautiful succession of single sounds produced, is no less ravishing to the ear than just symmetry or exquisite colours to the eye. The force of sound in alarming the passions is prodigious. Thus the noise of thunder, the shouts of war, the uproar of an enraged ocean, strike us with terror: so again there are certain sounds natural to joy, others to grief, or despondency, others to tenderness and love; and by hearing these, we naturally sympathize with those who either enjoy or suffer. Thus music, either by imitating these various sounds in due subordination to the laws of air [melody] and harmony, or by any other method of association ... does naturally raise a variety of passions in the human breast similar to the sounds which are expressed.'[8]

Throughout the eighteenth century music could claim little philosophical attention. Indeed, from Locke to Kant, music finds no serious consideration in the writings of philosophers, with the sole exception of Rousseau, whose contribution in this sphere can only be described as erratic. In his articles for the *Encyclopédie* and his own *Dictionnaire de Musique* (1768), Rousseau often shows what has been described as 'a deplorable lack of appreciation for music'.[9] He was basically opposed to non-vocal music, and always required music to function as the illustration of verbal ideas or physical actions. Composition, according to Rousseau,

'is the art of inventing and writing airs and of accompanying them with suitable harmony . . . we must be capable of collecting and forming the plan of a whole work, following its correspondence of every kind, and making ourselves acquainted with the mind of the poet, instead of amusing ourselves with running after the words . . . he [the composer] should consider music by its connection with the accents of the human voice.'[10]

It was melody which took on the main responsibility for expressing the meaning of the words: 'melody, by its immediate connection with the grammatical and oratorical account, is that which gives the character to all the rest'. 'What we endeavour to render by the melody,' he added, 'is the tone by which we express the sentiments which we wish to represent, and we ought . . . to follow the voice of nature, whose accents are without affectation, and without art' (p. 160). For Rousseau, then, the movement towards simplicity may be seen in its most extreme form, so that all techniques, except those of a single vocal line, delivering words in the rhythms of normal speech, and accompanied only by basic harmonies, are placed outside the boundaries of 'good taste'.

Although Hegel attached slightly more importance to music – 'music forms the centre of the Romantic arts as a whole. It thus constitutes the point of transition between the extended sensuousness of painting, and the higher spirituality of poetry'[11] – it is not until we reach Schopenhauer that the issue of musical aesthetics is given any extended examination. For Schopenhauer, 'music is the language of reason'.[12] Music, he says, 'stands alone, quite cut off from all the other arts. In it we do not recognize the copy or repetition of any idea in the world. Yet it is such a great and exceedingly noble art, its effect on the inmost nature of man is so powerful . . . [that] we must attribute to music a far more serious and deep significance connected with the inmost nature of the world and our own self' (p. 330). Music is 'entirely independent of the phenomenal world', and this is why it 'is so much more powerful and penetrating than the other arts, for they speak only of shadows, but it speaks of the thing [reality] itself' (p. 333).

In introducing the idea of music as a *language*, however, Schopenhauer was not thinking in the terms associated with the eighteenth-century theorists. They had attempted to develop the idea of a musical language with fixed connotations, or what may be described as 'dictionary meanings'. It may be recalled that Quantz thought that 'the passions change frequently in the Allegro just as in the Adagio. The performer must therefore seek to transport himself into each of these passions, and to express it suitably. Hence it is necessary to investigate whether the piece to be played consists entirely of gay ideas, or whether these are joined to others of different kinds.' He then proceeded to describe in fairly precise terms, how gaiety (das Lustige), majesty (das Prächtige), boldness (das Freche) and flattery (das Schmeichelnde) might be expressed by the composer (pp. 133ff).

Schopenhauer's 'language of feeling', however, 'reveals the inner nature of the world, and expresses the deepest wisdom', but not in terms that can be communicated in ordinary language, for music is a 'language which reason does not understand'. In contrast to the eighteenth century's fixed associations, music 'does not therefore express this or that particular and definite joy, this or that sorrow, or pain, or horror, or delight, or merriment, or peace of mind ... but their essential nature, without accessories, and therefore without their motives'. In complete contradiction of Rousseau, Schopenhauer believed that 'if music is too closely united to the words, and tries to form itself according to the events, it is striving to speak a language which is not its own'. Far from thinking in terms of music being added to words as a justification of the use of music, Schopenhauer believed that it was actually the reverse process which normally operated: words only served 'to embody it [the music] in an analogous example'. This he thought to be true of the song, and also of opera 'the text of which should therefore never forsake that subordinate position'. Music as a mere means of expressing words was 'a great misconception, and a piece of utter perversity'. Any attempt to make music representational was 'entirely to be rejected'.[13]

Music was a powerful independent art which 'attains its ends entirely with means of its own', and therefore did 'not stand in need of the words of the song or the action of the opera'.[14] Perhaps the final blow to eighteenth-century aesthetics came in the statement that 'the human voice is originally and essentially nothing else than a modified tone, just like that of any other instrument ... That this same instrument, as the organ of speech also serves to communicate conceptions is an accidental circumstance . . .'[15] Finally, 'the music of an opera . . . has a completely independent, separate, and as it were, abstract existence for itself, to which the incidents and persons of the piece are foreign, and which follows its own unchanging rules' (p. 233).

It is within the context of these changed circumstances that the ideas of Schumann and his contemporaries must be placed. 'The truly vital part of a work', wrote Schumann, 'cannot be pointed out in words; therefore those who would know it, must themselves play and listen' (I, p. 332). Throughout his critical writings, Schumann is constantly emphasizing the need for his readers to listen to the music, and form their own impressions. Like Schopenhauer, Schumann believed that music was able to communicate feelings, but that they were not feelings that could normally be expressed in words. 'I will not attempt to provide the symphony with a foil,' he wrote on one occasion, 'for the different generations choose very different words and pictures to apply to music. And the youth hears in a piece of music an event of world-wide importance, while the grown man sees only a local happening, and the musician thought of neither the one nor the other' (I, p. 124).

Schumann, however, had sufficient journalistic common sense to recognize that he could not fill up his periodical simply with exhortations to his readers to go away and listen to the music. It must always be remembered that before the days of recorded music, one of the principal tasks of the critic was, as often as not, simply to *describe* the music for those readers who were not familiar with it, just as the main task of the art critic before photography was also descriptive. Faced with this problem of trying to describe musical events in non-musical terms, Schumann employed words in what we have seen Schopenhauer describe as 'analogous example'. He therefore, like many generations of critics who followed him, employed the technique of metaphor to describe the impression that the music had made on him.

It is, perhaps, worth noting that Schopenhauer's views reflected and had most in common with the ideals of the classical instrumental forms of the symphony, sonata and quartet. Schumann and some of his colleagues had already moved slightly away from the classical tradition. While still believing himself that music did not need words to explain it, as it were, he did not seriously object to using descriptive titles, and even programmes, to help the listener approach the music more easily. He did, however, often emphasize that, at least in his own case, the titles had been added *after* the completion of the works, and that the words were meant to throw more light on the music, not the music to throw more light on the words. 'I always say,' he wrote, 'first of all let me hear that you have made beautiful music; after that I will like your programme too' (I, p. 120). Writing of a Berlioz programme symphony, he said:

'Whether a listener, unaware of the composer's intention, would see similar pictures in his mind's eye to those which Berlioz has designated, I cannot decide, as I read the programme before I heard the work. If the eye is once directed to a certain point, the ear can no longer judge independently. And if one asks whether music is capable of accomplishing that which Berlioz has demanded of it in his symphony, one should endeavour to attach different, opposite ideas to it. I confess that the programme at first spoiled my enjoyment, my freedom; but as this faded into the background, and my own fancy began to work, I found more than was set down, and almost everywhere in the music a warm, vital tone' (I, p. 250).

If Schumann, then, may be seen as sharing certain similarities with Schopenhauer, what of Wagner? Wagner claimed that he was much influenced by the philosopher, and the following comments by Wagner on words and music would certainly seem to underline such a view:

'We are all aware that music loses nothing of its character even when very different words are set to it; and this fact proves that the relation of music to the *art of poetry* is an entirely illusory one; for it holds true that when music is heard with singing added thereto, it is not the poetical thought, which, especially in choral pieces, can hardly be articulated intelligibly, that is grasped by the auditor; but, at best, only that element of it which, to the musician, seemed suitable for music, and which his mind transmuted into music.'[16]

Yet in general Wagner seems to contradict Schopenhauer at every turn. Wagner's lifelong interest was in music and drama, while as we have noted, Schopenhauer thought that in these circumstances, music was 'striving to speak a language which is not its own' (p. 308). Wagner claimed that the music and the drama should share equal significance, whereas Schopenhauer thought that the music should always be predominant. Wagner thought that music achieved its complete expression in relation to drama, whereas Schopenhauer thought that music 'attains its ends entirely within means of its own' (p. 309). Indeed it is arguable that Wagner had more in common with Rousseau than he did with Schopenhauer.

Nevertheless, Wagner, together with all the romantics, subscribed to the idea of music as a language, if not of ideas, then certainly of the emotions. This inevitably raised for the performer questions about his

role in the communication of these feelings: 'It is unusual,' wrote
Hummel,

'to discriminate between a correct and a beautiful performance. The
latter is frequently termed *expressive*, but as it appears to me, not with
sufficient accuracy. Correctness of performance relates to the
mechanism of playing, as far as it can be indicated by musical notation.
Beauty of performance supposes everything nicely rounded off, and
accurately suited to any given composition, and to every passage in it;
it includes whatever is tasteful, pleasing and ornamental. Expression
relates immediately to the feelings, and denotes in the player a capacity
and facility of displaying by his performance, and urging to the heart of
his audience, whatever the composer has addressed to the feelings in his
production, and which the performer must also feel after him; points
which can be initiated only by general terms, having but little precision
in them, and which usually are of service only to those who have these
things within them. If such be the case, it will follow that expression
may be awakened indeed, but properly speaking, that it can never be
taught nor acquired.'[17]

Hummel, then, is saying that the performer must capture the composer's feelings *as expressed in the music*, and by experiencing these
musical feelings himself, transmit them to this audience. This is characteristic of the composer's point of view, but not always of the performer's. Cramer, for example, felt that music had 'its purpose of
moving the passions and affections of the mind' (an echo of the mid
eighteenth century), and that therefore the performer had the duty 'of
giving its effect *according to the impulse of his own feelings*. Such a
performer, though defective in power of execution will always afford
pleasure to the listener.'[18] The 'interpretive' role of the performer is
one about which the composer often expresses concern, and one which
raises many questions related to the field of musical aesthetics. The
reason that it will not be pursued in the present discussion is, however,
straightforward: as far as the composers are concerned Hummel's
version of the situation is the only acceptable one.

If Schopenhauer was supported, but misunderstood, by Wagner, then
it is particularly ironic that his views should find their most complete
development in the work of Hanslick, who did not agree with Wagner's
aims, and who, as far as one can judge, made no reference to the
philosopher in his critical works. Hanslick was a music critic and a
teacher in the University of Vienna, and not a composer. There must

be special reasons, therefore, for including an analysis of his views in the present discussion. First, they bring into sharper focus many of the issues which had been raised by composers from Morley's to his own time; secondly, they lay the foundation for developments in musical aesthetics which took place in the first half of the twentieth century.

Hanslick's essay *Vom Musikalisch-Schönen*[19] was an attempt to clear up some of the issues in musical aesthetics that were to be found in mid-nineteenth-century musical circles. The fact that his views received a good deal of opposition did not prevent their wide circulation, as the large number of editions confirms. The essay forms only a very small part of Hanslick's output as a critic, and is a comparatively early document, since he was only twenty-nine when the first edition appeared. As Deas has suggested,[20] the constant demand for new editions must have proved something of an embarrassment, and Hanslick undoubtedly became tired of the controversy which surrounded it. Nevertheless, he did not shrink from defending his principal argument which was simply 'directed against the widely accepted doctrine that the office of music is *to represent the feelings*'.[21] His emphasis, of course, was on the word 'represent', not on feelings, as the whole essay shows. We may surely agree with Hanslick, when he added that 'it is difficult to see why this should be thought equivalent to "affirming that music is absolutely destitute of feeling"'.

Hanslick's positive proposition, that 'the beauty of a composition is specifically musical, i.e. it adheres in the combination of musical sounds and is independent of all alien, extramusical notions' (p. 5), is simply a restatement of Schopenhauer's view of music's independence. Hanslick regretted that this should be confused with the notion that music was 'meaningless', for he meant quite the opposite: that the beauty of music depended upon its *meaningfulness*, but that the more meaningful music was, the less could it be described in non-musical terms. Hanslick, then, is very much in line with Schumann's, and later Stravinsky's, view that musical criticism suffers severely from the limitation of trying to express musical ideas in other than a musical form.

It is important to establish the nature of Hanslick's proposition, for the misrepresentations of his views often appear to be more common than the real version. Even a hundred years later he was still being accused of 'denying the relevance of emotion to musical experience'.[22] What he was denying, of course, was the relevance of trying to verbalize musical feeling. 'The course hitherto pursued in musical aesthetics has nearly always been hampered by the false assumption that the object was not so much to enquire into what is beautiful in music as to describe the feelings which music awakens' (p. 7). Such information, he felt, might tell us something useful about the person who was listening to the music, but very little about the music, for the simple reason that people's responses to music vary, and may be determined by many factors and a very wide range of experiences. For Hanslick 'aesthetic investigations must above all consider the beautiful object, and not the perceiving subject' (p. 8). 'Far be it from us,' he wrote, 'to underrate the deep emotions which music awakens . . . it is only the unscientific procedure of deducing aesthetic principles from such facts against which we protest. Music may, undoubtedly, awaken feelings of great joy or intense sorrow; but might not the same or still greater effects be produced by the news that we have won the first prize in the lottery, or by the dangerous illness of a friend?' (p. 15).

It could not be the aim of music, he believed, to excite the emotions for 'the beautiful, strictly speaking, aims at nothing beyond itself . . . although the beautiful exists for the gratification of an observer, it is independent of him' (p. 9). If it can be said to have an aim beyond itself, it is on 'producing something beautiful which affects not our feelings, but the organ of pure contemplation, our imagination' (p. 11).

It would be possible to devote a great deal of space to the discussion of Hanslick's ideas, but this would not be appropriate at the present time. The following ten short extracts, however, may serve as a useful summary of his views:

(i) '. . . The nature of the beautiful in music . . . is specifically musical. By this we mean that the beautiful is not contingent upon nor in need of any subject introduced from without, but that it consists wholly of sounds artistically combined' (p. 47).

(ii) 'To the question: what is to be expressed with all this material? the answer will be: musical ideas. Now a musical idea reproduced in its entirety is not only an object of intrinsic beauty but also an end in itself, and not a means for representing feelings and thoughts' (p. 48).

(iii) 'The reason why people have failed to discover the beauties in which pure music abounds, is, in great measure, to be found in the underrating by the older systems of aesthetics of the sensuous element and in its subordination to morality and feeling . . .' (p. 49).

(iv) 'But our imagination, which is so constituted as to be affected by auditory impressions, delights in the sounding forms and musical structures and, conscious of their sensuous nature, lives in the immediate and free contemplation of the beautiful' (p. 49).

(v) 'The object of every art is to clothe in some material form an idea which has originated in the artist's imagination. In music this idea is an acoustic one; it cannot be expressed in words and subsequently translated into sounds. The initial force of a composition is the invention of some definite theme, and not the desire to describe a given emotion by musical means' (p. 52).

(vi) 'If, instead of looking for the expression of definite states of mind, or certain events in musical works, we seek music only, we shall then, free from other associations, enjoy the perfections it so abundantly affords' (p. 59).

(vii) '. . . wherever the question is a specifically musical one, all parallelisms with language are wholly irrelevant' (p. 70).

(viii) 'The sovereignty of the emotions . . . is nowhere more completely out of place than when it is supposed to govern the musician in the act of composing, and when the latter is regarded as a kind of inspired improvisation. The slowly progressing work of molding a composition . . . requires quiet and subtle thought such as none who have not actually essayed it can comprehend' (p. 72).

(ix) 'An aesthetic analysis can take no note of circumstances which lie outside the work itself' (p. 74).

(x) 'A critic does not substantiate the merit or subject of a symphony by describing his subjective feelings on hearing it, nor can he enlighten the student by making the feelings the starting point of his argument. This is of great moment, for if the connection between certain feelings and certain modes of musical expression were so well established as some seem inclined to think . . . it would be an easy matter to lead the young composer onward to the most sublime heights of his art' (p. 86).

Hanslick's ideas find articulation in England in part of a lengthy Victorian study by Gurney.[23] After much discussion of the nature of musical aesthetics, Gurney employs the following language in an attempt to clarify the position (Gurney's italics):

'The primary and essential function of music is to create beautiful *objective forms*, and to *im*press us with otherwise *un*known things, instead of to introduce and support particular *subjective moods* and to *ex*press for us *known* things' (p. 490).

The use of the word 'expressive', wrote Gurney,

'may fairly be called in question when the ideas and emotions conveyed have no assignable existence external to the phenomena so designated: however *im*pressive a phenomenon may be, it may be said, we have no right to call it *ex*pressive, unless we can say what it expresses; and to say what music expresses except in music is essentially impossible' (p. 125).

Music as an impressive rather than expressive art is a point of view which has many implications for musical education. It is appropriate, therefore, to investigate the form this idea took in the mind of a composer.

When, in 1935, Stravinsky wrote that 'music is, by its very nature, essentially powerless to *express* anything at all',[24] he was greeted with the same misunderstanding that had befallen Hanslick's use of 'meaning-less' seventy years before. 'Expression', Stravinsky continued,

'has never been an inherent property of music. That is by no means the purpose of its existence. If, as is nearly always the case, music appears to express something, this is only an illusion and not a reality. It is simply an additional attribute which by tacit and inveterate agreement, we have lent it, thrust upon it, as a label, a convention – in short, an aspect unconsciously or by force of habit, we have come to confuse with its essential being' (pp. 53–4).

Some thirty years later Stravinsky, in referring again to this statement, observed that 'I stand by the remark, incidentally, though today I would put it the other way around: music expresses itself.'[25] More important for Stravinsky was the idea that 'composition is something entirely new *beyond* what can be called the composer's feelings', or as Gurney put it, something 'to impress us with otherwise unknown things' (p. 490), or as Hanslick concluded, 'something beautiful which affects our imagination' (p. 100). His earlier statement had been 'simply a way of saying that music is supra-personal and super-real and as such beyond verbal meanings and verbal descriptions'.[26]

The many misunderstandings that occur in relationship to musical aesthetics, Stravinsky believed, 'arise from the fact that people will always insist upon looking in music for something that is not there. The main thing for them is to know what the piece expresses, and what the author had in mind when he composed it. They never seem to under-stand that music has an entity of its own apart from anything that it may suggest to them.'[27] In contrast to this situation, 'when people have learned to love music for itself, when they listen with other ears, their enjoyment will be of a far higher and more potent order, and they will be able to judge it on a higher plane and realize its intrinsic value'.[28] Clearly, then, Stravinsky, like Hanslick and Gurney before him, is not just playing with words. His concern is the listener's maximum enjoy-ment, and the allied belief that the listener will find a great deal of music unapproachable if he is constantly searching for associations which do not exist.

Stravinsky recognized that his listening 'with other ears' makes some demands upon the listener: 'Obviously such an attitude presupposes a certain degree of musical development and intellectual culture, but that is not very difficult of attainment.'[29] As we have seen in previous chapters, he believed, as many other composers believed also, that the simplest developments of musicianship in the child helped him to listen 'musically'. 'Unfortunately,' he concluded, 'the teaching of music, with a few exceptions, is bad from the beginning. One has only to think of all the sentimental twaddle so often talked about Chopin, Beethoven and even about Bach' (p. 168). Talking *about* music had no place in schools for Stravinsky. 'What does it matter whether the *Third Symphony* was inspired by the figure of Bonaparte the Republican or Napoleon the Emperor? It is only the music that matters. But to talk music is risky, and entails responsibility. Therefore some find it preferable to seize on side issues. It is easy, and enables you to pass as a deep thinker' (p. 117).

It may be argued, then, that Stravinsky's aesthetics form part of a total pattern that had slowly taken shape during the nineteenth century, and which found its most complete expression in the first half of the twentieth century. It is therefore appropriate to look at the form it took in the hands of some other composers.

Busoni is strikingly similar to Stravinsky on this point. 'Music remains wherever and in whatever form it appears', he wrote, 'exclusively music and nothing else, and it only passes over into a special category through the description given to it by the title and the superscription, or the text to which it is put, and the situation in which one places it.'[30] Just how far he and his contemporaries had moved from the eighteenth-century point of view may be measured in the context of the performer:

Busoni:	C. P. E. Bach:
'... an artist, if he is to move his audience, must never be moved himself, lest he lose, at that moment, his mastery over the material.'[31]	'... a musician cannot move others unless he too is moved. He must of necessity feel all of the effects that he hopes to arouse in his audience, for the revealing of his own humour will stimulate a like humour in the listener' (p. 152).

Schoenberg also has a valuable contribution to make. In instrumental music, he said, 'there is no story, no subject, no object, no moral, no philosophy or politics which one might like or hate',[32] in the music itself. He recognized however, that people often did make such associations: 'There are relatively few people who are capable of understanding, purely in terms of music, what music has to say. The assumption that a piece of music must summon up images of one sort or another, and that if these are absent the piece of music has not been understood or is worthless, is as widespread as only the false and banal can be' (p. 1). It was therefore the duty of musical education to increase this number; again, not for the purpose of persuading people to agree with the finer points of a composer's philosophy, but for the very practical reason that acceptance of the 'false' doctrine cut them off from a very large sector of the musical repertoire, and severely limited their enjoyment of music as a whole. 'One cannot do justice to a work of art while allowing one's imagination to wander to other subjects, related or not. In the face of works of art one must not dream, but must try to grasp their meaning' (p. 147). The work of art, then, is an *object*, which in Gurney's sense, may impress itself upon the listener. 'According to my long experience, the *impression* of a work changes considerably with frequent listening.'[33] Since the object does not change, then what is changing is the listener's perception of the object.

The same topic was also discussed by Křenek. He blamed the doctrine of 'expressive aesthetics' as being responsible for the average listener's inability to listen, 'for he is totally unused to acting without such crutches',[34] that is, the crutches of verbal and visual image: 'the means of the musical creative process . . . are not basically accessible to the means of verbal language' (p. 131). So long as we fail to recognize the musical process as thought-process carried out in a self-contained medium exclusive to music, it is bound to remain tied to other kinds of values outside itself. It then appears to be an expression of historical, psychological or other factors and is unrecognizable as a musical process. What are the dangers, it may reasonably be asked, in such associations?

'This line of reasoning leads to the ideas that an age full of discord uses more dissonances in its music, a serene, peace-loving man writes more "harmonious" music, and so on and so forth. Even if few people would admit to holding this vulgar view of musical aesthetics, secretly it is much deeper rooted than might be thought, and this sometimes emerges involuntarily' (p. 133).

It doesn't matter, of course, whether this view is *vulgar* or not; what matters is whether such an ill-formed view might adversely affect the composer. Křenek's answer to this is yes, it can harm the circumstances in which a composer works:

'From this point of view it is only a step to the idea that one could make the age seem more harmonious by writing more tonal music, and that if only discontented types could be restrained from composing, the annoying and confusing transformation of the sound-language could be stopped. First, then, we must make it plain that music is autonomous with regard to other fields; only then can we grasp the importance of the changes taking place in the musical sphere itself' (p. 133).

It must be recognized, of course, that Křenek, together with Schoenberg, Hindemith and many other German composers, had suffered from just such intervention in their modes of composition, and that similar attempts to influence the style of composers had been characteristic of Stalinist Russia. Křenek's argument then takes this form:

'We are dealing with the *musical* thought, that is, a thought that belongs exclusively to the sphere of music and can only be expressed with musical means, which is identical with its realization in musical material and cannot be separated from it; it cannot be encountered, described, defined or even named in verbal language. It is necessary to get this quite clear because experience teaches that the average person, under the influence of expressive aesthetics, has only to hear the words "musical thought" to imagine that this is a metaphor, that music expresses a thought, or rather a feeling, that exists outside itself. By "musical thought" I mean something that is contained entirely in the musical medium and that we can only perceive through that medium, without the intervention of extra-musical considerations or translation into another medium' (p. 139).

To the question, does it matter if the listener uses metaphor, consciously or unconsciously, to describe his experience of music, Křenek's answer was that the associative approach might be acceptable *in so far as it succeeded* in bringing the listener nearer the music, but once the 'habitual associative mechanism was not set in motion by it' (p. 157), and this was particularly characteristic of listening to new music, the listener was either cut off from the music, or forced to acquire the listening technique of the musician.

Hindemith takes up most of the points already mentioned. Like so many other composers, he does not deny that music can have onomatopoeic associations, but, like them, questions the value of employing such techniques: '. . . the value of onomatopoeia is greatly over-rated. Had its advocates asked the musicians about their methods instead of dealing with the listeners and their impressions they possibly would have abandoned their theory.'[35] He also questions the idea of music as a language: 'A composer who wanted to use music in the same sense a language is used could do so only by preparing a voluminous dictionary, in which each particle of musical form corresponds with a verbal equivalent . . .' (p. 35). In relation to expressive/impressive theories he makes the following points: if music is said to express feelings, '. . . whose are the feelings it expresses? Those of the composer, the performer, the individual listener, or the audience? Or does it express feelings of a general character, the specification of which is left to the members of any of these groups?' (p. 35). His answer is that it can't be the composer's feelings, for much the same reason that Stravinsky suggested, that is, a composition is essentially new, *beyond* his feelings; nor can it be the performers', for 'in reality they are, in respect to the current that flows from the composer's brain to the listener's mind, nothing but an intermediate station, a roadside stop, a transformer house, and their duty is to pass along what they received from the generating mind' (p. 37). We are therefore left with the *impressive* theory once again. Stanford, whose influence on music in England should never be underestimated, said that 'music may be divided into two classes – absolute music, when the art speaks for itself by sound alone, and descriptive music when it illustrates words or drama . . . There can be no question that music which speaks for itself is not only the purest, but also the most all-embracing form of art.'[36] Vaughan Williams, one of his pupils, bluntly observed:

'A lot of nonsense is talked nowadays about the "meaning" of music. Music indeed has a meaning though it is not one that can be expressed in words. Mendelssohn used to say that the meaning of music was too precise for words. The hearer may, of course, narrow the meaning of music to fit words or visual impressions . . but this particularization limits the scope of music.'[37]

Copland set out the discussion in the following way:

'Basically two opposing theories have been advanced by the aestheticians as to music's significance. One is that the meaning of music, if there is any meaning, must be sought in the music itself, for music has no extra-musical connotation; and the other is that music is a language without a dictionary whose symbols are interpreted by the listener according to some unwritten esperanto of the emotions. The more I consider these two theories the more it seems to me that they are bound together more closely than is generally supposed.'[38]

He believed that not enough people were able to listen to music on what he called 'the sheerly musical plane', and most of his writings on music consisted of an attempt to increase that number. What was important was 'increasing one's awareness of what is going on'.[39] 'What is going on', however, meant what *musical* events were taking place, not what extra-musical associations could be invented: 'As for the popularizers, who first began by attaching flowery stories and descriptive titles to make music easier and ended by adding doggerel to themes from famous compositions – their "solution" for the listener's problems is beneath contempt' (p. 7).

Both Copland and his fellow American Sessions tend to favour the autonomous view of musical aesthetics – art as the realization of intrinsic principles and ideas – but their presentation of this view lacks the directness of the sources already cited. When Copland wrote that: 'This whole problem can be stated quite simply by asking, "Is there a meaning to music?" My answer to that would be, "Yes". And "Can you state in so many words what the meaning is?" My answer would be, "No". Therein lies the difficulty' (p. 12), he is, perhaps, being less than helpful. Sessions, on the other hand, talks of music as 'an independent and self-sufficient medium of expression', and thus commits himself to having to say what is expressed. His answer, 'the dynamics and the abstract qualities of emotion' or as he prefers, 'emotional energy', possibly raises more problems than it resolves.[40]

It would appear that statements which begin with the phrase: 'Music is the expression of . . .' only lead to obscurities such as '. . . a composer's encounter with, or creative impulse towards, sound-time phenomena'. The alternative is surely to avoid the idea of expression altogether (or at least leave the psycho-analysts to deal with it), and to concentrate on the idea of music as an *impressive* art. Psycho-analytic theories of musical aesthetics do not attempt to offer criteria for the evaluation of the *artistic* excellence of music, nor have most musicians pursued the many years of specialist training in psychology that would lead them to something more than amateur speculations about what is being 'expressed'.

Discussions about extrinsic and intrinsic meanings in music usually focus on purely instrumental forms, for it is clear that in vocal music, or in instrumental music with a descriptive title or programme, the music can be seen as acting as a form of illustration in relation to verbal or visual (as in the case of ballet) ideas. However, at some point the musician must face up to the following question: to what extent should he limit his judgement of vocal and descriptive music according to how successful the music is in conveying the meaning of the words? The answer that most composers have given is their own version of Schumann's dictum: 'First of all let me hear that you have made beautiful music; after that I will like your programme too.'[41] Indeed it is in this context that we must place Stravinsky's emphasis on music's intrinsic values, for as a composer he was more or less continually absorbed in theatrical problems, where there is the constant danger of extrinsic factors interfering with the composer's musical objectives.

Attempts to evaluate songs, operas, oratorios and the like by reference to the composer's ability to illustrate the words, can also lead to another sort of non-musical evaluation, which in Victorian England, for example, took a form roughly the opposite of Schumann's statement: 'first of all let me hear the words, and then I will tell you if I like the music . . .' Thus the factor of moral worth, that is the text's moral worth, became an element in musical aesthetics. Perhaps the clearest statement of the musician's point of view in relationship to this whole problem was made by Turner when he said:

'I am of the opinion that the whole ancient controversy about programme music was the result of a misconception and is a controversy about an illusion. The text of an opera, the words of a song, the programme of a symphony or tone poem, or whatever name in the future may be given to any composition is of *no importance or significance whatsoever*.'[42]

For the teacher of music, these general problems of musical aesthetics usually take the form of four particular questions: in what way does one's approach to musical aesthetics influence (a) what one teaches children to sing and play, (b) the way one teaches children how to sing and play, (c) what one selects for them to listen to, and (d) what assistance, if any, one gives them in their evaluation of the music? In searching for answers to these questions the teacher may find in the composers' writings more than one point of view. The close study of their arguments, however, may help to provide the appropriate background for the development of an informed opinion. Ignorance of even the most basic arguments in aesthetics is unfortunately often characteristic of the equipment of many musicians, and yet at every point in our teaching activities we are forced to exercise these faculties of evaluation and assessment in the context of aesthetic issues.

By way of conclusion, it is appropriate to consider an interesting example of the way in which popular expressionist aesthetics may confuse the issues raised in a musical composition. For many years Honegger's *Pacific 231* has been used, especially in the classroom, to show the way that music can express non-musical ideas, in this case the onomatopoeic expression of a train in motion. In fact, however, we have it from the composer himself that the title was *ex post facto*, and that his own original title for the work was simply *Mouvement Symphonique*, in which 'I was on the trail of a very abstract and quite ideal concept, by giving the impression of a mathematical acceleration of rhythm, while the movement itself slowed. Musically, I composed a sort of big, diversified chorale, strewn with counterpoint in the manner of J. S. Bach.'[43]

Notes

1. *The Principles of Practical Musick* (London, 1665), p. 140.
2. P. Hindemith, *A Composer's World*, p. 125.
3. *Poetics of Music*, p. 75.
4. In a letter to the Grand Duke Leopold of Tuscany (later Leopold II), in *Letters of Distinguished Musicians*, ed. L. Nohl, trans. Lady Wallace (London, 1867), p. 5.
5. *Treatise*, p. 2. (The same passage also appears in the author's *The Art of Playing on the Violin*.)
6. Ibid. pp. 3–4 (also in *The Art of Playing on the Violin*).
7. *Der Vollkomenne Kapellmeister*. Eng. trans. H. Lang, *Music in Western civilisation* (New York, 1941), p. 586. See also H. Lenneberg, 'Johann Mattheson on Affect and Rhetoric in Music', *JMT*, 2 (1958), pp. 47–84, 193–236.
8. C. Avison, *An Essay on Musical Expression* (London, 1752), pp. 2–4. See also J. B. Brocklehurst, *Charles Avison and His Essay on Musical Expression*, thesis (Sheffield, 1960).
9. A. P. Oliver, *The Encyclopaedists as Critics of Music* (New York, 1947), p. 66.
10. *A Complete Dictionary of Music*, trans. W. Waring (London, 2nd ed., 1779), pp. 76–7.
11. G. W. F. Hegel, *The Philosophy of Art*, trans. W. Hastie (London, 1886), pp. 42–3.
12. A. Schopenhauer, *The World as Will and Idea*, trans. R. B. Haldane and J. Kemp (London, 1896), Bk. III, p. 336.
13. *The World as Will and Idea*, Bk III, pp. 336–41.
14. III, p. 232. Cf. E. T. A. Hoffman, 'Beethoven's Instrumental Music' (1813) trans. O. Strunk, *Source Readings in Music History* (New York, 1950), p. 775: 'When we speak of music as an independent art, should we not always restrict our meaning to instrumental music, which, scorning every aid, every admixture of another art, gives pure expression to music's specific nature, recognizable in this form alone? It is the most romantic of all the arts – one might almost say, the only genuine romantic one – for its sole subject is the infinite.'
15. III, p. 232. Contrast Herbert Spencer's view, expressed in *Education: Intellectual, Moral and Physical* (London, 1861), p. 42: '... music is but an idealization of the natural language of emotion; and that consequently, music must be good or bad according as it conforms to the laws of this natural language. The various inflections of voice which accompany feelings of different kinds of intensities, are the germs out of which music is developed'.
16. *Beethoven*, trans. E. Dannreuther (London, 1870), p. 74.
17. *Complete Theoretical and Practical Course*, Bk 3, p. 39.
18. J. B. Cramer, *Studio per il pianoforte* (London, c. 1815), pp. 1–2.
19. E. Hanslick, *The Beautiful in Music* (Vienna, 1854), Eng. trans. G. Cohen, ed. M. Weitz (New York, 1957), from the 7th ed. (1885).
20. S. Deas, *In Defence of Hanslick* (London, 1940).
21. *The Beautiful in Music*, p. 4.
22. *Grove's Dictionary of Music and Musicians*, 5th ed. (London, 1954), Vol. 2, p. 532.
23. E. Gurney, *The Power of Sound* (London, 1880).
24. *Chronicle*, p. 53.
25. *Expositions and Developments* (New York, 1962), p. 101.
26. Ibid., p. 101.

27. *Chronicle*, p. 163. Cf. Hanslick: 'Although the beautiful exists for the gratification of an observer, it is independent of him.' (op. cit., pp. 9–10.)
28. *Chronicle*, p. 163.
29. *Chronicle*, p. 163.
30. F. Busoni, *The Essence of Music* (London, 1957), p. 1.
31. *Entwurf einer neuen Aesthetic der tonkunst* (Trieste, 1907); Eng. trans. S. Langer, in *Philosophy in a New Key* (Cambridge, Mass., 1942), 1951 ed. p. 223.
32. *Style and Idea* (New York, 1950), p. 183.
33. A. Schoenberg, *Letters* (New York, 1965), p. 234.
34. E. Křenek, 'Basic Principles of a New Theory of Musical Aesthetics' (1937), in *Exploring Music*, trans. M. Shenfield and G. Skelton (London, 1966), p. 130.
35. *A Composer's World*, p. 33.
36. *Musical Composition* (London, 1911), p. 155.
37. *The Making of Music* (New York, 1955), p. 3.
38. *Music and Imagination* (Cambridge, Mass., 1952), p. 12.
39. *What to Listen for in Music* (New York, 1939, rev. ed. 1957), p. 17.
40. R. Sessions, *The Musical Experience of Composer, Performer, Listener* (Princeton, 1950), p. 7.
41. *NZfM*, 18 (1843), p. 140, trans. L. B. Plantinga, *Schumann as Critic* (New York, 1967), p. 154.
42. W. J. Turner, *Berlioz: the Man and His Work* (London, 1934), p. 133.
43. A. Honegger, *I Am a Composer* (London, 1966), p. 101.

8
The Context of Music Education

'When hereafter you shall be admitted to the handling of the weighty affairs of the commonwealth you may discreetly and worthily discharge the offices whereunto you shall be called' (p. 299).

Thus Morley's Master bids farewell to his pupils, and the reader is reminded that, although the purpose of *A Plaine and Easie Introduction* is to produce musicians, this is not the same as saying that it attempts to equip its readers in the task of becoming professional musicians. Morley's rigorous training, then, has objectives which reach beyond musical considerations, and, at the same time, do not reach as far as the requirements of training a professional musician.

The difficulties of defining objectives in music education are increased by arguments which overlook its central aim, which must be to educate musicians, regardless of whether they may wish to devote their lives exclusively to music, or whether they may wish music to play just one part in their complex lives. Everyone may recognize that the training of specialists in any field requires facilities beyond those provided for general education, but few appear to understand there are levels of provision *below which* no worthwhile educational objectives can be achieved at all. In the preceding chapters the composers may appear to have set rather high minimum standards, and it must be remembered that at least until the last hundred years or so, they were writing for people who had the time and the money to devote part of their lives to making music. Nevertheless, it is clear that the composers, with some possible exceptions, were not writing for professional musicians, but for educated amateurs, and it is for such people that musical education today must aim to provide a coherent, structured pattern of growth. If the composer's minimum standards appear to be not merely rather higher than those with which we are familiar today, but utterly remote from them, then we may be forced to re-examine the principles on which our present teaching is based.

If composers can be said to offer us a considerable quantity of information on the matters of what to teach, and how to teach it, it is also apparent that they do not pursue very far the question of why we teach music, preferring on the whole to leave that question to the philosophers and to the theorists. There is a fundamental assumption in their writing that people can delight in the experience of music, and that it is the task of the musician to share his own delight in music with others. Beyond this lies speculation, and generally speaking, the only sort of speculation in which the composer is interested is of an intrinsically musical nature.

It may be valuable, however, to place some of the composers' attitudes within the context of broader issues, and so this final chapter attempts to take a brief look at the framework within which the composers were writing.

Morley and the Elizabethans worked in an atmosphere that in many respects was dominated by the educational ideas of Greek thought. The main arguments that were presented in favour of music taking an important part in education were that, on the one hand, music was *good* for the individual person, and on the other, music was needed by society for many of its social functions such as those associated with the church, the court, and with civic activities.

Plato believed strongly in the moral value of good music, 'for rhythm and harmony penetrate deeply into the mind and have a most powerful effect on it, and if education is good, bring balance and fairness . . .'[1] At the same time, however, he thought that bad music would have the opposite effect, that is, it would bring lack of balance, and lack of fairness. Bad music was characterized by the use of the wrong modes, and the wrong rhythms. Plato seems to be thinking of music essentially as song, for good rhythm is achieved where we can 'adapt the metre and tune to the appropriate words, and not the words to the metre and the tune' (p. 140). For Aristotle, music could be 'a stimulus to goodness, capable of having an effect on the character . . . and so capable of forming men who have the habit of right critical appreciating', and of contributing to 'intelligent and cultivated pastimes'.[2] To the question 'must they [the educated] learn to sing themselves and play instruments with their own hands?' Aristotle answers:

'It is impossible, or at any rate very difficult to produce good judges of musical performance from among those who have never themselves performed . . . since actual performance is needed to make a good critic, they should while young do much playing and singing, and then when they are older, give up performing; they will then, thanks to what they have learned in their youth, be able to enjoy music aright and give good judgements' (pp. 310–11).

Although Morley would not have agreed that people need 'give up performing', the general assumptions in *A Plaine and Easie Introduction* are clearly much closer to Aristotle than to Plato.

Elizabethan attitudes to education were, however, not exclusively Platonic or Aristotelian, and the effect of Reformation writers such as Erasmus and Vives can be seen in the educational works of Elyot,[3] Ascham[4] and Mulcaster.[5] As a general proposition Mulcaster observed that 'whosoever shall consider carefully the manner of bringing up children which is in favour within this realm, cannot but agree with me in wishing that it were improved'.[6] In respect of musical education his 'improvements' must be regarded as substantial, and very much in keeping with the ideas found in the writings of Morley and his colleagues.

Mulcaster sees the curriculum of elementary education being based on four subjects, reading, writing, drawing and music:

'Musicke maketh up the summe, and is devided into two partes, the voice and the instrument, whereof the voice resembleth reading: as yealding that to the eare, which it seeth with the eye: and the instrument writing, by counterfeting the voice, both the two in this age best to be begun, while both the voice and the joints be pliable to the traine.'[7]

Like Morley and the other writers, Mulcaster insists that a musical education demands training both in the use of the voice and in playing an instrument. The comparisons are interesting, and suggest that Mulcaster was used to thinking of children singing from notation, and not simply by rote. Again we encounter the demand for early training in music 'while both the voice and the joints be pliable to train'.

Mulcaster's next point is one that is only too familiar today: 'The voice craueth lesse cost to execute her part . . . The instrumente seemeth to be more costly, and claimes both more care in keping, and more charge in compassing' (p. 36). In four hundred years practically nothing has changed! It is still only a favoured minority of children who are given the opportunity to learn an instrument; for the majority, because 'the voice craveth less cost', the massed singing lesson is still the most familiar feature of school music.

'For the pleasauntnesse of Musick there is no man that doth doubt, bycause it seemeth in some degree to be a medicine from heauen, against our sorowes upon earth . . . and I must needes allow it which place it among those that I do esteeme the cheife principles for training up of youth' (p. 36).

In these terms Mulcaster introduces a fundamental principle: that a

musical education contributes vital ingredients to a general education.
He develops his argument with obvious enthusiasm and at some length,
pointing to the double purposes of 'learning' and 'exercise', which are
of general educational significance, and familiar to everyone. The value
of singing in order to 'keep open the hollow passages, and inward
pipes of the tender bulk' reminds us of William Byrd's 'since singing is
so good a thing, I wish all mean would learn to sing'. Music as therapy
was of great importance to the Elizabethans, and Mulcaster is quick to
underline its values:

'. . . that it is verie comfortable to the wearyed minde: a preparatiue to
perswasion: . . . that it is best learned in childehood, when it can do
least harme, and may best be had: that if the constitution of man doth
for bodie and soule, had not some naturall, and nighe affinitie with the
concordances of Musick, the force of the one, would not so soone
stirre up, the cosen motion in the other. It is wonderfull that is writen,
and strange that we see, what is wrought therby in nature of Physick,
for the remedying of some desperate diseases' (p. 37).

The strength of his attitude is summed up in the central statement: if
music is 'considerately applied' in education, and given the chance to
have 'obtained the favourable use of their [the learners'] ears', then its
influence will be 'a very forcible strength to try and to touch the
inclination of the mind'.

The sensuous qualities of music were not always met with approval
by puritan elements in Elizabethan society, but Mulcaster's final
statement on this matter is typically well balanced:

'Musick will not harme thee, if thy behauiour be good, and thy conceit
honest, it will not miscary thee, if thy eares can carie it, and sorte it as
it should be. Appoint thou it well, it will serue thee to good perpose: if
either thy manners be naught, or thy judgement corrupt it, it is not
musick alone which thou doest abuse . . .' (p. 38).

However, the position in Mulcaster's schools must not be thought of
as representative. In spite of the growth of music in the sixteenth
century in England, Watson was forced to conclude that 'the interest
in the Grammar School concentrated on Renaissance classical studies'.[8]
Referring to the failure of these schools to teach music, he adds, 'It may
be justly said that this is one of the instances in which the Grammar
School placed itself out of touch with the social activities of the time'
(p. 216). In conclusion he points to the fact that 'the English music of

the 16th and 17th centuries is a remarkable object-lesson of a culture-development in a particular direction on a voluntary basis in which the school played scarcely any appreciable part, and academic guidance but little stimulus' (p. 221). Le Huray reinforces this idea when he states that: 'The manifest failure of the Universities to adapt themselves to contemporary needs may in some measure at least help to explain why music studies were so lightly regarded in the Grammar Schools.'[9]

It is also somewhat surprising that the private tutors of the aristocracy appear to give only mild support to the teaching of music, especially as the example from the court in the form of the musical activities of Henry VIII and Elizabeth I could not have been bolder. It is true that Sir Thomas Hoby's translation of Castiglione's *Il Cortegiano* and Sir Thomas Elyot's *The Boke named the Governour* both support the teaching of music, but it is by no means at the centre of their ideas. Characteristic of the approach is that of Roger Ascham, author of *Toxophilus* (1545) and *The Scholemaster* (1570):

'Some wits, moderate enough by nature, be many times marred by over much study and use of some sciences, namely, music, arithmetic and geometry. These sciences as they sharpen mens wits over much, so they change men's manners over sore, if they be not moderately mingled, and wisely applied to some good use of life.[10]

'Therefore to ride comely, to run fair at the tilt or ring, to play at all weapons, to shoot fair in bow, or surely in gun, to valt lustily, to run, to leap, to wrestle, to swim, to dance comely, to sing, and play of instruments cunningly, to hawk, to hunt, to play at tennis, and all passtimes generally, which be joined with labour, used in open place, and on the day light, containing either some exercise for war, or some pleasant passtime for peace, be not only comely and decent, but also very necessary for a courtly gentleman to use.'[11]

Nor did writers such as Lyly, Cleland, Peacham or Milton contribute very much to the musical aspects of education in their time, although they are often quoted. Since they are writing general books on education they generally cannot devote too much time to the problems of teaching music, and although they contribute some entertaining aphorisms, they cannot be said to have offered much help to the aspiring musician.

Peacham's *Compleat Gentleman* is an example of the confusion which these sources tend to create:

'... I desire not that any noble or gentleman should (save at his private recreation and leasureable hours) prove a master in the same, [musicianship] or neglect his more weighty employment; though I avouch it a skill worthy the knowledge and exercise of the greatest prince.'[12]

Either it is 'worthy' or it is not, so why does Peacham hesitate to recommend it to a gentleman? While it is understandable that Peacham does not wish to tell his aristocratic readers how to become professional musicians, it is not clear how they are going to achieve all that Peacham requires of them without considerable effort: 'I desire no more in you than to sing your part sure, and at the first sight, withall, to play the same upon your viol, or the exercise of the lute, privately to yourself' (p. 100). Good sight singing and good sight reading on an instrument: these accomplishments are certainly not acquired overnight, even with the help of Morley's book!

Peacham also makes the same claims for singing that we have met before:

'The physicians will tell you that the exercise of music is a great length-ener of life, by stirring and reviving of the spirits, holding a secret sympathy with them; besides the exercise of singing openeth the breast and pipes; it is an enemy to melancholy and dejection of the mind . . . Yea, a curer of some diseases . . . it is a most ready help for a bad pronunciation, and distinct speaking . . .' (p. 97).

He adds little to the ideas on this point that we have already met in Byrd and Dowland. There is, however, a passage that is particularly interesting to us; Peacham provides a list of 'whom among other authors you should imitate and allow for the best . . .', which includes the names of the principal composers of the period working in England and Italy. As a supplement to Morley's list it makes very interesting reading.

Peacham's book was followed in 1636 by Charles Butler's *Principles of Musik*. Butler almost certainly saw himself as a conservator: 'The art of music, for the important and manifold uses thereof, is found so necessary in the life of man, that even in this giddy and new-fangled times, it is still retained by the best, and in some measure, respected by all' (p. i). In the *Dedication* Butler makes a number of points which are of interest to us:

'There is nothing that more conduceth to the prosperity and happiness of a Kingdom, than the good education of youth and children: in which the philosopher requireth three arts especially to be taught them (Grammar, Music, Gymnastic); this last for the exercise of their limbs in activity and feats of arms; the other two for the ordering of their voices in speech and song' (p. ii).

The simple phrase 'ordering of voices' clearly needs explanation and expansion, and Butler goes on to say:

'Merely to speak and to sing, are of Nature: and therefore the rudest swains of the most barborous nations do make this double use of their articulate voices: but to speak well, and to sing well, are of Art: so that among the best wits of the most civilized people, none may attain unto perfection in either faculty without the rules and precepts of art, confirmed by the practice of approved authors' (p. ii).

Butler's propositions are familiar enough to us: 'prosperity and happiness' are among the aims of education; education demands standards; standards in music are artistic standards; artistic standards are established and 'confirmed by the practice of approved authors'.

When Butler goes on to say: 'And for music itself, the philosopher [Quintilian] concludeth the special necessity thereof in breeding of children, partly from its natural delight, and partly from the efficacy it hath in moving affections and virtues' (p. iii), he is making claims for the inclusion of music in the curriculum which are surprisingly familiar to teachers of today. His use of the phrase 'liberal arts' is also in tune with present fashions, though one doubts the possibility of its companion study being so regarded: '. . . these two associated sisters [Music and Grammar], these two liberal arts, necessary in the liberal education of youth . . .' (p. v).

The eighteenth-century essayists were concerned about the failure of many of their contemporaries to recognize the value of music education. Quantz points out that: 'Although music is a science that can never be studied and investigated too thoroughly, it does not have the good fortune of other sciences . . . of being taught publicly. Some cloudy-minded modern philosophers do not . . . consider knowledge of it a necessity' (p. 15). We cannot be certain which 'cloudy-minded philosophers' he had in mind, but there had certainly been a decline in intellectual respect for music during the seventeenth and eighteenth centuries. There is a passage in the writings of John Locke which illustrates the point:

'Music is thought to have some affinity with dancing, and a good hand upon some instruments, is by many people mightily valued. *But it wastes so much of a young man's time, to gain but a moderate skill in it*; and engages often in such odd company, that many think it much better spared; and I have, amongst men of parts and business, so seldom heard any one commended or esteemed for having an excellency in music, that amongst all those things that ever came into the list of accomplishments, I think I may give it the last place.'[13]

Recreation should be 'in some exercise of the body, which unbends the thought, and confirms the health and strength.'

This type of observation may well have been quite influential in eighteenth-century England, but in Berlin, with Frederick the Great himself devoting much of his time to music, the position was very different. Nevertheless the failure to achieve a proper place in 'being taught publicly',[14] is one that the eighteenth-century society shared with the twentieth, or at least until very recently. If we can easily ignore Locke's sneers at musicians, we must investigate with much greater care his central point – 'it wastes so much of a young man's time to gain but a moderate skill in it'.

For some time writers on education had been describing music as a 'spare time activity' of somewhat less value than athletic pursuits: 'Amongst all these [curriculum for 13–19s], I have not mentioned Musick, Vocall and Instrumentall, by itself, because it is a part of the Mathematicks, and the practice thereof is to be insensibly at spare times brought in use as part of their recreations.'[15] Apart from the reference to music as 'a part of mathematics', this is not far removed from the views of many modern administrators who tend to 'fit in' music on the school timetable when they have given enough time to everything else. Where the provision of time is less than adequate we cannot help but agree with Locke, for a 'moderate skill' in music does take a very long time to acquire. The logical position might well appear to be as follows: if there is a minimum allocation of time necessary for the teaching of a subject, then to pretend that worthwhile teaching can be pursued in a time allocation below that minimum is to deceive oneself as a teacher, and to waste the time of the learners who might be much better occupied doing something else.

Locke therefore challenges us to reconsider a fundamental educational issue, the total pattern of the curriculum. Most educational systems, at least in the democracies, are based on a very large proportion of compromises. Behind the compromises is the assumption that a 'good' education is a broadly based education. But as everyone knows, a little of everything often means not enough of anything.

We have seen that many composers outline for us what they feel is demanded of music education. One of the things that we have to consider in the light of their observations may, perhaps, be expressed in the following question: would the achievement of the aims particular to a musical education have values, that is educational values, of a general nature? Or, to put it another way, could a properly educated musician be properly educated in the general sense? Let us ignore, for the present, the fact that there is very little agreement on what the phrase 'properly educated' might mean, and simply accept that the *possibility* of a 'proper education' is what all educational discussion assumes. If the answer is no, because 'it wastes so much of a young man's time', and produces an adult unaware of surroundings, people, and problems that are not directly connected with music, then there is no music education, but only music training. But if the answer is yes, then we can concentrate on the demands made by music, and set aside, for the present, the illusive concept of a 'general' education.

Of course the eighteenth-century essayists do not ignore the wider implications of a music education, and Quantz makes a particularly interesting observation on this point:

'Serious counsel must be given to young people who dedicate themselves to music that they endeavour not to remain strangers at least to those sciences mentioned above [mathematics, philosophy, poetry and oratory], and some foreign languages besides, even if time does not permit them to engage in all academic studies. And for those who propose to make composition their goal, a thorough knowledge of acting will not be unserviceable' (p. 25).

The last reference is undoubtedly connected with the eighteenth-century enthusiasm for opera, although there may be a more general implication, as was suggested in the previous chapter, that the musician needs to understand how to convey (sometimes physically) the 'passions' or 'affections' to his audience in a way similar to that employed by an actor.

Mathematics, philosophy, poetry, oratory and 'some foreign languages' may seem a fairly heavy load, but it is not dissimilar to the sort of requirements for entrance to a university course in music today. Moreover many universities insist that students following a main course in music should also pursue some related aspects of study in other fields. Furthermore, in specialist music schools both in this country and abroad a pattern of studies grouped around the main course in music has generally proved successful.

In deciding upon the requirements of music first, and then forming the rest of the curriculum pattern, there can be a reasonable expectation that both the principal study and the related studies will be properly provided for. The same, no doubt, would also be true for the study of other subjects. In England, however, there has been a great deal of sympathy with the idea of the 'general' education, even when, as is the case with music, the failure to specialize at a reasonably early age means that the child is effectively denied the opportunity of properly developing his musical abilities.

As has already been indicated, music education in eighteenth-century England had to struggle against the opposition of the Locke-Chesterfield point of view, and the acceptance of Rousseau's enthusiastic, if confused, support for music education was not really felt in this country until the nineteenth century. In Rousseau's writing on education one might expect, in relation to his background of musical interests, to find a keener awareness of the problems of music education. This, however, seems not to be the case. We may point to a number of places where he elaborates important principles: the need for an adequate background of musical experience before reading is attempted, the value of composition by pupils and the importance of enjoyment; and yet, as a body of writing, *Émile*[16] lacks the coherence and sense of direction that we associate with the composer's writing on music education.

At one point Rousseau warns us to 'beware of giving anything they [children] need today if it can be deferred without danger till tomorrow'.[17] What danger? The danger of disrupting a coherent development within a structured learning scheme? If so, the advice seems rather pointless. The more positive 'beware of putting off anything till tomorrow which can be learnt today' would seem the more appropriate. The process of music education is a very slow and lengthy one; what is not achieved today may never be achieved at all.

However, the significant point for music education is that Rousseau recognized in music the important contribution that it could make to social, moral and aesthetic education of children. The gradual acceptance of this view, even in England, is an important characteristic of nineteenth-century developments.

The English Reformation saw the great popularization of the skill of reading music. Day's version of the Sternhold and Hopkins *The Whole Book of Psalms* (1562) contained sixty-five tunes and an 'Introduction to learn to sing'. It was followed by a succession of music teaching methods whose main purpose was the development of congregational participation in church services. The main psalters all contained teaching material, and include Este's (1592), Ravenscroft's (1621), Playford's (1677) and Tate and Brady's 'New Version' (1696).[18]

For most people before the nineteenth century the only contact with musical notation was through the church. Moreover, Curwen's efforts in the 1840s and afterwards had, as their chief purpose, the promotion of hymn singing, and of songs with a strong and obvious moral purpose. The teaching of music in the English state-aided schools of the period started from the proposition that the children should learn music in order to participate in psalm singing: the sub-title to John Turner's *Manual of Instruction in Vocal Music* (1833) is 'chiefly with a view to psalmody'. As Rainbow points out in his detailed study of English music teaching in the nineteenth century, '... Turner and many of his fellow pioneers chose to advocate the teaching of music rather for its capacity to act as an attractive vehicle for the repetition of maxims and "improving" verses, than for its intrinsic worth.'[19] William Hickson's *Singing Master* (1836), however, has a rather different emphasis. The didactic element was still very strong, but it was not linked with psalm singing in the Turner manner. Hickson's views were neatly summarized in a speech he made to the Central Society of Education in 1837: 'The moral influences of music are of two kinds: it has a tendency to wean the mind from vicious and sensual indulgences; and, if properly directed, it has a tendency to incline the heart to kindly feelings, and just and generous emotions.'[20]

The English Tonic Solfa pioneers, Sarah Glover and John Curwen, similarly taught musical notation for religious and moral purposes: the title of Miss Glover's main book was a *Scheme to render Psalmody Congregational* (1835), and Curwen's interest was as a Congregational minister initially searching for ways of improving the singing in Sunday Schools. For Curwen, music provided 'the indirect means of aiding worship, temperance, and culture, of holding young men and women among good influences, of reforming character, of spreading Christianity'.[21]

Curwen often spoke of his indebtedness to Pestalozzi, whose ideas on the teaching of music had been spread through the work of Michael Pfeiffer and H. G. Naegeli. In a letter to J. H. Greaves, Pestalozzi writes that he:

'will not let the opportunity pass by without speaking of one of the most effective aids to moral education. You are aware that I mean music, and you are not only acquainted with my sentiments on that subject, but you have also observed the very satisfactory results which we have obtained in our schools ... But it is not this proficiency which I would describe as a desirable accomplishment in education. It is the marked and most beneficial influence of music on the feelings, which I have always thought and always observed to be most efficient in preparing, or attaining the mind for the best impressions ...'[22]

We thus encounter again the use of music as a tool in the moral educa-tion of the child.

When in 1839 the Privy Council set up a special Committee of Council to watch over state-financed education in Britain it appointed Dr James Kay as its Secretary. Kay undoubtedly had a real interest in the teaching of music, and, characteristically, he valued the teaching of singing for its moral and social consequences: it was 'an important means of forming an industrious, brave, loyal, and religious people'.[23] The enormous growth in massed choral singing that was a feature of the mid nineteenth century, and which was developed by the work of John Hullah (1812–84) and Joseph Mainzer (1801–51), was closely connected with political, religious and social purposes.

Politically speaking, choral music was undoubtedly a cheap method of providing music for large numbers of people: 'Vocal music,' wrote Hickson, 'is the kind best adapted for the working classes.'[24] As an adjunct to religious activities, massed choral singing, particularly in non-conformist circles, had a significantly moral purpose. From a social point of view, the large choral society can also be seen to have exercised a valuable influence. Having pointed out the dangers of confusing the 'moral' influence of music with that of the words actually sung, Mackerness offers a valuable observation on an important side effect:

'There is, however, one obvious sense in which music may be said to exert a good moral influence . . . Any sort of genuinely co-operative action is likely to have a beneficial effect on the men and women who take part in it; and even if (as was unquestionably the case) the innumerable choral groups which were formed as a result of the Hullah and Tonic Sol-Fa propaganda did not always turn their attention to music of the very highest quality, it can hardly be denied that the practice of vocal music imbued habits of forbearance and "give-and-take" which are in some degree "moral".'[25]

The moral values associated with singing are also emphasized by Ruskin, who wrote that

'not to be able to sing should be more disgraceful than not being able to read or write. For it is quite possible to lead a virtuous and happy life without books, or ink; but not without wishing to sing when we are happy; nor without meeting with continual occasions when our song, if right, should be a kind of service to others'.[26]

Ruskin, however, like so many other nineteenth-century writers, seemed totally incapable of separating music from words.

One of the principal arguments, then, which influenced music
education in the nineteenth century and which continued to have a
powerful effect in the twentieth century, was that music had an important part to play in the moral education of the young, and of society in
general. Since, however, there appeared to be some uncertainty about
the moral implications of music which did not employ words, it is
essential, it was argued, that vocal music, and particularly *choral* music,
should play a prominent part in education.

Another argument which was often employed to help in the evaluation of music in general, but particularly in relation to instrumental
forms, concerned the moral-social acceptability of the composer. In its
crudest form it suggested, simply, that if a society could not approve
absolutely of a composer's personal life, it could not be expected to find
any virtue in his music.[27]

Not everyone, however, shared these curious ideas, and in Gurney
we may recognize a restatement of Mulcaster's view that: 'Musick will
not harme thee if they behaviour be good ...':

'On this question of morality it is important to avoid confusion
between the effects of music when produced and the causes that bear
on its production. Morality tells in the *production* of all work; and of
course a naturally-gifted musician is failing in duty if through a failure
of earnestness he shirks his responsibilities and writes down to his
public, as though a schoolmaster should bring up his pupils on fairy-
tales: but the fact that his public are satisfied is the result of their being
children, not the cause of their being naughty children ... We see, as
a matter of fact, all sorts of people, good, bad and indifferent, caring
about all sorts of music; the good turn this, like all other enjoyment, to
good moral purpose, the bad do not; but the morality is concerned with
the use that is made of the pleasure, not with the stage of receiving it.'[28]

This direct attack upon the idea that moral virtue could be located
within a piece of music, as if one only had to be exposed to it in order
to become a better person, was no doubt frowned upon by all those
who saw in music an instrument of moral enlightenment. Moreover,
despite all the evidence against it, it is a view which is still occasionally
encountered even today. Gurney, however, in presenting the contrary
view, is not only recalling Mulcaster's admirably sensible observations,
but is also essentially reinforcing the autonomous concept of musical
aesthetics which was discussed in the previous chapter. It was Copland
who put the idea in perhaps its most simple form: 'A concert is not a
sermon. It is a performance – a reincarnation of a series of ideas implicit
in a work of art.'[29]

If a concert is not a sermon, it is also unlikely to prove a very effective means of communicating political ideas. Nevertheless, there can be very little doubt that national songs have been used as a powerful weapon in, for example, attempts to establish national identities, and that composers have often lent their support to such activities.[30] It must be recognized, however, that such expressions of national, or even party-political, interests have always taken place in music with explicit verbal associations, either in songs, operas and choral works, or in instrumental works with descriptive titles or with quotations of known national folk songs.

No one would attempt to deny that music can be used for all sorts of purposes, whether it be in support of selling detergents, calming the nervous, exciting the indolent, providing a rhythm for labour, a distraction from reality, or whatever else. For the composer, however, it is the music which interests him, and it is upon the music which music education must concentrate.

Notes

1. Plato, *The Republic*, trans. H. D. F. Lee (London, 1955, reprint 1972), p. 142.
2. Aristotle, *The Politics*, trans. T. A. Sinclair (London, 1962, reprint 1970), p. 306.
3. Sir Thomas Elyot, *The Boke named the Governour* (London, 1531).
4. Roger Ascham, *Toxophilus* (London, 1545) and *The Scholemaster* (London, 1570).
5. Richard Mulcaster (1532–1611), headmaster of Merchant Taylor's School, and later of St Paul's School; author of *Positions* (London, 1581), and *The Elementarie* (London, 1582).
6. *The Educational Writings of Richard Mulcaster*, ed. J. Oliphant (London, 1903), p. 1. Music teaching was, however, properly established in a few schools during Morley's life. John Howes, writing about the curriculum of Christ's Hospital School in 1587, said: '... children should learn to sing, to play upon all sorts of instruments, as to sound the trumpet, the cornett, the recorder or flute, to play upon shagbolts [sackbuts] shalms [shawms] and all other instruments that are to be played upon ...' (Quoted in F. Watson, *The English Grammar Schools to 1660* (London, 1908), p. 214.)
7. R. Mulcaster, *Positions*, ed. R. H. Quick (London, 1888), p. 36.
8. *The English Grammar Schools to 1660*, p. 205.
9. P. Le Huray, 'The Teaching of Music in 16th Century England', *MEd*, 30 (1966), p. 75.
10. *The Scholemaster* (London, 1570), ed. E. Arber (London, 1870), p. 34.
11. Ibid., p. 64.
12. H. Peacham, *Compleat Gentleman* (London, 1622), ed. G. S. Gordon (London, 1906), p. 98.
13. *Some Thoughts Concerning Education*, ed. J. L. Axtell (London, 1968), p. 311. Cf. F. Gasparini, *L'Armonico pratico al cembalo* (Venice, 1708), trans. F. S. Stillings and D. L. Burrows (London, 1963), p. 10: 'There are an infinite number of nobles, gentlemen, ladies and princes, who feel an inclination toward music, but should they start in it, it is certain that, because of their customary preoccupation with studies of literature or other gentlemanly exercises, a generation, so to speak, would not suffice them to arrive at the playing of four notes.'
14. C. P. E. Bach, *Essay*, p. 173.

15. J. Drury, 'The Reformed School', in *The Educational Writings of Samuel Hartlib*, ed. C. Webster (London, 1970), p. 165.
16. *Émile, ou de l'éducation* (Paris, 1762).
17. W. Boyd (ed.), *Emile for Today* (London, 1956), p. 82.
18. See J. Stainer, 'On the Musical Instruction found in Certain Musical Psalters', *PMA*, 27 (1900), pp. 1–50.
19. B. Rainbow, *The Land without Music* (London, 1967), p. 31.
20. Quoted by A. Mower, in 'On Vocal Music Considered as a Branch of National Education', *Central Society of Education* (1837), p. 307.
21. B. Rainbow, op. cit., p. 141.
22. B. Rainbow, op. cit., p. 81.
23. Ibid., p. 120.
24. A. Mower, op. cit., p. 307.
25. E. D. Mackerness, *A Social History of English Music* (London, 1964), pp. 164–5.
26. J. Ruskin, *Rock Honeycomb* (Bibliotheca Pastorum, Vol. 2) (London, 1876–85), Preface, p. iii.
27. See J. A. Mussulman, *Music in the Cultured Generation: a Social History of Music in America 1870–1900* (Evanston, USA, 1971). Referring to Mendelssohn, he writes that (p. 62): 'It was assumed that so perfect a man as he would naturally produce the noblest music conceivable, and it in turn would elevate and purify the souls of all Americans. He was an ideal for all aspiring American musicians to emulate, and the cultured class desired all American musicians to resemble him.'
28. E. Gurney, *The Power of Sound* (London, 1880), p. 366.
29. A. Copland, *Music and Imagination* (Cambridge, Mass., 1952), p. 17.
30. Kodály was particularly interested in this aspect of musical education.

Appendix

Selected list of compositions written especially for children by composers of the period 1900–1950.

BARTÓK
Ten Easy Pieces for piano (1908).
For Children, for piano. Vol. 1 based on Hungarian folktunes, Vol. 2.
based on Slovakian folktunes (1908, rev. 1945).
The First Term at the Piano (1913).
Nine Little Piano Pieces (1926).
Forty-four Duos for two violins (1931).
Twenty-seven Choruses for 2-, 3-part children's voices (1935).
Mikrokosmos, 153 progressive pieces for piano (1926–39).

BLOCH
Enfantines, 10 pieces for children, for piano (1923).

BRITTEN
Three 2-part Songs, for boys' voices and piano (1932).
Friday Afternoons, 12 songs for children's voices and piano (1934).
A Ceremony of Carols, for treble choir and harp (1942).
The Young Person's Guide to the Orchestra (for listening, not performing) (1946).
The Little Sweep, opera for children (1949).
Noye's Fludde, opera/oratorio for children (1958).
The Golden Vanity, a vaudeville for boys and piano (1968).

DEBUSSY
Children's Corner, for piano (1906–8).

DELIUS
Two songs for a children's album (1913).

HINDEMITH
Schulwerk für Instrumental-Zusammenspiel (1927).
Spruch eines Fahrenden, for children's voices (1928).
Wir bauen eine Stadt ('Let's build a town'); play for children (1930); arr. piano pieces for children (1931).

HOLST
The Idea, Operetta for children (1898).
St Paul's Suite, for strings (1913).
Two Partsongs for Children (1917).
Brook Green Suite, for small orchestra (1933).
Four Partsongs for Children with piano (1910).

JANÁČEK
Nursery Rhymes, 19 rhymes for children's voices (1927).

KODÁLY
Bicinia Hungarica, 180 progressive 2-part songs (1937–41).
15 2-part Exercises (1941).
Let Us Sing Correctly, 107 2-part exercises (1941).
333 Elementary Exercises in Sight Singing (1943).
Songs for Schools, Vols. I and II (1943).
Song Book for Primary Schools (1943).
Sol-Mi, 8 volumes of educational works (1945).
Twenty-four Little Canons on the Black Notes, for piano (1945).
Children's Dances, 12 dances for piano (1945).
Pentatonic Music, Vols. I–IV (1945–8).
Epigrams (1954).
55 2-part Exercises (1954).
44 2-part Exercises (1954).
Tricinia, 29 progressive 3-part songs (1954).
33 2-part Exercises (1954).
Fifty Nursery Songs with a range of five notes (1926).
66 2-part Exercises (1963).
22 2-part Exercises (1965).
77 2-part Exercises (1967).

MARTINŮ
Six Simple Songs (1917*).
Eight Lullabies (Children's Songs) (1916–18*).
Children's Songs, Vols. 1 and 2 (1925*).
Three Little Songs for Children (1931*).
Suite Miniature, 7 easy pieces for 'cello (1931).
Four Children's Songs and Rhymes (1932*).
Songs for Four Children's Voices, set to Czech folk song texts (1959*).
Piece for children: duo for two 'cellos (1959).

NIELSEN
Song Book for the People's High School (1922).
Denmark: Song Book (1924).
Ten Little Danish Songs (1926).
Piano Music for Young and Old, 24 five-finger pieces (1930).

POULENC
Villageoises, 6 children's pieces for piano (1933).
Petites Voix, 5 easy choruses for 3-part children's *a cappella* choir (1936).

PROKOFIEV
Music for Children, 12 easy piano pieces for children (1936).
Three Children's Songs, for voice and piano (1937).

RAVEL
Ma Mère l'Oye, children's pieces for piano, four hands (1908).

SIBELIUS
Folk School Children's March, for children's voices (1910).
The Way to School, for children's voices (1925).

* Unpublished.

STRAVINSKY
Three Easy Pieces for piano, four hands (1914–15).
Five Easy Pieces, for piano, four hands (1916–17).
Les Cinq Doigts, 8 easy pieces for piano (1921).

VAUGHAN WILLIAMS
Three Children's Songs for a Spring Festival (1929).
Six Teaching Pieces for piano (1934).
Folk Songs for Schools, arr. unison voices and piano (1912).

Bibliography

AGRICOLA, J. F.
Anleitung zur Sinkunst (Berlin, 1757): 'The Art of Singing', a translation from Tosi, P. F., *Opinioni de' cantori* (Arte del canto figurato) (Bologna, 1723).

ALBRECHTSBERGER, J. G.
Gründliche Anweisung zur Composition (Leipzig, 1790 and 1818). Eng. trans. *Methods of Harmony, Figured Base, and Composition, adapted for self-instruction,* trans. Merrick, A. (London, 1834).

ALSTEDT, J. H.
Templum musicum: or, the musical synopsis . . . being a compendium of the rudiments both of the mathematical and the practical part of musick: of which subject not any book is extant in our English tongue, trans. John Birchensa (London, 1664); facs. edn. (New York, 1964). (Trans. from Alstedt's *Scientiarum omnium Encyclopaedia,* 1610.)

ANGLEBERT, J. H. d'
'Principes de l'accompagnement', *Pièces de clavecin* (Paris, 1689); facs. ed. (New York, 1965).

ARNE, THOMAS
The Compleat Musician (London, 1760). Arne only provided the musical examples to an anonymous text.

ARNOLD, F. T.
The Art of Accompaniment from a Thorough Bass (London, 1931); reprinted with an introduction by Dennis Stevens (New York, 1965).

ARRESTI, G. C.
Diagolo tra un maestro et un discepolo desideroso d'approfitare nel contrapunto (Bologna, 1663).

ASCHAM, ROGER
Toxophilus (London, 1545, reprint 1969), ed. Wright, W. A. (London, 1970). *The Scholemaster* (London, 1570); ed. Ryan, L. V. (New York, 1968); ed. Wright, W. A. (London, 1970).

AVISON, CHARLES
An Essay on Musical Expression (London, 1752, 1753, 1775).
SEE ALSO:
Brocklehurst, J. B.: *Charles Avison and His Essay on Musical Expression,* unpub. thesis (Sheffield, 1960).
Edwards, C.: 'Charles Avison, English Concerto-writer Extraordinary', *MQ,* LIX (1973), pp. 399–410.
Holsey, P. M.: 'Charles Avison: the Man and his Milieu', *ML,* 55/1 (1974), pp. 5–23.

BACH, C. P. E.
Versuch über die wahre Art das Clavier zu Spielen (Berlin, Part 1 1753, Part 2 1762);
Eng. trans. Mitchell, W. J. (with an introduction), *Essay on the True Art of Playing Keyboard Instruments* (London, 1949).
Autobiography (Hamburg, 1773), ed. Nohl, L., trans. Lady Wallace (London, 1867).
SEE ALSO:
Kirkpatrick, R.: 'C. P. E. Bach's Versuch Recollected', *Early Music*, 4/4 (October, 1976), pp. 384–92.

BACH, J. C. and RICCI, F. P.
Méthode ou recueil de connaissances élémentaires pour le forte-piano ou clavecin (Paris, 1786); facs. ed. (Geneva, 1973).

BACH, J. S.
Notenbuchlein für Anna Magdelene Bach (Leipzig, 1725); 'Some Most Necessary Rules of Thorough Bass', trans. David, H. T., and Mendel, A., *The Bach Reader* (London, 1946).
Vorschriften und Grundsätze zum vierstimmigen spielendes General basses (Leipzig, 1738); 'Precepts and Principles for Four-part Playing of Thorough-bass', trans. David, H. T. and Mendel, A., *The Bach Reader* (London, 1946).

BANCHIERI, ADRIANO
Cartella musicale nel canto figurato fermo et contrapunto (Venice, 1614).
L'organi suanarino (Venice, 1605).

BANNARD, Y.
'Composer Critics', *ML*, v (1924), pp. 264–69.

BARTÓK, BÉLA
Rumanian Folk Music, Vols. 1–3, ed. Suchoff, B. (The Hague, 1967).
'Das Problem der neuen Musik', *Helos*, 1 (1920), pp. 107ff.: Eng. trans. *Tempo*, 14 (1949), pp. 16ff. 'Selbstbiographie' (1918); Eng. trans. *Tempo*, 13 (1949), p. 3ff.
Béla Bartók: Letters, ed. Demery, J., Eng. trans. (London, 1971).
Béla Bartók: Essays, ed. Suchoff, B. (London, 1976).
A magyar nepdal (Budapest, 1924); Eng. trans. *Hungarian Folk Music*, Calvocoressi, M. D. (London, 1931).
'Revolution and Evolution in Art', *Tempo*, 103 (1972), pp. 4–7.
SEE ALSO:
Foldes, A.: 'Béla Bartók', *Tempo*, 43 (1957), pp. 22ff.
Novik, Y.: 'Teaching with Mikrokosmos', *Tempo*, 83 (1967), pp. 12ff.
Ogdon, J.: 'Bartók's Mikrokosmos', *Tempo*, 65 (1963), pp. 2ff.
Suchoff, B.: *Guide to Bartók's Mikrokosmos* (London, 1971).
'BB's Contribution to Musical Education', *Tempo*, 60 (1961), pp. 37–43; *JRME*, 1 (1961), p. 3.
Ujfalussy, J. *BB* (Budapest, 1971); Eng. trans. Pataki and West.

BATHE, WILLIAM
A Briefe Introduction to the True Art of Music (London, 1584?).
A Briefe Introduction to the Skill of Song (London, c. 1596).

BARZUN, J.
The Pleasures of Music (New York, 1952).

BEMETZRIEDER, ANTON
Leçons de clavecin (Paris, 1771).

BENNETT, WILLIAM STERNDALE
See: Bennett, J. R. S.: *The Life of William Sterndale Bennett* (Cambridge, 1907).

BERG, ALBAN
Letters to His Wife, ed. and trans. Grun, B. (London, 1971).
SEE ALSO:
Reich, W.: *The Life and Work of Alban Berg* (London, 1965), which contains articles by Berg.

BERLIOZ, HECTOR
Voyage musical en Allemagne et en Italie (Paris, 1843).
Études sur Beethoven, Gluck et Weber (Paris, 1843).
Les Soirées de l'orchestre (Paris, 1852). Eng. trans. Roche, C. E. (London, 1929); Barzun, J. (New York, 1956); Fortesque, C. R. (London, 1963).
Le chef d'orchestre, théorie de son art (Paris, 1855). Eng. trans. '*The art of the Conductor*', Broadhouse, J. (London, 1917).
A travers chants (Paris, 1862).
A Critical Study of Beethoven's Nine Symphonies (extract from 'A travers chants'), trans. Evans, E. (London, 1913).
Gluck and His Operas (from 'A travers chants'), trans. Evans, E. (London, 1915).
Mozart, Weber and Wagner (from 'A travers chants'), trans. Evans, E. (London, 1920).
Mémoires (Paris, 1870); Eng. trans. 1884, 1903; rev. ed. Cairns, D. (London, 1969).
La grande traité d'instrumentation et d'orchestration (Paris, 1843); Eng. ed. 1856, trans. Clarke, M. C., and 1882; enlarged German ed. (ed. Richard Strauss), 1904.
SEE ALSO:
Turner, W. J.: *Berlioz: The Man and His Work* (London, 1934).
Roberts, W. W.: 'Berlioz the Critic', *ML*, VII (1926), pp. 63–72 and 133–42.

BERNHARD, CHRISTOPH
Von der Singe-Kunst (Dresden, 1649); Eng. trans. Hilse, W., 'The Treatises of Christoph Bernhard', *The Music Forum*, III (1973), pp. 13–25.
Tractatus Compositionis augmentatus (Dresden, c. 1652); Eng. trans. Hilse, W., op. cit., pp. 31–179.

BESARD, JEAN-BAPTISTE
Thesaurus harmonicus (Cologne, 1603) includes a section on how to play the lute – 'De modo in testudine libelus'. These instructions were translated in Robert Dowland's *Varietie of Lute-lessons*. Besard later revised them, and included them in his *Novus Partus* (Augsburg, 1617); the German translation of the instructions was published in the same year under the title *Isagoge in artem testudinarium* (Augsburg, 1617).
SEE ALSO:
Sutton, J.: "The Music of J. B. Besard's *Novus Partus*, 1617', *JAmMSoc*, XIX (1966), pp. 182–204.
'The Lute Instructions of J. B. Besard's *Novus Partus*, 1617', *MQ*, 51 (1965), pp. 345–62.

BEVIN, ELWY
A Briefe and Short Introduction to the Art of Musicke, to teach how to make discant, of all proportions that are in use: very necessary for all such as are desirous to attains to knowledge in the art; and may by practice, if they can sing, soone be able to compose three, foure, and five parts: and also to compose all sorts of cannons that are usuall, by these directions of two or three parts in one, upon the plain-song (London, 1631).

BLOW, JOHN
Rules for Playing of Thorough-bass upon organ and harpsicon (MS.n.d.) BL Add.
34072. Published in Arnold, F. T.: *The Art of Accompaniment from a Thorough-bass*
(London, 1931).

BONAVIA, F. (ed.)
Musicians on Music (London, 1956).

BONONCINI, GIOVANI MARIA
*Musico prattico, che breuement dimostra il modo di giungere all perfetta cognizione di
tutte quelle cose, che concorrono alla composizione de i canti, e di ciò ch'all'arte del
contrapunto si ricerca* (Bologna, 1673, Venice, 1678); Ger. trans. (Stuttgart, 1701);
facs. ed. (Cassel, 1969).

BORGEOIS, LOYS
Le droict chemin de musique (Geneva, 1550); facs. ed. (Cassel, 1954).

BOYD, M. C.
Elizabethan Music and Musical Criticism (Philadelphia, 1962); 2nd ed. (1973).

BRAHMS, JOHANNES
See: Henschel, G.: *Personal Recollections of Johannes Brahms* (London, 1907).

BRAITHWAITE, RICHARD
*The English Gentleman: containing sundry excellent rules, or exquisite observations,
tending to the direction of every gentleman of selecter ranke and qualitie* (London,
1630).

BRITTEN, BENJAMIN
On Receiving the Aspen Award: A Speech (London, 1964).

BROSSARD, S. DE
Dictionnaire de musique (Paris, 1703), reprint of 1705 ed. (The Hague, 1966).

BRUCKNER, ANTON
Vorlesangen über Harmonielehre und Kontrapunkt, ed. Schwanzara, E. (Vienna, 1950).

BRUNER, J.
The Process of Education (Cambridge, Mass., 1960).
Toward a Theory of Education (Cambridge, Mass., 1966).

BUKOFZER, M.
Music in the Baroque Era (London, 1948).

BURNEY, CHARLES
Dr Burney's Musical Tours of Europe, ed. Scholes, P. A. (London, 1959).
A General History ... (London, 1776–89), ed. Mercer, F. (London, 1935).

BUSONI, FERRUCCIO
Entwurf einer neuen Aesthetic der Tonkunst (Trieste, 1907); Eng. trans. Baker, T.,
Sketch of a New Aesthetic of Music (New York, 1911); repr. (New York, 1962).
Letters to His Wife, trans. Ley, R. (London, 1938).
The Essence of Music (London, 1957).
'On the Nature of Music', *MR* (November, 1956), pp. 282ff.

BUTLER, CHARLES
*The Principles of Musick, in singing and setting: with the two-fold use thereof,
Ecclesiasticall and Civil* (London, 1636).

BYRD, WILLIAM
A Gratification unto Master Case (London, 1586?). [Music by Byrd, words by Thomas Watson] (See below, Case, J.: *The Praise of Musicke*).
Preface to *Psalms, Sonnets and Songs* (London, 1588).

CACCINI, GIULIO
Nuovo musiche (Florence, 1601), trans. Hitchcock, H. W. (Madison, USA, 1971).

CALCOTT, JOHN WALL
Explanation of the Notes, Marks, Words, etc. Used in Music (London, 1792).
A Musical Grammar, in 4 parts (London, 1806).

CALVISIUS, SETH
Melopoeia (Erfurt, 1592).
Compendium Musicae (Leipzig, 1594).
Exercitationes musicae duae (Leipzig, 1600).
Musicas artis (Jena, 1612).
SEE ALSO:
Livingstone, E. F.: 'The Place of Music in German Education around 1600', *JRME*, XIX (1971), pp. 144–67.

CAMBINI, G. G.
Nouvelle méthode théorique et pratique pour le violon (Paris, 1763; facs. ed. Geneva, 1972).

CAMPION, THOMAS
New Ways in Making foure parts in Counter-point, by a most familiar, and infallible rule. Secondly, a necessary discourse of keyes, and their proper closes. Thirdly, the allowed passages of all concords perfect, or imperfect, are declared. Also by way of preface, the nature of the scale is expressed, with a briefe method teaching to sing (London, *c.* 1614); also contained in Playford's *An Introduction to the Skill of Musick* in editions dating from 1654; and in Davis, W. R. (ed.), *The Works of Thomas Campion* (London, 1969), pp. 319–56.
SEE ALSO:
Atcheson, W.: 'Key and Mode in 17th Century Music Theory Books', *JMT*, 17 (1973), pp. 204–32.
Cohen, A. (ed.): 'National Predilections in 17th Century Music Theory', *JMT*, 16 (1972), pp. 2–71.

CARISSIMI, GIOVANI GIACOMO
Ars cantandi (Rome? 1639?); original version lost; German trans. (Augsburg, 1693); Engl. trans. (of German ed.), Douglas, J. R., *Thesis*; Union Theological Seminary, New York (1949).

CARNER, M.
'Composers as Critics', in *Of Men and Music* (London, 1944).

CARPENTER, N. C.
Music in the Medieval and Renaissance Universities (New York, 1972).

CARTER, ELLIOTT
'Music as a Liberal Art', *Modern Music*, XXII (1944), p. 12.

CASE, JOHN
The Praise of Musicke: wherin besides the antiquitie, dignitie, delectation, and use thereof in civill matters, is also declared the sober and lawful use of the same in the congregation and church of God (Oxford, 1586).
Apologia Musices (Oxford, 1588).

SEE ALSO:
Barnett, H. B.: 'John Case – an Elizabethan Music Scholar', *ML*, 50 (1969), pp. 252–66.

CASELLA, ALFREDO
Music in My Time: Memoirs, trans. and ed. Norton, S. (Norman, USA, 1955).

CASTIGLIONE, BALDASSARE
Il cortegiano (Rome, 1528); Engl. trans. Hoby, Sir Thomas: *The Boke of the Courtier* (London, 1561); ed. Raleigh, W. (London, 1900).
SEE ALSO:
Lowinsky, E. E.: 'Music in the Culture of the Renaissance', *JHI*, 15 (1954),pp. 509–53.

CERONE, D. P.
El melopeo y maestro (Naples, 1613); facs. ed. (Bologna, 1968).
SEE ALSO:
Hannas, R.: 'Cerone, Philosopher and Teacher', *MQ*, XXI (1935),' pp. 408ff.

CHARLES, S. R.
A Handbook of Music and Music Literature in Sets and Series (New York, 1972).

CHARLTON, K.
Education in Renaissance England (London, 1965).

CHARPENTIER, MARC–ANTOINE
Règles de composition (MS., Paris, *c*. 1692); facs. Eng. trans. Ruff, M., 'M. A. Charpentier's "Règles de composition"', *The Consort*, 24 (1967), pp. 233–70.

CHÁVEZ, CARLOS
Toward a New Music, trans. Weinstock, H. (New York, 1937).
Musical Thought (Cambridge, Mass., 1961).

CHERUBINI, M. L. C. Z. S.
Cours de contrepoint et de fugue (Paris, 1837). Eng. trans. Hamilton, J. A. *A Course of Counterpoint and Fugue* (London, 1837).

CHESTERFIELD, LORD
Letters to His Son (London, 1774); ed. Root, R. K. (London, 1929).

CHEVÉ, E. (with PARIS, N.)
Méthode générale élémentaire de musique (Paris, 1838).

CLELAND, JAMES
Institution of a Young Gentleman (London, 1607).

CLEMENTI, MUZIO
Gradus ad Parnassum (Leipzig, 1817–26).
Selection of Practical Harmony (London, *c*. 1840).
Introduction to the Art of Playing on the PianoForte (London, 1801, reprint New York, 1974).

COCLICO, ADRIAN PETIT
Compendium musices (Nuremburg, 1552); facs. ed. (Cassel, 1954).
SEE ALSO:
Bray, R.: 'Musical Compendium by Adrian Petit Coclico', review in *ML*, 55/3 (1974), pp. 344–5.

COOVER, J.
'Music Theory in Translation: a Bibliography', *JMT*, 13 (1969), pp. 230–48.

COPERARIO, GIOVANI
Rules How to Compose (MS. *c.* 1614); facs. ed. Bukofzer, M. (Los Angeles, 1952).

COPLAND, AARON
What to Listen for in Music (New York, 1938).
Our New Music (New York, 1941).
Music and Imagination (Cambridge, Mass., 1952).
Copland on Music (New York, 1960).

COUPERIN, FRANÇOIS
Règles pour l'accompagnement (MS. Paris, *c.* 1698); ed. Cauchie, M., *Complete Works*, Vol. 1 (Paris, 1933), pp. 13–17.
L'art de toucher le clavecin (Paris, 1716); Eng. trans. Roberts, M. (Leipzig, 1933); trans. Halford, M. (London, 1974).
SEE ALSO:
Kirkpatrick, R.: 'On re-reading Couperin's l'Art de toucher . . .', *Early Music*, 4/1 (Jan. 1976), pp. 3–11.

CRAMER, J. B.
Studio per il Pianoforte (London, *c.* 1815).

COWELL, HENRY
New Musical Resources (New York, 1930).

CROTCH, W.
Elements of Musical Composition, comprehending the rules of thorough bass and the theory of tuning (London, 1812).

CRÜGER, JOHANNES
Praecepta musicae practicae figuralis (Berlin, 1625).
Synopsis musica (Berlin, 1630).
Questiones musicae practicas (Berlin, 1650).

CURWEN, JOHN
Singing for Schools and Congregation (London, 1843).
Grammar of Vocal Music (London, 1848).
The Standard Course (London, 1848).
The Teacher's Manual (London, 1875).

CZERNY, CARL
Complete Theoretical and Practical Pianoforte School, from the first rudiments of playing to the highest and most refined state of cultivation, with the requisite examples newly and expressly composed for the occasion, trans. Hamilton, J. A. (London, 1839).
School of Practical Composition, or complete treatise on the composition of all kinds of music, both instrumental and vocal (London, 1848).
Letter to a Young Lady on the Art of Playing the Pianoforte, trans. Hamilton, J. A. (London, 3rd ed. 1848).
SEE ALSO entries under Pleyel and Reicha.

DALCROZE, E. JAQUES
Le rythme, la musique et l'éducation (Paris, 1920, 2nd ed. 1935). Trans Rothwell, F., ed. Cox, C. (London, 1930); rev. ed. Rubenstein, H. F. (London, 1967).

DALLAPICCOLA, LUIGI
'Sulla strada della dodecafonia', Eng. trans. 'On the Twelve Tone Road', *Music Survey*, IV (1951), pp. 318ff.
'Musique et humanité', *Journal of the International Folk Music Council*, XVI (1964), pp. 8ff.
Pages from a Diary, trans. Waterhouse, C. G. (London, 1972).

DART, R. T.
The Interpretation of Music (London, 1954).

DEBUSSY, CLAUDE
M. Croche, anti-dilettante (Paris, 1921); Eng. trans. (New York, 1928 and 1962).
SEE ALSO:
Abraham, G.: 'Debussy as a Critic', *Musical Standard*, 19 (1927), pp. 178ff.

DEMUTH, N.
An Anthology of Musical Criticism (London, 1947).

DENTICE, LUIGI
Duo dialoghi della musica . . . delli qualill'uno tratta della theorica e l'attro della pratica (Naples, 1552, and Rome, 1553).

DESCARTES, RENÉ
Musicae compendium (Amsterdam, 1618); Eng. trans. *Renatus Des-Cartes excellent compendium of musick:* with necessary and judicious animadversions thereupon. By a person of honour (William, Viscount Brouncker?), (London, 1653); trans. Robert, W. (Rome, 1961).
SEE ALSO:
Locke, A. W.: 'Descartes and 17th Century Music', *MQ*, 21 (1935), pp. 423ff.

DIEREN, BERNARD VAN
Down Among the Dead Men (London, 1935).

D'INDY, VINCENT
Cours de composition musicale (Paris, 1903–33).

DIRUTA, GIROLAMO
Il transilvano, diagolo sopra el vero modo di sonar organi & instomenti da penna (Venice, 1593 and 1597);
Seconda parte del Transilvano (Venice, 1609 and 1622).
SEE ALSO:
Falvy, Z.: 'Diruta – Il transilvano 1593', *Studia Musicologica*, XI (1969), pp. 123–31.

DOLMETSCH, A.
The Interpretation of the Music of the XVII and XVIIIth Centuries (London, 1946).

DONI, G. B.
Annotazioni sopra il compendio de' generi e de' modi della musica (Rome, 1640).
Compendio del trattato de' generie de' modi della musica (Rome, 1635).

DONINGTON, R.
The Interpretation of Early Music (London, 1963).

DOWLAND, JOHN
Andreas Ornithoparcus, his micrologus, or introduction; containing the art of singing. Digested into foure bookes. Not only profitable, but also necessary for all that are studious of musicke (London, 1609); ed. Poulson, D., *John Dowland* (London, 1972). Reprint of Latin and English texts (New York, 1973).

DOWLAND, ROBERT
Varietie of Lute-lessons: viz. fantasies, pavins, galliards, almains, corantoes and volts: selected out of the best approved authors, as well beyond the seas as of our owne country. Whereunto is annexed certaine observations belonging to lute-playing by John Baptisto Besardo of Visconti. [*See also* entry under *Besard J. B.*] Also a short treatise thereunto appertayning by John Dowland, batchelor of musicke (London, 1610); facs. ed. (London, 1958).

DUKAS, PAUL
Écrits sur la musique (Paris, 1948).

DUSSEK, J. L.
See Pleyel, I. J.

EINSTEIN, A.
Music in the Romantic Era (New York, 1947).
Preface to Eng. trans. of Leopold Mozart's *Versuch einer grunflichen Violinschule*, trans. Knocker, E. (London, 1951).

ELGAR, EDWARD
Letters and Other Writings, ed. Young, P. M. (London, 1956).
A Future for English Music and Other Lectures, ed. Young, P. M. (London, 1968).
SEE ALSO:
Moore, J. N.: 'Elgar as University Professor', *MT*, CI (1960), pp. 630ff and 690ff

ELIOT, T. S.
Selected Prose (London, 1953).

ELYOT, SIR THOMAS
The Boke Named the Governour (London, 1531).

FAURÉ, GABRIEL
Opinions musicales (Paris, 1930).

FÉTIS, F.-J.
Traité de contrepoint et de la fugue (Paris, 1824 and 1846).
Traité complet de la théorie et de la practique de l'harmonie (Paris, 1844).
Biographie universelle des musiciens (Paris and Brussels, 1835–44).
–and MOSCHELES, J. *Méthode des méthodes de piano* (Paris, 1840).

FINCK, HERMANN
Pratica musica (Wittenburg, 1556); facs. ed. (Bologna, 1969).

FOND, J. DE LA
A New System of Music both theoretical and practical, and yet not mathematical (London, 1725).

FRESCOBALDI, G.
Preface, Bk. 1, *Toccatas and Partitas* (Rome, 1614).

FROEBEL, F.
A Collection of His Writings, ed. Lilley, I. M. (London, 1967).

FUX, J. J.
Gradus ad Parnassum (Vienna, 1725); Eng. trans. (London, 1944).

GALIN, P.
Exposition d'une nouvelle méthode (Paris, 1818).

GALILEI, VINCENZO
Dialogo della musica antica e della moderna (Florence, 1581).
Discorso intorno (Florence, 1589).

GASPARINI, F.
L'Armonico pratico al cembalo (Venice, 1708); Eng. trans. Stillings, F. S., and Burrows, D. L. (London, 1963).
SEE ALSO:
Thackray, R.: 'Music Education in 18th Century Italy', *Studies in Music* (1975), pp. 1–7.

GEMINIANI, F.
The Art of Playing on the Violin (London, 1751).
Rules for Playing in a True Taste on the Violin, German flute, 'cello and Harpsichord (London, 1739?).
Guida Armonica, being a sure guide to harmony (London, 1742).
The Entire Tutor for the Violin (London, 1747).
A Treatise of Good Taste in the Art of Music (London, 1749).
L'Art de bien accompagner du clavecin (Paris, 1754); Eng. trans. (London, 1755).
SEE ALSO:
Boydon, D. D.: *The History of Violin Playing from its Origin to 1761* (London, 1965).

GERVAIS, L.
Méthodes pour l'accompagnement du clavecin (Paris, 1734).

GLOVER, S.
Scheme to Render Psalmody Congregational (London, 1835).

GLUCK, C. W.
The Collected Correspondence and Papers of C. W. Gluck, ed. Mueller von Asow, H. and E. H., trans. Thomson, S. (London, 1962).

GRAF, M.
Composer and Critic (London, 1947).

GRASSINNEAU, J.
A Musical Dictionary (London, 1740).

GRÉTRY, A.
Méthode simple pour apprendre à préluder (Paris, 1801).

GURNEY, E.
The Power of Sound (London, 1880); reprint (London, 1966).

HANDEL, G. F.
See: Mann, A. 'Artist and teacher', *Current Musicology*, 9 (1969), pp. 141–146.

HANALICK, E.
Vom Musikalisch-Schönen (Vienna, 1854); Eng. trans. Cohen, G., ed. Weitz, M. (New York, 1957), *The Beautiful in Music*.
SEE ALSO:
Deas, S.: *In defence of Hanslick* (London, 1940).
Fubini, E.: 'Music Aesthetics and Philosophy', *IntRMAesthSoc* (1970), pp. 94–6.
Howard, V. A.: 'On Musical Expression', *Brit J Aesth*, II (1971), pp. 268–80.
Howes, F.: 'The Foundations of Musical Aesthetics', *PMA*, 83 (1957), pp. 75–87.
Leahy, M. P. T.: 'The Vacuity of Musical Expressionism', *Brit J Aesth* (1976), pp. 144–56.

HAWKINS, J.
A General History of the Science and Practice of Music (London, 1776).

HAYDN, F. J.
Collected Correspondence and London Note Books, ed. Robbins Landon, H. C. (London, 1959).

HEGEL, G. W. F.
The Philosophy of Art, trans. Hastie, W. (London, 1886).

HEINICHEN, J. D.
Der Generalbass in der composition (Dresden, 1728); Eng. trans. Buelow, G. J., *Thorough-bass Accompaniment* (Los Angeles, 1966).

HELM, E. E.
Music at the Court of Frederick the Great (Norman, U.S.A., 1960).
Composer, Performer, Public (Florence, 1970).

HELMHOLTZ, H. L. F.
Lehre von den Tonemofindungen als physiologische Grundlage für die Theorie der Musik (Brunswick, 1863); Eng. trans. Ellis, A. J., *On the Sensations of Tone as a Physiological Basis for the Theory of Music* (London, 1875, repr. New York, 1954).

HICKSON, W. E.
The Singing Master (London, 1836).
Vocal Music as a Branch of National Education (London, 1838).

HILLER, J. A.
Wöchentliche Nachrichen ... die Musik (Leipzig, 1766ff., periodical).
Anweisung zum Violonspielen (Leipzig, 1792).

HINDEMITH, PAUL
Unterweisung im Tonsatz (Mainz, 1937); Eng. trans. Mendel, A., and Ortmann, O., *The Craft of Musical Composition* (New York, 1941–2).
A Concentrated Course in Traditional Harmony (London, 1943).
Elementary Training for Musicians (New York, 1946).
A Composer's World: Horizons and Limitations (Cambridge, Mass., 1952).

HOFFMAN, E. T. A.
Musikalische schriften (Ratizbon, 1919; Munich, 1963).

HOLST, GUSTAV
'The Education of a Composer', *Composer*, 52 (1974) pp. 7–12 (reprinted from *The Beacon*, 1/1 (1921).)
Heirs and Rebels (with Vaughan Williams) (London, 1959).
SEE ALSO:
Imogen Holst, *The Music of Gustav Holst* (2nd ed., 1968).

HONEGGER, ARTHUR
Je suis compositeur (Paris, 1951); Eng. trans. Clough, W. O. (London, 1966).

HOOK, JAMES
Guida di musica; being a complete book of instructions for beginners on the harpsichord or piano-forte (London, c. 1785).

HORNER, V.
Music Education, Background of Research and Opinion (Sydney, 1965).

HOTTETERRE, J.
Princeps de la flûte traversière (Paris, 1707); Eng. trans. (London, 1729) and Lascocki, D. (London, 1968), facs. ed. (Geneva, 1973).

HULLAH, JOHN
Wilhem's Method of Teaching Singing (London, 1842 and 1849).

HUMMEL, J. F.
Ansführliche theoretische practische Anweisung zum Pianoforte-spiel (Vienna, 1827); Eng. trans. anon., *Complete theoretical and practical course of instructions on the art of playing the pianoforte, commencing with the simplest elementary principles, and including every information requisite to the most finished style of performance* (London, N. D.).

JANÁČEK, LEOŠ
The Teaching of Singing (Brno, 1899).
A Complete Harmony Book (Brno, 1912, 2nd ed., 1920).
SEE ALSO:
Vogel, J.: *Leos Janáček*, trans. Thomsen-Muchova, G. (London, 1962); esp. Ch. 19, 'Teacher and Theoretician', pp. 159–66.

KABALEVSKY, D.
'The Composer's Education', *Composer*, 45 (1972), pp. 1–4.

KALODIN, V. (ed.)
The Critical Composer (New York, 1940).

KANT, E.
Critique of Judgement, 1790, trans. Bernard, J. H. (London, 1892).
SEE ALSO:
Churton, A. *Kant on Education* (London, 1892).

KASSLER, J. C.
British Writings on Music 1760–1830, unpub. thesis (Columbia University, 1971).

KELLER, HERMAN
Thorough Bass Method, trans. and ed. Parrish, C. (London, 1966).

KELLNER, D.
Treulicher Unterricht im General-bass (Hamburg, 1732); second ed. (1737) contains preface by Telemann.

KIRNBERGER, J. P.
Die Kunst des reimen Satzes (Berlin, 1771–9); (developed from Fux's *Gradus ad Parnassum*).

KODÁLY, ZOLTÁN
A magyar népzene (Budapest, 1937); Eng. trans. *Folk Music of Hungary* (London, 1960; rev. ed. 1971).
Mein weg zur Musik (Zurich, 1966).
For translations from extracts of articles, etc. *see:*
'Folk Music and Art Music in Hungary', *Tempo*, 63 (1963), pp. 28–36.
'Folksong in Hungarian Music Education', *IntMEd.*, 15 (1967).
SEE ALSO:
Eösze, L.: *Zoltán Kodály*, Eng. trans. Farkas, I., and Gulyás, C. (London, 1962).
Frigyes, S.: *Musical Education in Hungary* (London, 1966).
Murphy, W.: 'Kodály', *MEd.*, 28 (July 1964), pp. 154–61.
Szönyi, E.: *Kodály's Principles in Practice* (London, 1973).

Vajda, C.: 'The Kodály Way of Music Education', *EdT* (Summer 1971), pp. 37–46.
Young, P. M.: 'Kodály as Educationist', *Tempo*, 3 (1962), pp. 38ff.

KOLLMAN, A. F. C.
An Essay on Musical Harmony, according to the nature of that science and the principles of the greatest musical authorities (London, 1796).

KŘENEK, ERNST
Music Here and Now, trans. Fles, B. (New York, 1939).
Studies in Counterpoint (New York, 1940).
Exploring Music, trans. Shenfield, M., and Skelton, C. (London, 1966).
'Extents and Limits of Serial Techniques', *MQ*, 46/2 (1960), pp. 210–32.

KUHNAU, J. *Der musikalische Quack Salber* (Dresden, 1700); ed. Boundorf, K. (Berlin, 1900).

LAMBERT, CONSTANT
Music Ho! (London, 1934).

LAMBERT, M. DE ST.
Les princepes du clavecin (Paris, 1702); facs. ed. (Geneva, 1972).
Nouveau traité d'accompagnement de clavecin (Paris, 1707); facs. ed. (Geneva, 1972).

LAMPE, J. F.
The Art of Music (London, 1740).
A Plain and Compendious Method of Teaching Thorough-bass (London, 1737).

LANG, P. H.
Music in Western Civilisation (New York, 1941).

LANGER, S. K.
Philosophy in a New Key (Cambridge, Mass., 1942).
Feeling and Form (Cambridge, Mass., 1953).

LISZT, FRANZ
Gesammelte Schriften (Leipzig, 1880–83).
Frederick Chopin (Paris, 1852); trans. Waters, E. N. (London, 1963); and Broadhouse, J. (London, 1899).
SEE ALSO:
Gervers, H. 'Franz Liszt as Pedagogue', *JRME*, XVIII (1970), pp. 377–84.

LOCKE, JOHN
The Educational Writings of John Locke, ed. Axtell, J. L. (London, 1968).

LOCKE, MATTHEW
Observations upon an Essay to the advancement of musick by Thomas Salmon (London, 1672).
The Present Practice of Musick Vindicated (London, 1673).
Melothesia, or certain rules of playing upon a continued-bass (London, 1673).

LOCKSPEISER, E.
The Literary Clef, an anthology of letters and writings by French composers (London, 1958).

LOULIÉ, E.
Musique théorique et practique (Paris, 1722).
Eléments ou principes de musique mis dans un nouvel ordre (Paris, 1696); trans. and ed. Cohen, A. (New York, 1965); facs. ed. (Geneva, 1971).

MACE, THOMAS
Musick's Monument, or a remembrance of the best practical musick, both divine and civil, that has ever been known to have been in the world (London, 1676).

MACFARREN, G. A.
Rudiments of Harmony (London, 1860).
Six Lectures on Harmony (London, 1867).

MACKERNESS, E. D.
A Social History of English Music (London, 1964).

MAINZER, J.
Singing for the Million (London, 1841).
Music and Education (London, 1848).

MAHLER, GUSTAV
Briefe, 1897–1911 (Berlin, 1924); Eng. trans. Creighton, B., *Memories and Letters* (London, 1946).

MANFREDINI, VINCENZO
Regole armoniche (Venice, 1775 and 1797).

MARBECK, JOHN
A Booke of Notes and Common Places, with their expositions, collected and gathered out of the workes of divers singular writers, and brought alphabetically into order (London, 1581).

MARPURG, F. W.
Der critischen Musicas an der Spree ('The critical musician along the River Spree') (Berlin, 1750ff., periodical).
Historischen-Kritische Beyträge zur Aufnahme der Musik ('Historical-critical contributions to the appreciation of music') (Berlin, 1754ff., periodical).
Kritische Briefe über die Tonkunst ('Critical letters on music') (Berlin, 1759ff., periodical).
Handbuch bei dem Generalbasse (Berlin, 1755).
Die Kunst das Clavier zu spielen (Berlin, 1750, repr. 1969). Fr. ed. 1756 (repr. Geneva, 1973).
Anleitung zur Musik und Singkunst (Berlin, 1763).
Anfangsgruende der theoretischen musik (Leipzig, 1757).
SEE ALSO:
Mekeel, J.: 'The Harmonic Theories of Kimberger and Marpurg', *JMT*, 4 (1960), pp. 169–93.

MARSENNE, MARIN
Harmonie universelle (Paris, 1636–7); Eng. trans. (in part), Chapman, R. E., *The books on Instruments* (London, 1957).
SEE ALSO:
Mace, D. T.: 'Marin Marsenne on Language and Music', *JMT*, 14 (1970), pp. 2–34.

MARTINI, G. B.
Esemplere osia saggio fondamentalo pratico di contrapunto sopra il canto formo (Bologna, 1774, repr. Ridgewood, USA, 1965).

MATTHESON, J.
General Bass (Hamburg, 1719).
Das Forschends Orchestre (Hamburg, 1721).

Grosse General-bass schule (Hamburg, 1731).
Kleine General-bass schule (Hamburg, 1735).
Der Volkommene Kapellmeister (Hamburg, 1739); facs. ed.(Cassel, 1954).
Critica Musica (Hamburg, periodical).
SEE ALSO:
Buelow, G. J.: 'Music, Rhetoric and the Concept of the Affections: a Selective Bibliography', *Notes*, 30 (1973), pp. 250–59.
Cannon, B. C.: *Johann Mattheson, Spectator in Music* (New Haven, USA, 1947).
Kivy, P.: 'What Mattheson Said', *MR*, 34/2 (1973), pp. 132–40.
Lenneberg, H.: 'Johann Mattheson on Affect and Rhetoric in Music', *JMT*, 2 (1958), pp. 47–85 and 193–236.

MENDELSSOHN, FELIX
Briefe 1830–47 (Leipzig, 1861–63); Eng. trans. Lady Wallace (London, 1863), and Selden-Goth, G. (London, 1946).
SEE ALSO:
Mussulman, J. A.: *Music in the Cultured Generation: a Social History of Music in America 1870–1900* (Evanston, USA, 1971).

MESSIAEN, OLIVIER
Technique de mon langage musicale (Paris, 1944); Eng. trans. (Paris, 1950).

MILHAUD, DARIUS
Notes sans Musique (Paris, 1949); Eng. trans. Evans, D., *Notes without Music*, (London, 1952).

MILTON, JOHN
Tractate of Education (London, 1644).

MIZLER, L. C.
Neu eröffnete musikalische Bibliothek ('Newly established musical library') (Leipzig, 1736ff., periodical).

MONTÉCLAIR, M. P. DE
Nouvelle méthode (Paris, 1709).
Petite méthode pour apprendre la musique aux enfants (Paris, c. 1730), Eng. trans. Pincherle, M., 'Elementary Musical Instruction in 18th Century', *MQ*, 34 (1948), pp. 61–7.
Principes de musique (Paris, 1736), facs. ed. (Geneva, 1972).

MORGENSTERN, S.
Composers on Music (New York, 1956; London, 1958).

MORLEY, THOMAS
A Plaine and Easie Introduction to Practicall Musicke, set downe in forme of a dialogue: devided into three partes, the first teacheth to sing with all things necessary for the knowledge of prickt-song. The second treateth of descante and to sing two parts in one upon a plainsong or ground, with other things necessary for a descanter. The third and last part entreateth of composition of three, four, five or more parts with many profitable rules to that effect. With new songs of 2, 3, 4, and 5 parts (London, 1597 and 1608); facs. ed. (London, 1957); ed. Harman, R. A. (London, 1597 and 1608); facs. ed.(London, 1937); ed. Harman, R. A. (London, 1952, 2nd ed. 1963).
SEE ALSO:
Harris, D. G. T.: 'Musical Education in Tudor Times (1485–1603)', *PMA*, 65 (1939), pp. 109–39.

Le Huray, P.: 'The Teaching of Music in Sixteenth-century England', *MEd*, 30 (1966), pp. 75–7.

MOWER, A.
'On Vocal Music Considered as a Branch of National Education', *Central Society of Education* (1837), pp. 307ff.

MOZART, LEOPOLD
Versuch einer grunflichen Violinschule (Salzburg, 1756), Eng. trans. Knocker, E., *A Treatise on the Fundamental Principles of Violin Playing* (London, 1951). Fr. trans. Valentin Roesser (Paris, 1770, *c.* 1783, *c.* 1788, 1800).

MUFFAT, GEORG
An Essay on Thorough Bass (1699), ed. Federhofer, H. (American Iist. Musicology, 1961).

MULCASTER, RICHARD
Positions, wherein those primitive circumstances be examined that are necessarie for the training up children (London, 1581); ed. Quick, P. H. (London, 1888); ed. DeMolen, R. L. (London, 1973).
First Part of the Elementarie (London, 1582); ed. Campagnac, E. T. (London, 1925).
SEE ALSO:
Oliphant, J.: *The Educational Writings of Richard Mulcaster* (London, 1903).
Simon, J.: *Education and Society in Tudor England* (London, 1966).

NIELSEN, CARL
Living Music, trans. Spink, R. (London, 1953).

NIVERS, G. G.
Traité de la composition de musique (Paris, 1667); trans. and ed. Cohen, A. (New York, 1961).

NOHL, L. (ed.)
Letters of Distinguished Musicians, trans. Lady Wallace (London, 1867).

NORTH, ROGER
The Musicall Grammarian (MS. *c.* 1726), ed. Andrews, H. (London, 1925).
SEE ALSO:
Wilson, J. (ed.): *Roger North on Music* (London, 1959).
Bridge F.: 'A 17th Century View of Musical Education', *PMA*, 27 (1901), pp. 121–30.

OLIVER, A. P.
The Encyclopaedists as Critics of Music (New York, 1947).

ORFF, CARL
'Orff-Schulwerk: Past and Future', trans. Murray, M., *MEd*, 28 (1964), pp. 209ff.
SEE ALSO:
Blackburn, M.: 'Orff Schulwerk', *Teachers' World*, nos. 3017–19, (1967).
Siemens, M. T.: 'A Comparison of Orff and Traditional Instrumental Methods in Music', *JRME*, XVII (1969), pp. 272–85.
Keetman, G.: *Elementaria* (London, 1974).

PARRY, C. H. H.
The Evolution of the Art of Music (London, 1893).
Style in Musical Art (Oxford, 1900).

Johann Sebastian Bach (London, 1909).
Training in Music (London, 1922).

PARIS, N. (with CHEVÉ, E.)
Méthode générale élémentaire de musique (Paris, 1838).

PASQUALI, NICOLO
Thorough-Bass Made Easy (Edinburgh, 1757).

PEACHAM, HENRY
The Compleat Gentleman, fashioning him absolute in the most necessary and commendable qualities concerning minde or bodie that may be required in a noble gentleman (London, 1622).

PEPUSCH, J. C.
A Short Treatise on Harmony (London, 1730).

PESTALOZZI, J. H.
See: Naegeli, H. G.: *Die Pestalozzische Gesangbildunglehre* (Zurich, 1809).

PINCHERLE, M.
'Elementary Musical Education in the 18th Century', *MQ*, 34 (1948), pp. 61–7.

PISTON, WALTER
Harmony (New York, 1941).
Counterpoint (New York, 1947).
Orchestration (New York, 1955).

PLAYFORD, JOHN
A Breife Introduction to the Skill of Musick (London, 1654); 19th ed., 1730; 12th ed., 1694, 'corrected and amended by Henry Purcell' (facs. ed., New York, 1973).
SEE ALSO:
Colles, H. C.: 'Some Musical Instruction Books of the Seventeenth Century', *PMA*, 55 (1928), pp. 31–49.
Spink, I.: 'Playford's Directions for Singing after the Italian Manner', *MMR*, lxxxix (1959), pp. 31–49.

PLEYEL, I. J.
J. Pleyel's 'Klavierschule', newly arranged and augmented with additional exercises by C. Czerny (London, N.D.).
–and DUSSEK, J. L. *Instructions on the Art of Playing the Pianoforte or Harpsichord* (London, 1796).

POULENC, FRANCIS
'Feuilles américaines', *Table ronde* xxx (1950), pp. 66ff., partly trans. Morgenstern, S., *Composers on Music* (New York, 1956), p. 514.
Correspondance (Paris, 1967).

PRAETORIUS, MICHAEL
Syntagma musicum: I, Musicae artis analecta (Wittenburg, 1614–15); II, De organographia (Wolfenbüttel, 1619); III, Termini musici (Wolfenbüttel, 1619); facs. ed. (Cassel, 1958); Part II trans. and ed. Bluenfeld (New York, 1949).

PROKOFIEV, SERGEI
See: Sabaneer, L.: 'Two More Russian Critiques: Sergei Prokofiev and the Composer-Critic', *ML*, viii (1927), pp. 425–36.

PURCELL, HENRY
See: Playford: A breife introduction . . . 12th ed. (1694), '. . . corrected and amended by Henry Purcell'. Barclay Squire, W.: 'Purcell as Theorist', QMIMS, VI (1905), pp. 521–67.

QUANTZ, J. J.
Versuch einer Anweisung die Flöte traversiere zu spielen (Berlin, 1752); also Berlin, 1789. Fr ed., Essai d'une methode . . . (Berlin 1752). Eng. ed., Easy and Fundamental Instructions . . . (London 1770).
Ed. Reilly, E. R., On Playing the Flute (London, 1966). Facs. ed. of Berlin 1789 edition (Cassel, 1953).

RACHMANINOV, SERGE
'Beware of the Indifferent Piano Teacher', Musician (Feb. 1925), pp. 11ff.

RAINBOW, B.
The Land Without Music (London, 1967).
'The Historical and Philosophical Background of School Music Teaching', Handbook for Music Teachers (London, 1968), pp. 21–32.

RAMEAU, J. P.
Traité de l'harmonie (Paris, 1722); Eng. trans. Gossett, P. (London, 1971); Bk 3 only, A Treatise of Musick (London, 1737, 52).
Nouveau système du musique théorique (Paris, 1726).
Génération harmonique (Paris, 1737).
Demonstration du princeps de l'harmonie (Paris, 1750).
Nouvelles réflexions sur sa demonstration (Paris, 1752).
Observations sur notre instinct musical (Paris, 1754).
Code de musique pratique (Paris, 1760).

RAVENSCROFT, THOMAS
A breife discourse of the true (but neglected) use of charact'ring the degrees by this perfection, imperfection, and diminution in measurable musicke, against the common practise and custom of these times. Examples whereof are exprest in the harmony of 4 voyces, concerning the pleasure of 5 usuall recreations: 1 hunting, 2 hawking, 3 dauncing, 4 drinking, 5 enamouring (London, 1614).

RAYNOR, H.
A Social History of Music (London, 1972).

REESE, G.
Four Score Classics of Music Literature (New York, 1957).
Music in the Renaissance (New York, rev. ed., 1959).

REGER, MAX
Beiträge zur modulationslehre (Leipzig, 1903). 24th ed., 1952.

REICHA, ANTON
Traité de melodie (Paris, 1814).
Cours de composition musicale (Paris, 1818); Eng. trans. Merrick, A., ed. Bishop, J., Course of Musical Composition (London, 1854).
Traité complet de la théorie et de la pratique de l'harmonie (Paris, 1844).
Anton Reicha's Theoretical Works on Harmony, Melody, Counterpoint and Dramatic Composition, trans. from the original French, and accompanied with numerous remarks and additional examples by C. Czerny, 5 vols. (London, N.D.).

REILEY, M. W.
'A Tentative Bibliography of Early Wind Instrument Tutors', JRME, 6 (1958), pp. 3–24.

RIMSKY-KORSAKOV, N.
Principles of Orchestration (St Petersburg, 1912); Eng. trans. (Berlin, 1922).
Treatise on Practical Harmony (St Petersburg, 1885); Eng. trans. (New York, 1930).

ROBINSON, THOMAS
The Schoole of Musicke: wherein is taught the perfect method of true fingering of
the lute, pandora, orpharion, and viol de gamba; with most infallible rules, both
easie and delightfull. Also a method, how you may be your owne instructor for
prick-song, by the help of your lute, without any other teacher: with lessons of all
sorts, for your further and better instruction (London, 1603).

ROUSSEAU, JEAN
Traité de la viole (Paris, 1687); facs. ed. (Geneva, 1975).
Méthode claire, certaine et facile, pour apprendre à chanter la musique (Paris, 1683); facs.
ed. (Geneva, 1976).

ROUSSEAU, J. J.
Émile, ou de l'éducation (Paris, 1762); Eng. trans. Foxley, B. (London, 1911).
Projet concernant de nouveau signes pour la musique (Geneva, 1742).
Dissertation sur la musique moderne (Geneva, 1743).
Dictionnaire de musique (Paris, 1768); Eng. trans. Waring, W., *A Complete Dic-
tionary of Music consisting of a copious explanation of all words necessary to a true
knowledge and understanding of music* (London, 2nd ed. 1779).
Traité sur la musique (Geneva, 1781?).
SEE ALSO:
Boyd, W.: *Emile for Today, the Emile of J-J. Rousseau* (London, 1956).
Lessem, A.: 'Imitation and Expression: Opposing French and British View in the
18th Century', *JAMS*, xxvii/2 (1974), pp. 325–30.
Somerset, H. V. F.: 'J-J Rousseau as a Musician', *ML*, xvii (1936), pp. 37ff. and
218ff.
Taylor, E.: 'Rousseau's Conception of Music', *ML*, xxx (1949), pp. 231–42.

RUBBRA, EDMUND
Counterpoint (London, 1960).

RUSKIN, J.
Bibliotheca Pastorum (London, 1876–83).

SAINT-SAËNS, C.
Harmonie et Mélodies (Paris, 1885).
Outspoken Essays on Music (London, 1922).

SALMON, THOMAS
An Essay to the Advancement of Musick, by casting away the perplexity of different
cliffs, and uniting all sorts of musick . . . in one universal character (London, 1672).
A Vindication of an Essay . . . from Mr Matthew Locke's observations by enquiring
into the real nature and most convenient practice of that science (London, 1672).

SCHAFER, M.
British Composers in Interview (London, 1963).

SCHEIBE, J. A. (and TELEMANN, C. P.)
Der critische musicus (Hamburg, 1737ff., periodical).

SCHENKER, HEINRICH
Neue musikalische theorien und phantasien (Vienna, 1906–35); Vol. 1, Eng. trans.
Jonas, O., and Borgese, E. M. (Chicago, 1954).

SCHOENBERG, ARNOLD
Harmonielehre (Vienna, 1911); Eng. trans., abridged, *Theory of Harmony* (New York, 1948).
Models for Beginners in Composition (New York, 1943).
Style and Idea, ed. Newlin, D. (New York, 1950); ed. Stein, L. (London, 1974).
Structural Functions of Harmony, ed. Searle, H. (London, 1950); ed. Stein, L. (New York, 1954).
Briefe, ed. Stein, E. (Mainz, 1958); Eng. trans. *Letters* (New York, 1965).
Preliminary Exercises in Counterpoint, ed. Stein, L. (London, 1963).
Fundamentals of Musical Compositions (London, 1967).
SEE ALSO:
Newlin, D.: 'Schönberg in America', *Music Survey*, 1 (1949), pp. 128–31 and pp. 185–9. (Includes a discussion of Schoenberg's career as a teacher in the USA.)

SCHOLES, P. A.
The Mirror of Music (London, 1947).

SCHOPENHAUER, A.
The World as Will and Idea (Leipzig, 1818); Eng. trans. Haldane, R. B., and Kemp, J. (London, 1896).
SEE ALSO:
Barford, P.: 'Music in the Philosophy of Schopenhauer', *Soundings*, 5 (1975), pp. 29–43.

SCHUMANN, ROBERT
Briefe: neue Folge, ed. Jansen, F. G. (Leipzig, 1886); Eng. trans. Bryant, H. (London, 1907).
Gesammelte Schriften (Leipzig, 1854); Eng. trans. Ritter, F. R. *Music and Musicians* (London, 1877–80); Rosenfeld, R., ed. Wolff, K. (London, 1947); *see also*:
The musical world of Robert Schumann – a selection from his writings, trans. and ed. Pleasants, H. (London, 1965).
SEE ALSO:
Lippmann, E. A.: 'Theory and Practice in Schumann's Aesthetics', *JAmMSoc*, 17 (1964), pp. 310–45.
Plantinga, L. B.: *Schumann as Critic* (New York, 1967).

SCHUMANN, WILLIAM
'On Teaching the Literature and Materials of Music', *MQ*, Vol. 34 (1948), pp. 155–68.

SCOTT, CYRIL
The Influence of Music on History and Morals (London, 1928).

SEARLE, HUMPHREY
Twentieth Century Counterpoint (London, 1954).

SESSIONS, ROGER
'New Vistas in Musical Education', *Modern Music*, XI (1934), pp. 115–20.
The Musical Experience of Composer, Performer, Listener (Princeton, USA, 1950).
Questions about Music (Cambridge, Mass., 1970).
Harmonic Practice (New York, 1951).

SHIELD, W.
Introduction to Harmony (London, 1814).

SIMPSON, A.
'A Short List of Printed English Instrumental Tutors up to 1800', *RMAResC*, 6 (1966)

SIMPSON, CHRISTOPHER
The Division Viol (London, 1659).
The Principles of Practical Musick (London, 1665).
A Compendium of Practical Musick in five parts: teaching by a new and easie method, 1. The rudiments of song, 2. The principles of composition, 3. The use of discords, 4. The form of figurate descant, 5. The contrivance of canon (London, 1667); ed. Lord, P. J. (Oxford, 1970).

SIMPSON, K.
'Some Great Music Educators', *Music Teacher* (Sept. 1967), pp. 14–15; (Oct. 1967), p. 16; (Nov. 1967), pp. 12–13; (Dec. 1967), pp. 10–12; (Jan. 1968), pp. 21ff.; (June 1969), pp. 15–16; (July 1969), pp. 17–18. Collected ed. (1976).

SOUHAITTY, JEAN JACQUES
Essai du chant d'église par la Nouvelle Méthode des nombres (Paris, 1679).

SPENCER, H.
'On the Origin and Function of Music', *Essays on Education* (London, 1911), pp. 310–30.
Education: Intellectual, Moral and Physical (London, 1861).

SPOHR, L.
Violinschule (Vienna, 1831); Eng. trans. *Violin School*, Bishop, J. (London, 1848).
Autobiography, Eng. trans. anon. (London, 1865 and 1878).

STAINER, J.
Theory of Harmony (London, 1871).

STANFORD, C. V.
Musical Composition (London, 1911).
Pages from an Unwritten Diary (London, 1914).

STERNFELD, F. W.
'Music in the Schools of the Reformation', *MD*, 2 (1948), pp. 99–122.
Music in the Modern Age (London, 1973).

STRAUSS, RICHARD
'The Artistic Testament of Richard Strauss', trans. (with an introduction) Alfred Mann, *MQ*, Jan. 1950, pp. 1ff.
Betrachtungen und Erinnerungen (Zurich, 1949); Eng. trans. Lawrence, L.J., *Recollections and Reflections* (London, 1953).

STRAVINSKY, IGOR
Chroniques de ma vie (Paris, 1935); Eng. trans. (New York, 1936).
Poétique musicale (Cambridge, Mass., 1942); Eng. trans. Knodel, A., and Dahl, I. *Poetics of Music* (Cambridge, Mass., 1947).
(and Craft, R.), *Conversations* (New York, 1959).
(and Craft, R.), *Memories and Commentaries* (New York, 1960).
(References in the text to *Conversations* and to *Memories* are to the combined English edition *Stravinsky in Conversation with Robert Craft* (London, 1962)).
(and Craft, R.), *Expositions and Developments* (New York, 1962).
(and Craft, R.), *Dialogues and a Diary* (New York, 1963; London, 1968).
(and Craft, R.), *Themes and Conclusions* (London, 1972).

SEE ALSO:
Asenjo, F. G.: 'The Aesthetics of Igor Stravinsky', *JAesthArtCr*, Vol. XXVI (1968), pp. 297–306.
Perrin, M.: 'Stravinsky in a Composition Class', *The Score*, 20 (1957), pp. 44–6.

STRUNK, O.
Source Readings in Music History (London, 1950).

SUK, JOSEPH
Studies and Reminiscences (Prague, 1935).

SUZUKI, S.
Nurtured by Love: a New Approach to Education (New York, 1969).
SEE ALSO:
Cook, C. A.: *Suzuki Education in Action* (New York, 1970).

SWEELINK, J. P.
Compositions-regeln, MS, no date; see *Complete works* (Amsterdam, 1895–1903), Vol. x.

TARTINI, GUISEPPE
Trattato di musica (Padua, *c.* 1754); Eng. trans. Stillingfleet, B., *Principles and Power of Harmony* (London, 1771); Jacobi, R. (New York, 1961); French trans. *Traité des Agréments de la musique* (Paris, 1771); Facs. ed. (Geneva, 1977).
Lettera alla Signora Maddalena Lombardini (Padua?, 1770); Eng. trans. Burney, C., *A letter from the late Signor Tartini to Signora Maddalena Lombardini, published as an important lesson to performers on the violin* (London, 1771); Girdlestone, C. (1961, as appendix to Jacobi's ed.); Babitz, S. *JRME*, Vol. IV (1956), pp. 75–102; Fr. trans. (Paris, 1771); Ger. trans. (Leipzig, 1784).
SEE ALSO:
Planchart, A. E.: 'A Study of the Theories of G. Tartini', *JMT*, 4 (1960), pp. 32–61.

TCHAIKOVSKY, P. I.
Guide to the Practical Study of Harmony (Moscow, 1871). Eng. trans. Krall, E., and Liebling, J., from the German ed. (Leipzig, 1900).

TELEMANN, G. P.
Der getreue Musikmeister ('The faithful music-master'), (Hamburg, 1728ff., periodical).
Singe-, spiel- und generalbass übungen (Hamburg, 1733).

TIPPETT, MICHAEL
Moving into Aquarius (London, 1959).

TOSI, P. F.
Opinioni de' cantori antichi e moderni (Bologna, 1723). Eng. trans. Galliard, J. E. *Observations on the Florid Song* (London, 1743 and 1926); facs. ed. (Geneva, 1977).

TOVEY, DONALD
A Musician Talks (London, 1941).
Essays in Musical Analysis (London, 1935–9).
Essays and Lectures on Music (London, 1949).

TÜRK, D. G.
Anweisung zum Generalbass spielen (Halle, 1800), facs. ed. (Amsterdam, 1971).

TURRENTINE, E. M.
'Historical Research in Music Education', *BCResMEd*, 33 (1973).

VARÈSE, EDGARD
'A Communication', *MQ*, LXI (1955), p. 574.

VAUGHAN WILLIAMS, RALPH
National Music (London, 1935).
Some Thoughts on Beethoven's Choral Symphony, with Writings on Other Musical Subjects (London, 1953).
The making of music (New York, 1955).
and Gustav Holst, *Heirs and Rebels* (London, 1959).
SEE ALSO:
Martin, J. M.: 'Vaughan Williams in the Classroom', *MEd*, 21 (1957), pp. 79–113.

VINCENTINO, NICOLO
L'antica musica ridotta alla moderna prattica (Venice, 1555); facs. ed. (Cassel, 1959).

WAGNER, R.
Gesammelte Schriften, 10 vols. (Berlin, Leipzig, 1871–83); Eng. trans. Aston Ellis, W., *Prose Works*, 8 vols. (London, 1892ff.).
Beethoven, Eng. trans. Dannreuther, E. (London, 1870).
Uber das dirigiren, Eng. trans. *On Conducting*, trans. Dannreuther, E. (London, N.D.).
SEE ALSO:
Goldman, A., and Sprinchorn, E.: *Wagner on Music and Drama* (London, 1970).

WALSH, W.
The Use of the Imagination (London, 1959).

WATSON, F.
The English Grammar Schools to 1660 (London, 1908).

WEBER, C. M. VON
Ausgewählte Schriften, ed. Altmann, W. (Ratisbon, 1937).
SEE ALSO:
Abraham, G.: 'Weber as Novelist and Critic', *MQ*, XX (1934), pp. 27–38.

WEBER, GOTTFRIED
Versuch einer geordneten Theorie der Tonsetzkunst (Mainz, 1817–21); Eng. trans. Warner, J. F., *Attempt at a Systematically Arranged Theory of Musical Composition* (Boston, USA, 1841ff., and London, 1846); ed. Bishop, J., *The Theory of Musical Composition Treated with a View to a Naturally Consecutive Arrangement of Topics* (London, 1851).

WEBERN, ANTON
Der Weg zur Neuen Musik, ed. Reich, W., Eng. trans. Black, L., *The Path to the New Music* (Bryn Mawr, USA, 1963).
SEE ALSO:
'Towards a New Music', *The Score*, 28 (1961), p. 29; *Arnold Schonberg* (Munich, 1912).

WESTRUP, J. A.
An Introduction to Musical History (London, 1955).

WIDOR, C. M. J. A.
The Technique of Modern Orchestration (Paris, 1904), trans. Suddand, E. (London, 1906); rev. ed. (London, 1946).

WILHEM, L. G. B.
Manuel Musical (Paris, 1841).

WILLEY, B.
The Eighteenth-Century Background (London, 1953).

WILLIAMS, D. R.
A Bibliography of the History of Music Theory (New York, 2nd ed., 1971).

WOLF, HUGO
Musikalische Kritiken (Leipzig, 1912).

WOODFILL, W. L.
Music in the English Society from Elizabeth to Charles I (Princeton, 1953).

YORKE TROTTER, T. H.
The Making of Musicians (rev. ed., London, 1930).
Music and Mind (London, 1924).

YOUNG, C. W.
'School Music in 16th Century Strasbourg', *JRME*, x (1962), pp. 129–38.

ZACCONI, LODOVICO
Prattica di musica (Venice, 1592).
Prattica di musica seconda parte (Venice, 1622).

ZARLINO, GIOSEFFE
Le institutioni harmoniche (Venice, 1558); Part three, Eng. trans. Marco, G. A., and Palisca, C. V.: *The Art of Counterpoint* (London, 1968).
Dimonstrationi harmoniche (Venice, 1571).
Sopplimente musicale (Venice, 1588).

ANON
The Pathway to Musicke, an introduction to musicke, how to learn to sing, contayning sundrie familiar and easie rules for the readie and true understanding of the scale, or gamma-ut . . . (London, 1596).

Index